WEST'S LAW SCHOOL
ADVISORY BOARD

THE LAW AND POLICY OF SENTENCING AND CORRECTIONS

IN A NUTSHELL

Seventh Edition

By

LYNN S. BRANHAM

Professor of Law
Thomas M. Cooley Law School

Mat #40340923

COPYRIGHT © 1976, 1983, 1988 WEST PUBLISHING CO.
© West, a Thomson business, 1998, 2002
© 2005 Thomson/West
        610 Opperman Drive
        P.O. Box 64526
        St. Paul, MN 55164–0526
        1–800–328–9352
Printed in the United States of America

ISBN 0–314–15937–1

Dedicated

to

Dawn Beachnau,

A fount of light, a friend forever,
a blessing to all

*

PREFACE

This book is designed to provide students with a general overview of the law and policy of sentencing and corrections. The book covers a broad range of subjects. The first nine chapters cover sentencing-related topics, including the purposes of criminal sanctions, guilty pleas, the rights defendants have during the sentencing process, different ways to structure sentencing systems, community-based sanctions, the death penalty, Eighth Amendment constraints in noncapital cases, parole release, probation and parole revocation, and the collateral sanctions and consequences that attend a criminal conviction. Chapters 10 through 17 focus on the constitutional rights that prisoners have while they are incarcerated. The final two chapters of the book discuss the mechanics of litigating § 1983 suits and the remedies available to inmates whose constitutional rights have been violated.

The book is not confined to a discussion of current law and policy, but also looks towards the future. The book, for example, discusses some key proposals for making the nation's sentencing and corrections systems more cost-effective, equitable, and just. Some of these proposals include the adoption by each state and the federal government of a comprehensive community-corrections act, the implementation of capacity-based sentencing guidelines that provide for the imposition of community sanctions on most defendants convicted of nonviolent crimes, and the incorporation of restorative-justice mechanisms, such as victim-offender mediation programs, into jurisdictions' sentencing and corrections systems.

In writing the first three editions of this Nutshell, Sheldon Krantz laid the important groundwork for this book. I have attempted to build on this foundation by writing a Nutshell geared to the needs of students who must assimilate an extensive amount of information on sentencing and correctional law and policy. Because many of these students will be taught in courses using the casebook that I have co-authored, The Law and Policy of Sentencing and Corrections (West Law School 2005), this Nutshell tracks the format of that casebook.

I am grateful to my secretary, Chris Ducsay, whose skills and natural ebullience facilitated the completion of this book. And I am thankful for the support and encouragement I have received from my husband and four boys over the years as I pursue my work to promote the understanding and improvement of the nation's sentencing and corrections systems.

LYNN S. BRANHAM

August, 2005

OUTLINE

Page

PREFACE -- V
TABLE OF CASES --- XIII

PART ONE.   THE LAW AND POLICY OF SENTENCING

Chapter 1.   Introduction to Sentencing ---   1
A. The Purposes of Criminal Sentences --------   2
B. Proposals for Reform ----------------------------   11

Chapter 2.   Guilty Pleas and Plea Bargaining --   14
A. Intelligent and Voluntary Guilty Pleas ------   16
B. Breaches of Plea Agreements ------------------   29
C. Constraints on the Government in Offering Incentives to Plead Guilty --------------   33

Chapter 3.   The Sentencing Process --------   45
A. Rights During Sentencing -----------------------   45
   1. The Right to Counsel-------------------------   45
   2. The Rights to Have Access to and to Rebut the Presentence Investigation Report --   49
   3. The Rights to Make a Statement to the Sentencer and to Present Evidence   53

Page

Chapter 3. The Sentencing Process—
Continued

    4. The Rights to Confrontation and Cross–
       Examination ------------------------------- 56

    5. The Right to a Statement of Reasons
       for the Sentence Imposed ---------------- 57

    6. Standard of Proof/Jury Trial-------------- 59

    7. Double Jeopardy ----------------------------- 66

B. Factors Considered at Sentencing ------------ 68

    1. Criminal Conduct and Convictions ------ 69

    2. First Amendment Limitations------------- 73

    3. False Information --------------------------- 74

    4. Unconstitutional Convictions-------------- 75

    5. Illegally Obtained Evidence --------------- 79

    6. Victim–Impact Statements ---------------- 80

Chapter 4. Sentencing Statutes and
    Guidelines -------------------------------- 85

A. Indeterminate Sentencing Statutes ---------- 86

B. Determinate Sentencing Statutes------------- 88

    1. Determinate Discretionary Sentencing-- 89

    2. Presumptive Sentencing ------------------- 91

    3. Mandatory Sentences ----------------------- 92

C. Sentencing Guidelines----------------------------- 95

D. *Ex Post Facto* Laws-------------------------------- 103

Chapter 5. Community–Based Sanctions 107

A. Community–Based Sentencing Options------ 109

    1. Probation ------------------------------------- 109

    2. Day Reporting Centers --------------------- 111

    3. Home Confinement and Electronic
       Monitoring-------------------------------- 112

    4. Economic Sanctions ------------------------- 114

    5. Community Service -------------------------- 122

B. Comprehensive and Integrated Corrections
    Systems -------------------------------------- 123

                                                        Page
Chapter 6.   The Death Penalty -------------   130

**Chapter 7.   Cruel and Unusual Punish-
             ment and Noncapital Cases** ------------   148
A. Disproportionality Claims ----------------------   148
B. Challenges Regarding the Nature of a
    Criminal Sanction ----------------------------   159
    1. Shame Sentences ----------------------------   160
    2. Medical Interventions -----------------------   162

**Chapter 8.   Parole Release and Proba-
             tion and Parole Revocation** ------------   163
A. Probation and Parole Revocation -------------   165
    1. Due Process -----------------------------------   165
    2. The   Fifth   Amendment   Privilege
        Against Self–Incrimination --------------   174
    3. The Fourth Amendment --------------------   178
    4. Policy Issues ----------------------------------   184
B. Parole Release----------------------------------   184

**Chapter 9.   Collateral   Sanctions   and
             Consequences** --------------------------   195
A. The Reintegration of Released Prisoners
    Into Society: Practical Obstacles -----------   195
B. The Reintegration of Released Prisoners
    Into Society: Legal Obstacles ----------------   197
    1. Employment Restrictions and Restric-
        tions on Government Benefits----------   198
    2. Restrictions on Political Rights -----------   199
    3. Restrictions on Sex Offenders: Notifica-
        tion, Registration, and Civil-Commit-
        ment Laws ----------------------------------   201

Page

Chapter 9. Collateral Sanctions and Consequences—Continued
C. Restoration of Rights and Other Steps to Limit Collateral Sanctions and Consequences 209

PART TWO. THE LAW AND POLICY OF CORRECTIONS

Chapter 10. Prisoners' Rights: An Introduction 213
A. History of Prisoners' Rights—A General Overview 214
B. The Purposes of Incarceration 219

Chapter 11. First Amendment Rights 223
A. Freedom of Speech 223
B. Freedom of Association 239
C. Freedom of Religion 244

Chapter 12. Right of Access to the Courts 252

Chapter 13. Prison Disciplinary Proceedings 270
A. Procedural Due Process 270
B. *Miranda* and the Privilege Against Self–Incrimination in the Correctional Context 279

Chapter 14. Transfers, Classification, and Disparity in Programming Opportunities 283
A. Procedural Due Process 283
   1. Liberty Interests 284
   2. Procedural Safeguards 294

Page

Chapter 14. Transfers, Classification, and Disparity in Programming Opportunities—Continued

B. The Fifth Amendment Privilege Against Self–Incrimination ----------------------------- 307
C. Equal Protection of the Law-------------------- 309

Chapter 15. Searches, Seizures, and Privacy Rights---------------------------------- 317
A. The Fourth Amendment----------------------- 318
B. Right of Privacy --------------------------------- 325

Chapter 16. Due-Process Claims for Personal Injuries and Property Deprivations; Restrictions on Inmate Labor --- 337
A. Due Process--------------------------------------- 337
B. Restrictions on Inmate Labor ----------------- 343

Chapter 17. Cruel and Unusual Punishment--- 347
A. Medical and Psychiatric Care ----------------- 348
   1. The Right to Receive Medical Treatment --- 348
   2. The Right to Refuse Medical Treatment 354
B. Conditions of Confinement --------------------- 357
C. Use of Force and the Protection of Inmates 365

PART THREE. PRISONERS' RIGHTS LITIGATION

Chapter 18. The Mechanics of Litigating Inmates' § 1983 Suits --------------------- 373
A. Filing a § 1983 Complaint ---------------------- 373
   1. Elements of a Cause of Action Under § 1983--- 374
   2. *Bivens* Actions-------------------------------- 380

Page

Chapter 18.   The Mechanics of Litigating Inmates' § 1983 Suits—Continued

    3. Jurisdiction 381
    4. Filing Fees 382
    5. Sufficiency of the Complaint 384
    6. The PLRA's "Three–Strikes" Provision 386
    7. Appointed Counsel 387
B. Affirmative Defenses 388
    1. Immunity 388
       a. Sovereign Immunity 388
       b. Personal Immunity 391
    2. Statute of Limitations 396
    3. Mootness 397
    4. Exhaustion of Remedies 398

Chapter 19.   Remedies 399
A. § 1983 Suits 399
    1. Damages 399
    2. Equitable Relief 403
    3. Attorney's Fees 412
       a. General Rules 412
         i. Prevailing Party 412
         ii. Reasonable Attorney's Fee 414
       b. Restrictions Under the Prison Litigation Reform Act 417
B. Modifying and Terminating Court Orders .. 419
C. Enforcing Court Orders Through Contempt Proceedings and Other Means 430
D. Other Remedies 431

INDEX 435

TABLE OF CASES

References are to Pages

Acosta, United States v., 303 F.3d 78 (1st Cir.2002), *79*

Addonizio, United States v., 442 U.S. 178, 99 S.Ct. 2235, 60 L.Ed.2d 805 (1979), *75*

Ake v. Oklahoma, 470 U.S. 68, 105 S.Ct. 1087, 84 L.Ed.2d 53 (1985), *56*

Alabama v. Shelton, 535 U.S. 654, 122 S.Ct. 1764, 152 L.Ed.2d 888 (2002), *46*

Alabama v. Smith, 490 U.S. 794, 109 S.Ct. 2201, 104 L.Ed.2d 865 (1989), *38, 40*

Almendarez–Torres v. United States, 523 U.S. 224, 118 S.Ct. 1219, 140 L.Ed.2d 350 (1998), *65, 66*

Apprendi v. New Jersey, 530 U.S. 466, 120 S.Ct. 2348, 147 L.Ed.2d 435 (2000), *62, 64, 65, 66*

Arizona v. Rumsey, 467 U.S. 203, 104 S.Ct. 2305, 81 L.Ed.2d 164 (1984), *67*

Atkins v. Virginia, 536 U.S. 304, 122 S.Ct. 2242, 153 L.Ed.2d 335 (2002), *143, 144*

Avery v. Perrin, 473 F.Supp. 90 (D.N.H.1979), *328*

Bagley v. Watson, 579 F.Supp. 1099 (D.Or.1983), *328*

Bajakajian, United States v., 524 U.S. 321, 118 S.Ct. 2028, 141 L.Ed.2d 314 (1998), *159*

Baker v. Welch, 2003 WL 22901051 (S.D.N.Y.2003), *331*

Ball v. United States, 163 U.S. 662, 16 S.Ct. 1192, 41 L.Ed. 300 (1896), *66*

Bass by Lewis v. Wallenstein, 769 F.2d 1173 (7th Cir.1985), *351*

Baxter v. Palmigiano, 425 U.S. 308, 96 S.Ct. 1551, 47 L.Ed.2d 810 (1976), *280, 281, 282*

Bearden v. Georgia, 461 U.S. 660, 103 S.Ct. 2064, 76 L.Ed.2d 221 (1983), *117, 118, 119*

Bell v. Wolfish, 441 U.S. 520, 99 S.Ct. 1861, 60 L.Ed.2d 447 (1979), *230, 231, 320, 321, 322, 323, 324, 358, 361, 423*

Bell–Bey v. Williams, 87 F.3d 832 (6th Cir.1996), *254*

Benchimol, United States v., 471 U.S. 453, 105 S.Ct. 2103, 85 L.Ed.2d 462 (1985), *31, 33*

Benjamin v. Fraser, 264 F.3d 175 (2nd Cir.2001), *293*

Bivens v. Six Unknown Named Agents of Federal Bureau of Narcotics, 403 U.S. 388, 91 S.Ct. 1999, 29 L.Ed.2d 619 (1971), *380*

Blackledge v. Perry, 417 U.S. 21, 94 S.Ct. 2098, 40 L.Ed.2d 628 (1974), *34, 35, 38*

Blakely v. Washington, 542 U.S. 296, 124 S.Ct. 2531, 159 L.Ed.2d 403 (2004), *63, 64, 65, 68, 103*

Blanchard v. Bergeron, 489 U.S. 87, 109 S.Ct. 939, 103 L.Ed.2d 67 (1989), *417*

Blevins v. Brew, 593 F.Supp. 245 (W.D.Wis.1984), *312*

Block v. Rutherford, 468 U.S. 576, 104 S.Ct. 3227, 82 L.Ed.2d 438 (1984), *239, 240, 242, 320*

Blystone v. Pennsylvania, 494 U.S. 299, 110 S.Ct. 1078, 108 L.Ed.2d 255 (1990), *140*

Boag v. MacDougall, 454 U.S. 364, 102 S.Ct. 700, 70 L.Ed.2d 551 (1982), *397*

Boardman v. Estelle, 957 F.2d 1523 (9th Cir.1992), *55*

Board of County Com'rs of Bryan County, Oklahoma v. Brown, 520 U.S. 397, 117 S.Ct. 1382, 137 L.Ed.2d 626 (1997), *380*

Board of Educ. of Oklahoma City Public Schools, Independent School Dist. No. 89, Oklahoma County, Okl. v. Dowell, 498 U.S. 237, 111 S.Ct. 630, 112 L.Ed.2d 715 (1991), *427*

Board of Pardons v. Allen, 482 U.S. 369, 107 S.Ct. 2415, 96 L.Ed.2d 303 (1987), *186, 188*

Board of Trustees of University of Alabama v. Garrett, 531 U.S. 356, 121 S.Ct. 955, 148 L.Ed.2d 866 (2001), *389*

Boerne, City of v. Flores, 521 U.S. 507, 117 S.Ct. 2157, 138 L.Ed.2d 624 (1997), *250*

Booker, United States v., ___ U.S. ___, 125 S.Ct. 738, 160 L.Ed.2d 621 (2005), *65, 68, 102, 103*

Booth v. Churner, 532 U.S. 731, 121 S.Ct. 1819, 149 L.Ed.2d 958 (2001), *398*

Booth v. Maryland, 482 U.S. 496, 107 S.Ct. 2529, 96 L.Ed.2d 440 (1987), *80, 80, 82, 83*

Bordenkircher v. Hayes, 434 U.S. 357, 98 S.Ct. 663, 54 L.Ed.2d 604 (1978), *34, 35, 36, 37, 40*

Bounds v. Smith, 430 U.S. 817, 97 S.Ct. 1491, 52 L.Ed.2d 72 (1977), *253, 262, 263, 264*

Bowling v. Enomoto, 514 F.Supp. 201 (N.D.Cal.1981), *328*

Bowring v. Godwin, 551 F.2d 44 (4th Cir.1977), *353*

Boykin v. Alabama, 395 U.S. 238, 89 S.Ct. 1709, 23 L.Ed.2d 274 (1969), *17, 18*

Brady v. Maryland, 373 U.S. 83, 83 S.Ct. 1194, 10 L.Ed.2d 215 (1963), *20, 23*

Brady v. United States, 397 U.S. 742, 90 S.Ct. 1463, 25 L.Ed.2d 747 (1970), *19, 27*

Broce, United States v., 488 U.S. 563, 109 S.Ct. 757, 102 L.Ed.2d 927 (1989), *25*

Broussard v. Johnson, 253 F.3d 874 (5th Cir.2001), *278*

Brunet, State v., 174 Vt. 135, 806 A.2d 1007 (Vt.2002), *174*

Buckhannon Bd. and Care Home, Inc. v. West Virginia Dept. of Health and Human Resources, 532 U.S. 598, 121 S.Ct. 1835, 149 L.Ed.2d 855 (2001), *414*

Bullington v. Missouri, 451 U.S. 430, 101 S.Ct. 1852, 68 L.Ed.2d 270 (1981), *67*

Bullock, People v., 440 Mich. 15, 485 N.W.2d 866 (Mich.1992), *156*

Burlington, City of v. Dague, 505 U.S. 557, 112 S.Ct. 2638, 120 L.Ed.2d 449 (1992), *416*

Burns v. United States, 501 U.S. 129, 111 S.Ct. 2182, 115 L.Ed.2d 123 (1991), *53*

Calhoun v. DeTella, 319 F.3d 936 (7th Cir.2003), *332*

California v. Ramos, 463 U.S. 992, 103 S.Ct. 3446, 77 L.Ed.2d 1171 (1983), *141*

California Dept. of Corrections v. Morales, 514 U.S. 499, 115 S.Ct. 1597, 131 L.Ed.2d 588 (1995), *104*

California Motor Transport Co. v. Trucking Unlimited, 404 U.S. 508, 92 S.Ct. 609, 30 L.Ed.2d 642 (1972), *253*

Callins v. Collins, 510 U.S. 1141, 114 S.Ct. 1127, 127 L.Ed.2d 435 (1994), *141*

Canedy v. Boardman, 16 F.3d 183 (7th Cir.1994), *332*

Canell v. Lightner, 143 F.3d 1210 (9th Cir.1998), *402*

Canton, Ohio, City of v. Harris, 489 U.S. 378, 109 S.Ct. 1197, 103 L.Ed.2d 412 (1989), *379*

Carey v. Piphus, 435 U.S. 247, 98 S.Ct. 1042, 55 L.Ed.2d 252 (1978), *399, 401*

Carlson v. Green, 446 U.S. 14, 100 S.Ct. 1468, 64 L.Ed.2d 15 (1980), *380*

City of (see name of city)

Cleavinger v. Saxner, 474 U.S. 193, 106 S.Ct. 496, 88 L.Ed.2d 507 (1985), *392, 393, 394*

Cochran v. State of Kansas, 316 U.S. 255, 62 S.Ct. 1068, 86 L.Ed. 1453 (1942), *253*

Cody v. Weber, 256 F.3d 764 (8th Cir.2001), *254*

Coker v. Georgia, 433 U.S. 584, 97 S.Ct. 2861, 53 L.Ed.2d 982 (1977), *142*

Colon v. Howard, 215 F.3d 227 (2nd Cir.2000), *292*

Connecticut Bd. of Pardons v. Dumschat, 452 U.S. 458, 101 S.Ct. 2460, 69 L.Ed.2d 158 (1981), *187*

Connecticut Dept. of Public Safety v. Doe, 538 U.S. 1, 123 S.Ct. 1160, 155 L.Ed.2d 98 (2003), *203*

Corbitt v. New Jersey, 439 U.S. 212, 99 S.Ct. 492, 58 L.Ed.2d 466 (1978), *40, 41*

Correctional Services Corp. v. Malesko, 534 U.S. 61, 122 S.Ct. 515, 151 L.Ed.2d 456 (2001), *381*

Cruz v. Beto, 405 U.S. 319, 92 S.Ct. 1079, 31 L.Ed.2d 263 (1972), *244, 248*

Custis v. United States, 511 U.S. 485, 114 S.Ct. 1732, 128 L.Ed.2d 517 (1994), *76, 77, 78*

Cutter v. Wilkinson, ___ U.S. ___, 125 S.Ct. 2113 (2005), *251*

Daniels v. United States, 532 U.S. 374, 121 S.Ct. 1578, 149 L.Ed.2d 590 (2001), *78*

Daniels v. Williams, 474 U.S. 327, 106 S.Ct. 662, 88 L.Ed.2d 662 (1986), *337, 338, 339, 340*

Dannenberg v. Valadez, 338 F.3d 1070 (9th Cir.2003), *419*

Danneskjold v. Hausrath, 82 F.3d 37 (2nd Cir.1996), *344*

Davidson v. Cannon, 474 U.S. 344, 106 S.Ct. 668, 88 L.Ed.2d 677 (1986), *339*

Davis v. Passman, 442 U.S. 228, 99 S.Ct. 2264, 60 L.Ed.2d 846 (1979), *380*

Dawson v. Delaware, 503 U.S. 159, 112 S.Ct. 1093, 117 L.Ed.2d 309 (1992), *73*

DeHart v. Horn, 227 F.3d 47 (3rd Cir.2000), *248*

DeWalt v. Carter, 224 F.3d 607 (7th Cir.2000), *268*

Diaz v. Collins, 114 F.3d 69 (5th Cir.1997), *248*

Doe v. Poritz, 142 N.J. 1, 662 A.2d 367 (N.J.1995), *203*

Dothard v. Rawlinson, 433 U.S. 321, 97 S.Ct. 2720, 53 L.Ed.2d 786 (1977), *333, 334, 335*

Dubose, United States v., 146 F.3d 1141 (9th Cir.1998), *119*

Dunnigan, United States v., 507 U.S. 87, 113 S.Ct. 1111, 122 L.Ed.2d 445 (1993), *70*

Duran v. Elrod, 713 F.2d 292 (7th Cir.1983), *404*

Edwards v. Balisok, 520 U.S. 641, 117 S.Ct. 1584, 137 L.Ed.2d 906 (1997), *410*

Employment Div., Dept. of Human Resources of Oregon v. Smith, 494 U.S. 872, 110 S.Ct. 1595, 108 L.Ed.2d 876 (1990), *249*

Enmund v. Florida, 458 U.S. 782, 102 S.Ct. 3368, 73 L.Ed.2d 1140 (1982), *143*

Estelle v. Gamble, 429 U.S. 97, 97 S.Ct. 285, 50 L.Ed.2d 251 (1976), *348, 351, 352, 367*

Estelle v. Smith, 451 U.S. 454, 101 S.Ct. 1866, 68 L.Ed.2d 359 (1981), *49*

Everson v. Michigan Dept. of Corrections, 391 F.3d 737 (6th Cir.2004), *335*

Ewing v. California, 538 U.S. 11, 123 S.Ct. 1179, 155 L.Ed.2d 108 (2003), *157, 158*

Ex parte (see name of party)

Farmer v. Brennan, 511 U.S. 825, 114 S.Ct. 1970, 128 L.Ed.2d 811 (1994), *349, 371*

Farrar v. Hobby, 506 U.S. 103, 113 S.Ct. 566, 121 L.Ed.2d 494 (1992), *415*

F.C.C. v. Beach Communications, Inc., 508 U.S. 307, 113 S.Ct. 2096, 124 L.Ed.2d 211 (1993), *386*

Felder v. Casey, 487 U.S. 131, 108 S.Ct. 2302, 101 L.Ed.2d 123 (1988), *381*

Fitzpatrick v. Bitzer, 427 U.S. 445, 96 S.Ct. 2666, 49 L.Ed.2d 614 (1976), *389*

Forbes v. Edgar, 112 F.3d 262 (7th Cir.1997), *388*

Ford v. Wainwright, 477 U.S. 399, 106 S.Ct. 2595, 91 L.Ed.2d 335 (1986), *146*

France v. Artuz, 1999 WL 1251817 (E.D.N.Y.1999), *29*

Freeman v. Pitts, 503 U.S. 467, 112 S.Ct. 1430, 118 L.Ed.2d 108 (1992), *426, 427*

Furman v. Georgia, 408 U.S. 238, 92 S.Ct. 2726, 33 L.Ed.2d 346 (1972), *130, 134, 138*

Gagnon v. Scarpelli, 411 U.S. 778, 93 S.Ct. 1756, 36 L.Ed.2d 656 (1973), *170, 171, 172, 173*

Garcia v. Singletary, 13 F.3d 1487 (11th Cir.1994), *281*

Gardner v. Florida, 430 U.S. 349, 97 S.Ct. 1197, 51 L.Ed.2d 393 (1977), *50, 51, 52, 53*

Garner v. Jones, 529 U.S. 244, 120 S.Ct. 1362, 146 L.Ed.2d 236 (2000), *105*

Gementera, United States v., 379 F.3d 596 (9th Cir.2004), *160, 161*

Georgia, United States v., ___ U.S. ___, 125 S.Ct. 2256 (2005), *390*

Giglio v. United States, 405 U.S. 150, 92 S.Ct. 763, 31 L.Ed.2d 104 (1972), *20*

Gilmore v. Lynch, 319 F.Supp. 105 (N.D.Cal.1970), *263*

Gilmore v. People of the State of California, 220 F.3d 987 (9th Cir.2000), *429*

Glover v. Johnson, 478 F.Supp. 1075 (E.D.Mich.1979), *340*

Glover v. United States, 531 U.S. 198, 121 S.Ct. 696, 148 L.Ed.2d 604 (2001), *47*

Golomb, United States v., 754 F.2d 86 (2nd Cir.1985), *58*

Gomez v. Vernon, 255 F.3d 1118 (9th Cir.2001), *268*

Goodman, United States v., 165 F.3d 169 (2nd Cir.1999), *43*

Goodwin, United States v., 457 U.S. 368, 102 S.Ct. 2485, 73 L.Ed.2d 74 (1982), *37*

Grayson, United States v., 438 U.S. 41, 98 S.Ct. 2610, 57 L.Ed.2d 582 (1978), *70*

Green v. Georgia, 442 U.S. 95, 99 S.Ct. 2150, 60 L.Ed.2d 738 (1979), *56*

Green v. Polunsky, 229 F.3d 486 (5th Cir.2000), *248*

Green v. United States, 365 U.S. 301, 81 S.Ct. 653, 5 L.Ed.2d 670 (1961), *55*

Greenholtz v. Inmates of Nebraska Penal and Correctional Complex, 442 U.S. 1, 99 S.Ct. 2100, 60 L.Ed.2d 668 (1979), *185, 186, 188, 189, 190, 190, 192, 305*

Gregg v. Georgia, 428 U.S. 153, 96 S.Ct. 2909, 49 L.Ed.2d 859 (1976), *130, 133, 135*

Griffin v. California, 380 U.S. 609, 85 S.Ct. 1229, 14 L.Ed.2d 106 (1965), *72*

Griffin v. Wisconsin, 483 U.S. 868, 107 S.Ct. 3164, 97 L.Ed.2d 709 (1987), *178*

Griswold v. Connecticut, 381 U.S. 479, 85 S.Ct. 1678, 14 L.Ed.2d 510 (1965), *325*

Hahn, United States v., 359 F.3d 1315 (10th Cir.2004), *42*

Haines v. Kerner, 404 U.S. 519, 92 S.Ct. 594, 30 L.Ed.2d 652 (1972), *384*

Hakim v. Hicks, 223 F.3d 1244 (11th Cir.2000), *248*

Hamling v. United States, 418 U.S. 87, 94 S.Ct. 2887, 41 L.Ed.2d 590 (1974), *65*

Hans v. Louisiana, 134 U.S. 1, 10 S.Ct. 504, 33 L.Ed. 842 (1890), *388*

Harlow v. Fitzgerald, 457 U.S. 800, 102 S.Ct. 2727, 73 L.Ed.2d 396 (1982), *391, 394*

Harmelin v. Michigan, 501 U.S. 957, 111 S.Ct. 2680, 115 L.Ed.2d 836 (1991), *152, 153, 156, 157, 158*

Harris v. Angelina County, Texas, 31 F.3d 331 (5th Cir.1994), *404*

Harris v. United States, 536 U.S. 545, 122 S.Ct. 2406, 153 L.Ed.2d 524 (2002), *61*

Heck v. Humphrey, 512 U.S. 477, 114 S.Ct. 2364, 129 L.Ed.2d 383 (1994), *409, 410, 411, 412*

Helling v. McKinney, 509 U.S. 25, 113 S.Ct. 2475, 125 L.Ed.2d 22 (1993), *363*

Henderson v. Morgan, 426 U.S. 637, 96 S.Ct. 2253, 49 L.Ed.2d 108 (1976), *18*

Hensley v. Eckerhart, 461 U.S. 424, 103 S.Ct. 1933, 76 L.Ed.2d 40 (1983), *414, 415*

Hewitt v. Helms, 482 U.S. 755, 107 S.Ct. 2672, 96 L.Ed.2d 654 (1987), *397*

Hewitt v. Helms, 459 U.S. 460, 103 S.Ct. 864, 74 L.Ed.2d 675 (1983), *285, 287, 289, 294, 298, 299, 302, 303*

Higgason v. Clark, 984 F.2d 203 (7th Cir.1993), *28*

Higgins v. Carpenter, 258 F.3d 797 (8th Cir.2001), *387*

Hill v. Lockhart, 474 U.S. 52, 106 S.Ct. 366, 88 L.Ed.2d 203 (1985), *23*

Hill v. United States, 368 U.S. 424, 82 S.Ct. 468, 7 L.Ed.2d 417 (1962), *54*

Hitchcock v. Dugger, 481 U.S. 393, 107 S.Ct. 1821, 95 L.Ed.2d 347 (1987), *140*

Holloway v. Brush, 220 F.3d 767 (6th Cir.2000), *374*

Hope v. Pelzer, 536 U.S. 730, 122 S.Ct. 2508, 153 L.Ed.2d 666 (2002), *369, 392*

Hudson v. McMillian, 503 U.S. 1, 112 S.Ct. 995, 117 L.Ed.2d 156 (1992), *369, 370*

Hudson v. Palmer, 468 U.S. 517, 104 S.Ct. 3194, 82 L.Ed.2d 393 (1984), *318, 319, 321, 337, 341*

Hughes v. Rowe, 449 U.S. 5, 101 S.Ct. 173, 66 L.Ed.2d 163 (1980), *413*

Hull, Ex parte, 312 U.S. 546, 61 S.Ct. 640, 85 L.Ed. 1034 (1941), *253*

Hunter v. Underwood, 471 U.S. 222, 105 S.Ct. 1916, 85 L.Ed.2d 222 (1985), *200*

Hutto v. Davis, 454 U.S. 370, 102 S.Ct. 703, 70 L.Ed.2d 556 (1982), *150, 151*

Hutto v. Finney, 437 U.S. 678, 98 S.Ct. 2565, 57 L.Ed.2d 522 (1978), *361, 391*

Illinois v. Perkins, 496 U.S. 292, 110 S.Ct. 2394, 110 L.Ed.2d 243 (1990), *280*

Iowa v. Tovar, 541 U.S. 77, 124 S.Ct. 1379, 158 L.Ed.2d 209 (2004), *21*

Jackson, United States v., 390 U.S. 570, 88 S.Ct. 1209, 20 L.Ed.2d 138 (1968), *20, 41*

Jacobs v. West Feliciana Sheriff's Dept., 228 F.3d 388 (5th Cir.2000), *372*

Jeldness v. Pearce, 30 F.3d 1220 (9th Cir.1994), *315*

Johnson v. Avery, 393 U.S. 483, 89 S.Ct. 747, 21 L.Ed.2d 718 (1969), *258, 259, 260, 261*

Johnson v. California, ___ U.S. ___, 125 S.Ct. 1141, 160 L.Ed.2d 949 (2005), *310, 311*

Johnson v. Daley, 339 F.3d 582 (7th Cir.2003), *419*

Johnson v. Jones, 515 U.S. 304, 115 S.Ct. 2151, 132 L.Ed.2d 238 (1995), *395*

Johnson v. Mississippi, 486 U.S. 578, 108 S.Ct. 1981, 100 L.Ed.2d 575 (1988), *76*

Johnson v. United States, 763 A.2d 707 (D.C.2000), *173*

Jones v. North Carolina Prisoners' Labor Union, Inc., 433 U.S. 119, 97 S.Ct. 2532, 53 L.Ed.2d 629 (1977), *229, 230, 239, 315*

Jordan v. Gardner, 986 F.2d 1521 (9th Cir.1993), *333*

Kansas v. Crane, 534 U.S. 407, 122 S.Ct. 867, 151 L.Ed.2d 856 (2002), *206, 207*

Kansas v. Hendricks, 521 U.S. 346, 117 S.Ct. 2072, 138 L.Ed.2d 501 (1997), *204, 207*

Kentucky v. Graham, 473 U.S. 159, 105 S.Ct. 3099, 87 L.Ed.2d 114 (1985), *391*

Kentucky Dept. of Corrections v. Thompson, 490 U.S. 454, 109 S.Ct. 1904, 104 L.Ed.2d 506 (1989), *286, 287, 288*

Kincade, United States v., 379 F.3d 813 (9th Cir.2004), *181*

Klinger v. Department of Corrections, 31 F.3d 727 (8th Cir. 1994), *314*

Knights, United States v., 534 U.S. 112, 122 S.Ct. 587, 151 L.Ed.2d 497 (2001), *180*

Lackawanna County Dist. Attorney v. Coss, 532 U.S. 394, 121 S.Ct. 1567, 149 L.Ed.2d 608 (2001), *78*

Lankford v. Idaho, 500 U.S. 110, 111 S.Ct. 1723, 114 L.Ed.2d 173 (1991), *53*

Lee v. Downs, 641 F.2d 1117 (4th Cir.1981), *328*

Lee v. Washington, 390 U.S. 333, 88 S.Ct. 994, 19 L.Ed.2d 1212 (1968), *310*

Lewis v. Casey, 518 U.S. 343, 116 S.Ct. 2174, 135 L.Ed.2d 606 (1996), *256, 258, 262, 263, 265, 266, 404*

Lockhart v. Fretwell, 506 U.S. 364, 113 S.Ct. 838, 122 L.Ed.2d 180 (1993), *48*

Logan v. Zimmerman Brush Co., 455 U.S. 422, 102 S.Ct. 1148, 71 L.Ed.2d 265 (1982), *342*

Lynce v. Mathis, 519 U.S. 433, 117 S.Ct. 891, 137 L.Ed.2d 63 (1997), *104*

Mabry v. Johnson, 467 U.S. 504, 104 S.Ct. 2543, 81 L.Ed.2d 437 (1984), *31*

Madrid v. Gomez, 889 F.Supp. 1146 (N.D.Cal.1995), *351*

Madyun v. Franzen, 704 F.2d 954 (7th Cir.1983), *333*

Maher v. Gagne, 448 U.S. 122, 100 S.Ct. 2570, 65 L.Ed.2d 653 (1980), *413*

Maine v. Moulton, 474 U.S. 159, 106 S.Ct. 477, 88 L.Ed.2d 481 (1985), *255*

Manes v. State, 92 P.3d 289 (Wyo.2004), *159*

Mapp v. Ohio, 367 U.S. 643, 81 S.Ct. 1684, 6 L.Ed.2d 1081 (1961), *183, 217*

Mathews v. Eldridge, 424 U.S. 319, 96 S.Ct. 893, 47 L.Ed.2d 18 (1976), *50, 193, 298, 299, 300, 302, 303, 307*

Mathis v. United States, 391 U.S. 1, 88 S.Ct. 1503, 20 L.Ed.2d 381 (1968), *280*

Maynard v. Cartwright, 486 U.S. 356, 108 S.Ct. 1853, 100 L.Ed.2d 372 (1988), *137*

McCarthy v. Bronson, 500 U.S. 136, 111 S.Ct. 1737, 114 L.Ed.2d 194 (1991), *382*

McCleskey v. Kemp, 481 U.S. 279, 107 S.Ct. 1756, 95 L.Ed.2d 262 (1987), *135, 136*

McCoy v. Nevada Dept. of Prisons, 776 F.Supp. 521 (D.Nev. 1991), *314*

McKune v. Lile, 536 U.S. 24, 122 S.Ct. 2017, 153 L.Ed.2d 47 (2002), *178, 307, 308, 309*

McMann v. Richardson, 397 U.S. 759, 90 S.Ct. 1441, 25 L.Ed.2d 763 (1970), *22*

McMillan v. Pennsylvania, 477 U.S. 79, 106 S.Ct. 2411, 91 L.Ed.2d 67 (1986), *59, 61, 62*

Meachum v. Fano, 427 U.S. 215, 96 S.Ct. 2532, 49 L.Ed.2d 451 (1976), *284, 285, 286*

Mempa v. Rhay, 389 U.S. 128, 88 S.Ct. 254, 19 L.Ed.2d 336 (1967), *45*

Menna v. New York, 423 U.S. 61, 96 S.Ct. 241, 46 L.Ed.2d 195 (1975), *24, 25*

Meyers v. Gillis, 93 F.3d 1147 (3rd Cir.1996), *28*

Mezzanatto, United States v., 513 U.S. 196, 115 S.Ct. 797, 130 L.Ed.2d 697 (1995), *42*

Michenfelder v. Sumner, 860 F.2d 328 (9th Cir.1988), *195, 327, 328*

Miles v. Dorsey, 61 F.3d 1459 (10th Cir.1995), *37*

Miller v. Florida, 482 U.S. 423, 107 S.Ct. 2446, 96 L.Ed.2d 351 (1987), *103*

Miller v. French, 530 U.S. 327, 120 S.Ct. 2246, 147 L.Ed.2d 326 (2000), *429, 430*

Minnesota v. Murphy, 465 U.S. 420, 104 S.Ct. 1136, 79 L.Ed.2d 409 (1984), *174, 176*

Miranda v. Arizona, 384 U.S. 436, 86 S.Ct. 1602, 16 L.Ed.2d 694 (1966), *175, 217, 279, 280, 281*

Missouri v. Jenkins, 495 U.S. 33, 110 S.Ct. 1651, 109 L.Ed.2d 31 (1990), *405*

Missouri v. Jenkins by Agyei, 491 U.S. 274, 109 S.Ct. 2463, 105 L.Ed.2d 229 (1989), *415, 417*

Mitchell v. Forsyth, 472 U.S. 511, 105 S.Ct. 2806, 86 L.Ed.2d 411 (1985), *394*

Mitchell v. United States, 526 U.S. 314, 119 S.Ct. 1307, 143 L.Ed.2d 424 (1999), *29, 72*

Mitchell, United States v., 463 U.S. 206, 103 S.Ct. 2961, 77 L.Ed.2d 580 (1983), *388*

Monell v. Department of Social Services of City of New York, 436 U.S. 658, 98 S.Ct. 2018, 56 L.Ed.2d 611 (1978), *374, 378*

Monge v. California, 524 U.S. 721, 118 S.Ct. 2246, 141 L.Ed.2d 615 (1998), *67*

Monroe v. Pape, 365 U.S. 167, 81 S.Ct. 473, 5 L.Ed.2d 492 (1961), *217, 376*

Montanye v. Haymes, 427 U.S. 236, 96 S.Ct. 2543, 49 L.Ed.2d 466 (1976), *285*

Moody v. Daggett, 429 U.S. 78, 97 S.Ct. 274, 50 L.Ed.2d 236 (1976), *169*

Moore v. Carwell, 168 F.3d 234 (5th Cir.1999), *326*

Morrissey v. Brewer, 408 U.S. 471, 92 S.Ct. 2593, 33 L.Ed.2d 484 (1972), *166, 169, 170*

Muhammad v. Close, 540 U.S. 749, 124 S.Ct. 1303, 158 L.Ed.2d 32 (2004), *410*

Murray v. Giarratano, 492 U.S. 1, 109 S.Ct. 2765, 106 L.Ed.2d 1 (1989), *261*

Neitzke v. Williams, 490 U.S. 319, 109 S.Ct. 1827, 104 L.Ed.2d 338 (1989), *385*

Newport, City of v. Fact Concerts, Inc., 453 U.S. 247, 101 S.Ct. 2748, 69 L.Ed.2d 616 (1981), *395*

Newton, Town of v. Rumery, 480 U.S. 386, 107 S.Ct. 1187, 94 L.Ed.2d 405 (1987), *43, 44*

Ngiraingas v. Sanchez, 495 U.S. 182, 110 S.Ct. 1737, 109 L.Ed.2d 163 (1990), *375*

Nichols v. United States, 511 U.S. 738, 114 S.Ct. 1921, 128 L.Ed.2d 745 (1994), *46, 72*

North Carolina v. Alford, 400 U.S. 25, 91 S.Ct. 160, 27 L.Ed.2d 162 (1970), *27, 28*

North Carolina v. Pearce, 395 U.S. 711, 89 S.Ct. 2072, 23 L.Ed.2d 656 (1969), *34, 39, 58, 67*

O'Bryan v. Bureau of Prisons, 349 F.3d 399 (7th Cir.2003), *250*

Ohio Adult Parole Authority v. Woodard, 523 U.S. 272, 118 S.Ct. 1244, 140 L.Ed.2d 387 (1998), *187, 188*

Oklahoma City, City of v. Tuttle, 471 U.S. 808, 105 S.Ct. 2427, 85 L.Ed.2d 791 (1985), *378*

Olim v. Wakinekona, 461 U.S. 238, 103 S.Ct. 1741, 75 L.Ed.2d 813 (1983), *285*

Oliver v. Scott, 276 F.3d 736 (5th Cir.2002), *326*

O'Lone v. Estate of Shabazz, 482 U.S. 342, 107 S.Ct. 2400, 96 L.Ed.2d 282 (1987), *245, 248, 249*

Ortiz v. Stewart, 149 F.3d 923 (9th Cir.1998), *53*

Oses v. Fair, 739 F.Supp. 707 (D.Mass.1990), *371*

Overton v. Bazzetta, 539 U.S. 126, 123 S.Ct. 2162, 156 L.Ed.2d 162 (2003), *243, 363*

Owen v. City of Independence, Missouri, 445 U.S. 622, 100 S.Ct. 1398, 63 L.Ed.2d 673 (1980), *395*

Owens v. Okure, 488 U.S. 235, 109 S.Ct. 573, 102 L.Ed.2d 594 (1989), *397*

Paredez, State v., 136 N.M. 533, 101 P.3d 799 (N.M.2004), *19*

Parke v. Raley, 506 U.S. 20, 113 S.Ct. 517, 121 L.Ed.2d 391 (1992), *17*

Parratt v. Taylor, 451 U.S. 527, 101 S.Ct. 1908, 68 L.Ed.2d 420 (1981), *340, 341, 342*

Patsy v. Board of Regents of State of Florida, 457 U.S. 496, 102 S.Ct. 2557, 73 L.Ed.2d 172 (1982), *398*

Payne v. Tennessee, 501 U.S. 808, 111 S.Ct. 2597, 115 L.Ed.2d 720 (1991), *82, 84*

Peckham v. Wisconsin Dept. of Corrections, 141 F.3d 694 (7th Cir.1998), *326*

Pell v. Procunier, 417 U.S. 817, 94 S.Ct. 2800, 41 L.Ed.2d 495 (1974), *226, 227, 228, 229, 231, 233, 242*

Pennsylvania v. Finley, 481 U.S. 551, 107 S.Ct. 1990, 95 L.Ed.2d 539 (1987), *261*

Pennsylvania Bd. of Probation and Parole v. Scott, 524 U.S. 357, 118 S.Ct. 2014, 141 L.Ed.2d 344 (1998), *181, 183*

Penry v. Lynaugh, 492 U.S. 302, 109 S.Ct. 2934, 106 L.Ed.2d 256 (1989), *143, 144*

People v. _____ (see opposing party)

Peterson v. Shanks, 149 F.3d 1140 (10th Cir.1998), *269*

Pitts v. Thornburgh, 866 F.2d 1450, 275 U.S.App.D.C. 332 (D.C.Cir.1989), *315*

Plaut v. Spendthrift Farm, Inc., 514 U.S. 211, 115 S.Ct. 1447, 131 L.Ed.2d 328 (1995), *428, 429*

Ponte v. Real, 471 U.S. 491, 105 S.Ct. 2192, 85 L.Ed.2d 553 (1985), *272*

Preiser v. Rodriguez, 411 U.S. 475, 93 S.Ct. 1827, 36 L.Ed.2d 439 (1973), *408*

Procunier v. Martinez, 416 U.S. 396, 94 S.Ct. 1800, 40 L.Ed.2d 224 (1974), *223, 227, 228, 233, 236, 237, 253, 256, 257*

Procunier v. Navarette, 434 U.S. 555, 98 S.Ct. 855, 55 L.Ed.2d 24 (1978), *392*

Quern v. Jordan, 440 U.S. 332, 99 S.Ct. 1139, 59 L.Ed.2d 358 (1979), *389*

Ramos v. Lamm, 639 F.2d 559 (10th Cir.1980), *263*

Rauser v. Horn, 241 F.3d 330 (3rd Cir.2001), *269*

Reeves v. Pettcox, 19 F.3d 1060 (5th Cir.1994), *278*

Reno v. Koray, 515 U.S. 50, 115 S.Ct. 2021, 132 L.Ed.2d 46 (1995), *90*

Revere, City of v. Massachusetts General Hosp., 463 U.S. 239, 103 S.Ct. 2979, 77 L.Ed.2d 605 (1983), *351*

Rhodes v. Chapman, 452 U.S. 337, 101 S.Ct. 2392, 69 L.Ed.2d 59 (1981), *359, 361*

Richardson v. McKnight, 521 U.S. 399, 117 S.Ct. 2100, 138 L.Ed.2d 540 (1997), *396*

Richardson v. Ramirez, 418 U.S. 24, 94 S.Ct. 2655, 41 L.Ed.2d 551 (1974), *199, 200*

Ricketts v. Adamson, 483 U.S. 1, 107 S.Ct. 2680, 97 L.Ed.2d 1 (1987), *32, 33*

Ring v. Arizona, 536 U.S. 584, 122 S.Ct. 2428, 153 L.Ed.2d 556 (2002), *63*

Riverside, City of v. Rivera, 477 U.S. 561, 106 S.Ct. 2686, 91 L.Ed.2d 466 (1986), *418*

Roberts v. Louisiana, 431 U.S. 633, 97 S.Ct. 1993, 52 L.Ed.2d 637 (1977), *139*

Roberts v. State of Rhode Island, 239 F.3d 107 (1st Cir.2001), *325*

Roberts v. United States, 445 U.S. 552, 100 S.Ct. 1358, 63 L.Ed.2d 622 (1980), *71*

Robinson v. California, 370 U.S. 660, 82 S.Ct. 1417, 8 L.Ed.2d 758 (1962), *217*

Roe v. Flores–Ortega, 528 U.S. 470, 120 S.Ct. 1029, 145 L.Ed.2d 985 (2000), *26*

Roper v. Simmons, ___ U.S. ___, 125 S.Ct. 1183, 161 L.Ed.2d 1 (2005), *144, 145*

Royal v. Kautzky, 375 F.3d 720 (8th Cir.2004), *402*

Ruffin v. Commonwealth, 62 Va. 790 (Va.1871), *214*

Rufo v. Inmates of Suffolk County Jail, 502 U.S. 367, 112 S.Ct. 748, 116 L.Ed.2d 867 (1992), *420, 423, 424, 425, 427*

Ruiz, United States v., 536 U.S. 622, 122 S.Ct. 2450, 153 L.Ed.2d 586 (2002), *20, 21*

Rummel v. Estelle, 445 U.S. 263, 100 S.Ct. 1133, 63 L.Ed.2d 382 (1980), *148, 149, 150, 151, 153*

Sandin v. Conner, 515 U.S. 472, 115 S.Ct. 2293, 132 L.Ed.2d 418 (1995), *188, 189, 271, 289, 290, 291, 292, 294, 305, 308, 309*

Santobello v. New York, 404 U.S. 257, 92 S.Ct. 495, 30 L.Ed.2d 427 (1971), *30, 31, 32*

Saxbe v. Washington Post Co., 417 U.S. 843, 94 S.Ct. 2811, 41 L.Ed.2d 514 (1974), *228*

Schware v. Board of Bar Exam. of State of New Mexico, 353 U.S. 232, 77 S.Ct. 752, 1 L.Ed.2d 796 (1957), *212*

Scott v. Illinois, 440 U.S. 367, 99 S.Ct. 1158, 59 L.Ed.2d 383 (1979), *45, 46*

Seling v. Young, 531 U.S. 250, 121 S.Ct. 727, 148 L.Ed.2d 734 (2001), *208*

Shafer v. South Carolina, 532 U.S. 36, 121 S.Ct. 1263, 149 L.Ed.2d 178 (2001), *141*

Sharpe, United States v., 470 U.S. 675, 105 S.Ct. 1568, 84 L.Ed.2d 605 (1985), *323*

Shaw v. Murphy, 532 U.S. 223, 121 S.Ct. 1475, 149 L.Ed.2d 420 (2001), *267*

Silverman, United States v., 976 F.2d 1502 (6th Cir.1992), *57*

Simmons v. South Carolina, 512 U.S. 154, 114 S.Ct. 2187, 129 L.Ed.2d 133 (1994), *52*

Smith v. Campbell, 250 F.3d 1032 (6th Cir.2001), *268*

Smith v. Doe, 538 U.S. 84, 123 S.Ct. 1140, 155 L.Ed.2d 164 (2003), *203, 204*

Smith v. Wade, 461 U.S. 30, 103 S.Ct. 1625, 75 L.Ed.2d 632 (1983), *402*

Solem v. Helm, 463 U.S. 277, 103 S.Ct. 3001, 77 L.Ed.2d 637 (1983), *151, 153, 154, 155, 156, 158*

Somers v. Thurman, 109 F.3d 614 (9th Cir.1997), *331*

Sosna v. Iowa, 419 U.S. 393, 95 S.Ct. 553, 42 L.Ed.2d 532 (1975), *398*

Spaziano v. Florida, 468 U.S. 447, 104 S.Ct. 3154, 82 L.Ed.2d 340 (1984), *62*

Spencer v. Kemna, 523 U.S. 1, 118 S.Ct. 978, 140 L.Ed.2d 43 (1998), *411*

Stanford v. Kentucky, 492 U.S. 361, 109 S.Ct. 2969, 106 L.Ed.2d 306 (1989), *144*

State v. _____ (see opposing party)

Stewart v. Rhodes, 473 F.Supp. 1185 (S.D.Ohio 1979), *313*

St. Louis, City of v. Praprotnik, 485 U.S. 112, 108 S.Ct. 915, 99 L.Ed.2d 107 (1988), *378*

Strickland v. Washington, 466 U.S. 668, 104 S.Ct. 2052, 80 L.Ed.2d 674 (1984), *22, 47, 48*

Sumner v. Shuman, 483 U.S. 66, 107 S.Ct. 2716, 97 L.Ed.2d 56 (1987), *139*

Superintendent, Massachusetts Correctional Institution, Walpole v. Hill, 472 U.S. 445, 105 S.Ct. 2768, 86 L.Ed.2d 356 (1985), *277, 278*

Tate v. Short, 401 U.S. 395, 91 S.Ct. 668, 28 L.Ed.2d 130 (1971), *117*

Texas v. McCullough, 475 U.S. 134, 106 S.Ct. 976, 89 L.Ed.2d 104 (1986), *39, 58*

Texas State Teachers Ass'n v. Garland Independent School Dist., 489 U.S. 782, 109 S.Ct. 1486, 103 L.Ed.2d 866 (1989), *413*

Thornburgh v. Abbott, 490 U.S. 401, 109 S.Ct. 1874, 104 L.Ed.2d 459 (1989), *236, 238*

Timm v. Gunter, 917 F.2d 1093 (8th Cir.1990), *329, 329, 331, 332*

Tison v. Arizona, 481 U.S. 137, 107 S.Ct. 1676, 95 L.Ed.2d 127 (1987), *142*

Tollett v. Henderson, 411 U.S. 258, 93 S.Ct. 1602, 36 L.Ed.2d 235 (1973), *23, 24*

Tourscher v. McCullough, 184 F.3d 236 (3rd Cir.1999), *343*

Town of (see name of town)

Townsend v. Burke, 334 U.S. 736, 68 S.Ct. 1252, 92 L.Ed. 1690 (1948), *74, 75*

Tucker, United States v., 404 U.S. 443, 92 S.Ct. 589, 30 L.Ed.2d 592 (1972), *75, 76, 77*

Turner v. Safley, 482 U.S. 78, 107 S.Ct. 2254, 96 L.Ed.2d 64 (1987), *231, 232, 233, 235, 237, 240, 242, 244, 245, 246, 257, 266, 267, 311, 312, 313, 326, 355*

United States v. _____ (see opposing party)

Valentine v. Englehardt, 474 F.Supp. 294 (D.N.J.1979), *234*

Venegas v. Mitchell, 495 U.S. 82, 110 S.Ct. 1679, 109 L.Ed.2d 74 (1990), *417*

Vitek v. Jones, 445 U.S. 480, 100 S.Ct. 1254, 63 L.Ed.2d 552 (1980), *278, 285, 287, 296, 298, 299, 307, 397*

Walker v. Bain, 257 F.3d 660 (6th Cir.2001), *403*

Walton v. Arizona, 497 U.S. 639, 110 S.Ct. 3047, 111 L.Ed.2d 511 (1990), *59, 141*

Washington v. Harper, 494 U.S. 210, 110 S.Ct. 1028, 108 L.Ed.2d 178 (1990), *305, 306, 307, 311, 354, 355, 356, 357*

Washington v. Lee, 263 F.Supp. 327 (M.D.Ala.1966), *309*

Watson v. Graves, 909 F.2d 1549 (5th Cir.1990), *345*

Watts, United States v., 519 U.S. 148, 117 S.Ct. 633, 136 L.Ed.2d 554 (1997), *69*

Weaver v. Graham, 450 U.S. 24, 101 S.Ct. 960, 67 L.Ed.2d 17 (1981), *104*

Weekly, United States v., 118 F.3d 576 (8th Cir.1997), *56*

Wellman v. Faulkner, 715 F.2d 269 (7th Cir.1983), *351*

West v. Atkins, 487 U.S. 42, 108 S.Ct. 2250, 101 L.Ed.2d 40 (1988), *377*

White v. Morris, 832 F.Supp. 1129 (S.D.Ohio 1993), *313*

Whitford v. Boglino, 63 F.3d 527 (7th Cir.1995), *278*

Whitley v. Albers, 475 U.S. 312, 106 S.Ct. 1078, 89 L.Ed.2d 251 (1986), *365, 367, 369*

Wilkinson v. Dotson, ___ U.S. ___, 125 S.Ct. 1242, 161 L.Ed.2d 253 (2005), *292, 304, 411*

Will v. Michigan Dept. of State Police, 491 U.S. 58, 109 S.Ct. 2304, 105 L.Ed.2d 45 (1989), *375, 388, 395*

Williams v. Illinois, 399 U.S. 235, 90 S.Ct. 2018, 26 L.Ed.2d 586 (1970), *117*

Williams v. People of State of New York, 337 U.S. 241, 69 S.Ct. 1079, 93 L.Ed. 1337 (1949), *56, 69, 70*

Williams v. Taylor, 529 U.S. 362, 120 S.Ct. 1495, 146 L.Ed.2d 389 (2000), *48*

Wilson v. City of Kalamazoo, 127 F.Supp.2d 855 (W.D.Mich. 2000), *321*

Wilson v. Garcia, 471 U.S. 261, 105 S.Ct. 1938, 85 L.Ed.2d 254 (1985), *397*

Wilson v. Seiter, 501 U.S. 294, 111 S.Ct. 2321, 115 L.Ed.2d 271 (1991), *362, 364*

Wisconsin v. Mitchell, 508 U.S. 476, 113 S.Ct. 2194, 124 L.Ed.2d 436 (1993), *74*

Witte v. United States, 515 U.S. 389, 115 S.Ct. 2199, 132 L.Ed.2d 351 (1995), *67*

Wolff v. McDonnell, 418 U.S. 539, 94 S.Ct. 2963, 41 L.Ed.2d 935 (1974), *172, 190, 193, 213, 254, 260, 271, 272, 273, 274, 275, 277, 278, 289, 305*

Woodson v. North Carolina, 428 U.S. 280, 96 S.Ct. 2978, 49 L.Ed.2d 944 (1976), *137, 138, 139*

Young v. Harper, 520 U.S. 143, 117 S.Ct. 1148, 137 L.Ed.2d 270 (1997), *170*

Zablocki v. Redhail, 434 U.S. 374, 98 S.Ct. 673, 54 L.Ed.2d 618 (1978), *325, 326*

Zentmyer v. Kendall County, Illinois, 220 F.3d 805 (7th Cir. 2000), *352*

Zinermon v. Burch, 494 U.S. 113, 110 S.Ct. 975, 108 L.Ed.2d 100 (1990), *341*

*

THE LAW AND POLICY OF SENTENCING AND CORRECTIONS

IN A NUTSHELL

Seventh Edition

*

PART ONE

THE LAW AND POLICY OF SENTENCING

CHAPTER 1

INTRODUCTION TO SENTENCING

For most judges, some of the most difficult, and sometimes wrenching, decisions that they must make concern the sentences to be imposed on persons convicted of crimes. The difficulty of these decisions is compounded by the fact that in many jurisdictions, judges still have few sentencing options from which to choose. Their options are often confined to incarceration in prison or jail, probation, or a fine.

The problem with this type of simplistic sentencing structure is that criminal behavior often cannot be pigeonholed into one of only three slots. Crimes cover a wide spectrum of criminal behavior, which means that a wide array of criminal sanctions must be available if judges are to be able to impose the most appropriate penalty on a criminal offender. A fine may be an unsuitable sanction in a particular case because public-safety needs require that the offender be supervised and monitored for a defined period of time, whether in the community or in a correctional institution. Probation may be ill-advised because of the seriousness of the offender's crime or because the offender requires a level of supervision greater than that accompanying probation in its traditional form. But incarceration may be unnecessary under the circumstances, and in fact counterproductive because of its negative effects on incarcerated individuals and their families.

It is therefore critically important that sentencing systems be structured so that judges can impose the most appropriate sentence on convicted offenders. For what is ultimately at stake when devising the nation's sentencing systems is the public's safety, billions of dollars of taxpayers' money, and the very justness of the criminal-justice system.

A. THE PURPOSES OF CRIMINAL SENTENCES

What penalty or penalties should be imposed on an individual for a crime depends on the purpose or purposes of a criminal sentence. Traditionally, it has been said in this country that criminal sanctions have four principal purposes.

The first touted purpose of punishment is to deter future crimes. This deterrent objective has two dimensions—what is known as specific deterrence and general deterrence. The focus of specific deterrence is on the actual offender; the goal is to impose a punishment that will dissuade the offender from committing crimes in the future. On the other hand, general deterrence, as its name suggests, has a broader objective—inducing the public to refrain from criminal conduct by using the person sentenced for a crime as an example of what will befall a person who violates the law.

The deterrent rationale for punishment, particularly punishment in the form of incarceration, has increasingly come under attack in recent years. Critics point to the extremely high recidivism rates of individuals released from prison as evidence of the lack of success of specific deterrence. These critics also emphasize that it is the certainty of apprehension and punishment, rather than the amount of punishment, that has the greatest effect in deterring crimes.

The second purpose of criminal punishment is incapacitation, which entails making it physically difficult or impossible for a person convicted of a crime to commit further crimes—or at least crimes against the public—while serving a sentence. The primary means of incapacitation is incarceration, although some community-based sanctions, such as electronically-monitored home confinement, have some incapacitation benefits.

In recent years, incarceration proponents have embraced incapacitation as a primary purpose of incarceration. These proponents argue that because imprisonment averts many crimes that would otherwise have been committed had prisoners remained within the community, all that we need to do to be safer is incarcerate more criminals.

Others have decried what they consider a facile argument that exaggerates incarceration's incapacitative benefits while overlooking its drawbacks. According to these critics, to argue that we should just "lock them all up" ignores the fact that "they" are not all the same. A drug offender is not the same as a rapist, a thief is not the same as a murderer, and an embezzler is not the same as a pedophile in terms of the risks posed to the public's safety. So incapacitative benefits vary, depending on whom we are locking up. In addition, as the incapacitation net is expanded further, more marginal offenders, who would have committed relatively minor crimes, are caught in its web.

The incapacitative benefits of locking up certain types of criminals, particularly drug dealers, are also limited by what is called the "replacement effect." Because there is a market for drugs, the drug dealers who are imprisoned are typically replaced soon by others who fill their niche in the drug-dealing market.

The incarceration, for incapacitative purposes, of offenders who could be punished effectively in the community is also extremely costly, leading to the expenditure of billions of dollars to build and operate the prisons to hold these offenders. But the costs stemming from unnecessary incarceration are not solely financial. Incarceration exacts a human toll as well, having deleterious effects on the children of prisoners and sometimes leading to the disintegration of prisoners' families. Another, sometimes overlooked, cost of incapacitation-driven sentencing policies is that they actually may endanger the public's safety, depending on whom is incarcerated. Researchers have found, for example, that community-based drug treatment for drug offenders is much more effective than incarceration in reducing crime. *See, e.g.*, C. Peter Rydell & Susan S. Everingham, *Controlling Cocaine: Supply Versus Demand Programs* xvi (1994).

Finally, the argument for incarcerating more convicted criminals for incapacitation purposes gives short shrift to the problem of "false positives"— persons who are incarcerated for incapacitation purposes but who, in fact, would not have committed additional crimes, or would have committed relatively minor crimes, had they been punished in the community. The costs, both human and financial, incurred when persons who are "false positives" are incarcerated are high, while the benefits, from an incapacitation standpoint, are nil.

A third reason cited for imposing criminal sanctions is rehabilitation. A certain penalty is imposed on an offender, such as mandatory drug treatment, to assist the offender in overcoming criminal propensities.

The rehabilitative objective of criminal sanctions has proven to be controversial when offenders are sent to prison, supposedly for rehabilitation purposes. Critics argue that to pretend that prison is somehow good for a person ignores the negative effects of incarceration, including the criminogenic influences to which prisoners are exposed. In addition, in recent years correctional officials, both within and outside prisons, have balked at the notion that they can somehow rehabilitate offenders. These officials argue that if given adequate funds, they can, at most, provide offenders with the tools, such as an education and job skills, through which offenders can rehabilitate themselves.

The final purpose of punishment that is commonly invoked is retribution. Retribution is simply punishment for punishment's sake—punishment because the offender deserves to be punished. The proponents of retribution typically acknowledge that the retributive aim of punishment should be qualified by the limiting principle known as "just deserts." This principle directs that while offenders may be punished because they deserve to be punished, they should be punished no more than is warranted by the severity of the crimes of which they were convicted.

Another limiting principle that may affect both the implementation and execution of a criminal sentence is known as the "parsimony principle" or "least-restrictive-alternative principle." Under this principle, offenders should receive the least restrictive sanction that will meet the sentence's penological goal or goals. Thus, if either of two sanctions would penalize an offender in a way that is commensurate with the severity of his or her crime—in other words, in keeping with the principle of "just deserts," application of the parsimony principle would lead to imposition of the penalty that is the least restrictive. For example, if both work release and confinement in jail twenty-four hours a day were viable and appropriate sentencing options, the parsimony principle typically would direct that the judge sentence the defendant to work release.

This least-restrictive-alternative principle can be and is incorporated into corrections systems as well as sentencing systems. When applied in the correctional context, correctional officials place offenders in the least restrictive facilities and programs that are deemed appropriate for the offender. For example, application of the least-restrictive-alternative principle would dictate that a low-risk prisoner be housed in a minimum-security prison, not a medium- or maximum-security prison.

The retributive aim of criminal sanctions is to be contrasted with a fifth purpose of sentencing that has been espoused with increasing frequency in recent years, a purpose that is subsumed within the phrase, "restorative justice." The premise of restorative justice is that offenders should be held accountable for the harm caused by their crimes. Restorative justice therefore seeks to involve offenders in repairing the harm that they have caused victims, the community, themselves, and their families through their criminal behavior.

Victim-offender mediation programs are one of the primary means through which restorative-justice principles are implemented. During the mediation process, an offender and the victim of the offender's crime meet together in the presence of a trained mediator. During the mediation session or sessions, the victim is given the opportunity to explain to the offender how the crime has affected the victim. The victim can also ask the offender questions about the crime that may have been troubling the victim, such as why the offender chose the victim's home to burglarize or what the victim might have done to avert the crime. Finally, the offender is given the opportunity to discuss his or her views about the crime. This discussion will often culminate in an expression of remorse for the crime.

The victim and the offender will then try to reach an agreement about what the offender can and should do to redress the harm caused by the offender's crime. This agreement may, for example, require the offender to pay restitution to the victim, to perform work for the victim, or to perform community service. The agreement may also require the offender to take steps to resolve some of the offender's personal problems that may have contributed to the offender's criminal behavior. The offender may, for example, agree to obtain substance-abuse treatment or to secure a GED.

One of the chief advantages of victim-offender mediation programs is that they humanize the criminal-justice process. During a mediation session, offenders often realize, for the first time, the human impact of their crimes. They are then less able to rationalize, as they typically do, their criminal behavior. At the same time, victims see the human side of the person otherwise impersonally known as "the offender" and gain an understanding of what that person is like and of the factors that may have contributed to that person's criminal behavior.

Victim-offender mediation programs typically require that the participation of victims and offenders in the programs be voluntary. This requirement springs from the recognition that a mediation program's purposes would be undermined if victims and offenders were forced to participate in them. Forcing offenders to participate in them would run the risk of aggravating, rather than repairing, the harm caused by their crimes. In addition, forcing victims to participate in the mediation programs would augment the sense of loss of control felt by persons who have been victimized by crime. For additional information about victim-offender mediation programs, see Mark S. Umbreit, *The Handbook of Victim Offender Mediation* (2001).

Restorative justice is also effectuated through other means. For example, family group conferencing brings family members and friends, as well as the victim and the offender, into the mediation process. Some communities utilize community reparative boards, which discuss the effects of a crime with an offender, work with the offender to develop a sanctioning agreement that reflects reparative goals, and then monitor the offender's compliance with the agreement. Finally, victim-offender panels can be used for restorative purposes when either a victim or the offender refuses to participate in mediation. For example, several victims of drunk drivers can appear before a group of offenders convicted of drunk driving to discuss the impact of drunk driving on the victims and their families.

Restorative-justice programs can be integrated into various stages of the criminal-justice process. For example, victim-offender mediation may occur as part of a pretrial-diversion program that will enable the offender to avoid a criminal conviction. Alternatively, a victim-offender mediation program can be utilized following a conviction but before the sentencing of the offender, with the results of the mediation process informing the judge's sentencing decision. Finally, a convicted offender, including one incarcerated in prison, may participate in a victim-offender mediation program after having been sentenced.

Not all of the purposes of criminal sanctions meld together very well, and in fact, some of them are conflicting. For example, sending a person to prison for incapacitative purposes may undermine the rehabilitation that might occur were the offender to be punished in the community. And imposing sanctions to satisfy retributive urges to "get back" at offenders because of their crimes is at odds with the premise of restorative justice that what is most important is that offenders "give back" to victims and the community—to repair, to the extent possible, the harm caused by their crimes.

B. PROPOSALS FOR REFORM

Even a cursory look at the nation's sentencing and corrections systems reveals that something is amiss. In this country, we incarcerate more people *per capita* than any other country in the world. Billions of dollars have been, and are being, diverted from educational, health, and other governmental programs to pay the costs of building and operating a burgeoning number of prisons and jails. And what is the payoff for this enormous diversion of resources? When examined over time, crime rates appear largely unaffected by the level of incarceration. Recidivism rates are extremely high, and victims of crime feel unrequited and ignored by the criminal-justice system. Inappropriately lenient or stringent sentences are often the norm in many jurisdictions where judges are offered just two choices when sentencing criminal offenders—"slap them on the wrist" or "lock them up and throw away the key." And the system is rocked by charges that it is racist, punishing African Americans more severely than Caucasians.

This latter charge has prompted research to examine the racial disparity in the imposition of criminal punishments. According to one study whose results were published in 1995, one out of every three black men aged twenty through twenty-nine is, on any given day, in prison or jail, on probation, or on parole. By contrast, one out of every fifteen white men in that age group is under correctional supervision. Marc Mauer & Tracy Huling, *Young*

Black Americans and the Criminal Justice System: Five Years Later 1, 5 (1995). Researchers have identified multiple causes for this disparity, including both discrimination in the operations of the criminal-justice system and the disproportionate involvement of African–American men in certain types of crime. *See* Michael Tonry, *Malign Neglect: Race, Crime, and Punishment in America* 49–123 (1995).

A number of proposals have been propounded, and in some cases implemented, to make the nation's sentencing and corrections systems more equitable, accountable, and cost-effective. Some of these proposals include: (1) the adoption of comprehensive, community-corrections acts by each state and the federal government; (2) the utilization of sentencing guidelines that guide judges in the exercise of their sentencing discretion, encompass community-based sanctions, ensure that the criminal penalties imposed do not exceed the resources made available to the corrections system, and enable most nonviolent offenders to be punished in the community; (3) the repeal of mandatory-minimum sentencing provisions; and (4) the preparation and consideration of correctional-impact statements before legislation is ever enacted that increases the number of people subject to a particular sanction, such as imprisonment, or the duration of their sentences, whether incarcerative or community-based.

In ensuing chapters of this book, you will be reading about some of these proposals, which represent just a few examples of the many steps that have been recommended to improve the efficacy of the nation's corrections and sentencing systems. The reader should keep in mind, however, that even if the nation's sentencing and corrections systems are reformed to better protect the public's safety and to provide meaningful and cost-effective responses to crime, crime itself will not be eradicated. We must remember that there are limits to what the criminal-justice system can do to combat crime and that the solution to crime lies not in the criminal-justice system nor even within any other governmental program, but within our own families and ultimately, within ourselves.

CHAPTER 2

GUILTY PLEAS AND PLEA BARGAINING

A person charged with a crime can enter one of several different pleas to the charge—not guilty, guilty, or, in some jurisdictions, *nolo contendere.* A person who enters a plea of *nolo contendere* or "no contest" can be sentenced as if he or she had pleaded guilty to the crime. The principal distinction between a no-contest plea and a guilty plea is that the former type of plea cannot be introduced as evidence in a civil trial, such as one brought by a victim to obtain recompense for losses caused by the crime.

Understanding guilty pleas is critical to the understanding of the criminal-justice process, because guilty pleas play such a dominant role in that process. In fact, more than ninety percent of criminal convictions stem from guilty pleas. Bureau of Justice Statistics, U.S. Dep't of Justice, *State Court Sentencing of Convicted Felons, 2002* Table 4.2 (2005).

There are basically two types of guilty pleas— "blind pleas" and negotiated pleas. A "blind plea" is one that is entered without any promise of a concession from either the prosecutor or the judge.

14

A negotiated plea, on the other hand, reflects a *quid pro quo*. A defendant may enter a plea of guilty, for example, in return for the prosecutor's agreement to refrain from bringing additional charges, to drop other pending charges, or to make a certain sentencing recommendation to the court. Alternatively, as part of the plea agreement, the prosecutor may agree to let the defendant plead guilty to a crime that is less serious than the one with which he or she was charged initially.

The plea-bargaining process that can culminate in negotiated pleas has been castigated by critics. Some of the principal objections that have been levelled against plea bargaining include the following: (1) that the inducements offered to plead guilty pressure innocent defendants into entering pleas of guilty; (2) that the "rewarding" of those who plead guilty in effect penalizes those who exercise their constitutional right to go to trial; and (3) that public safety is jeopardized and correctional goals undermined by unduly lenient plea bargains. Critics have also noted that some prosecutors are much more willing to plea bargain when their cases are weak, thereby enhancing the risk of innocent persons being convicted.

Defense attorneys have been criticized for their role in the plea-bargaining process as well. "Quickly cop a plea and take the fee" seems to be the mantra of at least some defense attorneys. In addition, public defenders laboring under the demands of very heavy caseloads may be more likely to enter into plea bargains when it is not in their clients' best interests to do so.

Plea-bargaining proponents argue that many benefits follow from plea bargaining. Plea bargaining, for example, expedites the processing of criminal cases, preventing the breakdown of court systems that might occur if many more defendants insisted on going to trial. In addition, as cases are disposed of more quickly, defendants who are awaiting trial in jail simply because they do not have the money to post bail can be released sooner, a benefit not only to themselves and their families but to the taxpayers who are paying the expensive tab for their pretrial incarceration. Plea bargaining can also relieve the stress on victims, defendants, and their families caused by not knowing what the outcome of a criminal case will be, and it can help defendants, their families, and taxpayers avoid the expense of a criminal trial. Furthermore, plea bargaining can assist law enforcement as defendants provide information about the criminal activities of others in return for a favorable plea agreement. Finally, plea bargaining can temper the very harsh effects of certain sentencing statutes, such as those mandating imposition of a long prison sentence regardless of any facts mitigating the seriousness of the defendant's crime.

A.   INTELLIGENT AND VOLUNTARY GUILTY PLEAS

In order for a guilty plea to be constitutional, the defendant must have entered it intelligently and

voluntarily. Failure to meet either one of these
requirements violates the tenets of due process.

When a defendant is challenging the validity of a
guilty plea on appeal, a court cannot constitutionally presume that the defendant entered a valid plea.
Instead, the record must contain an "affirmative
showing" that the defendant's guilty plea was indeed rendered intelligently and voluntarily. *Boykin
v. Alabama* (S.Ct.1969).

By contrast, the Supreme Court has said that
when a defendant is challenging the validity of a
guilty plea in a collateral proceeding, one which
follows the exhaustion or relinquishment of direct
appeal rights, a court can properly presume that the
guilty plea was constitutional, at least to the extent
that the burden can be placed on the defendant to
introduce evidence of its unconstitutionality. *Parke
v. Raley* (S.Ct.1992). Whether the ultimate burden
of proof on the issue of a guilty plea's constitutionality can be placed on a defendant in a collateral
proceeding was not resolved by the Court in *Parke
v. Raley*, because the state statute whose constitutionality was at issue in that case placed the burden
of proof on the prosecution. The Court did, however, say that the preponderance-of-the-evidence standard that this statute required the prosecution to
meet clearly satisfied the requirements of due process. In other words, even if the government has the
ultimate burden of proof in a collateral proceeding
on the issue of a guilty plea's validity, the government can meet that burden by proving that it is

more likely than not that the defendant's plea was entered intelligently and voluntarily.

The Supreme Court has not fully answered the question of what is required for a guilty plea to be considered "intelligent" in the constitutional sense. From its discussion in *Boykin*, it appears as though the defendant must at least be aware of the crime with which he or she has been charged, of the potential penalties that can be imposed for that crime, and of the rights that are being surrendered through entry of the guilty plea—the right to a jury trial, the right to confront and cross-examine adverse witnesses, and the privilege not to be compelled to incriminate oneself.

In addition, in at least some circumstances, a defendant must be apprised of at least some of the elements of the crime with which he or she has been charged. In *Henderson v. Morgan* (S.Ct.1976), a defendant charged with first-degree murder pled guilty to second-degree murder. Later, he contended that his guilty plea was invalid because he was never told that to be guilty of second-degree murder, a defendant must have acted with an intent to kill the victim.

In striking down the defendant's guilty plea, the Supreme Court underscored that it was not necessarily holding that in all criminal cases in which defendants plead guilty, the defendants must first be apprised of the elements of the crime with which they have been charged. The Court noted, however, that in this case, intent to kill was "such a critical element" of the crime of second-degree murder that the defendant must have been made aware of this element for his guilty plea to meet constitutional requirements.

The Court went on to observe that ordinarily, a court might properly presume that a defendant's attorney had informed the defendant in sufficient detail of the nature of the charge to which the defendant was pleading guilty. In this case, however, such a presumption was unwarranted because the district court had specifically found that the defense attorney had not apprised the defendant of the intent-to-kill element.

Most courts have held that a defendant need not be apprised of the collateral consequences of a criminal conviction, such as that the defendant will forfeit voting rights if convicted or will be deported, in order to tender a guilty plea "intelligently" in the constitutional sense. *See State v. Paredez* (N.M. 2004) (listing cases). The distinction typically drawn between a direct consequence and collateral consequence of a conviction is that a direct consequence, such as placement on probation, is part of the defendant's sentence.

A defendant's guilty plea may be "intelligent" from a constitutional perspective even though the defendant is unaware of weaknesses in the government's case, including constitutional problems in the way in which the case has been prosecuted. In *Brady v. United States* (S.Ct.1970), a defendant pled guilty to a kidnapping that had culminated in the victim's death. The defendant entered the guilty plea at least in part to avoid the death penalty that could have been imposed under a federal statute if he went to trial and was convicted. The Supreme Court later ruled that this statute was unconstitutional. *United States v. Jackson* (S.Ct.1968). The Supreme Court, however, spurned the defendant's argument in *Brady* that his guilty plea was therefore invalid because he would not have pled guilty if he had known that the death-penalty statute was unconstitutional. The Court observed that when a defendant has admitted having committed a crime in open court, the defendant cannot then retract the plea simply because the defendant's attorney failed to predict a future change in existing law.

United States v. Ruiz (S.Ct.2002) is another case that illustrates that just because the disclosure of certain information might be useful to a defendant deciding whether to plead guilty does not mean that the disclosure is constitutionally mandated. In that case, the Court held that the prosecution's refusal to share at least certain kinds of exculpatory evidence with a defendant does not render a guilty plea invalid. By contrast, the government has a constitutional obligation, grounded in due process, to disclose exculpatory evidence to a defendant who goes to trial. *Giglio v. United States* (S.Ct.1972); *Brady v. Maryland* (S.Ct.1963).

The prosecutor in *Ruiz* had refused to disclose two kinds of exculpatory evidence to the defendant—evidence that supported any affirmative defense that the defendant might assert and impeachment evidence, which is evidence that discredits a prosecution witness's credibility. The Court emphasized that requiring the government to ferret out this information would defeat one of plea bargaining's primary advantages—the conservation of government resources, including prosecutors' time. In addition, the disclosure of impeachment evidence, which would often necessitate the revelation of a government informant's identity, could jeopardize the safety of witnesses and compromise ongoing criminal investigations. *Ruiz* left open whether the prosecutor's failure to disclose other exculpatory evidence to a defendant before entry of a guilty plea, such as evidence that someone other than the defendant committed the crime, would violate due process, rendering the guilty plea unconstitutional.

When a defendant entering a guilty plea is not represented by counsel, the court must ensure not only that the guilty plea is being entered voluntarily and intelligently, but that the defendant has validly waived the right to counsel accorded by the Sixth Amendment. In order for the defendant to tender a valid waiver of this right, the judge must first apprise the defendant of the "nature" of the charges that have been filed against the defendant, of the right to receive advice from an attorney before entering a plea, and of the range of penalties to which the defendant may be subject if the defendant pleads guilty. *Iowa v. Tovar* (S.Ct.2004). However, the judge does not have to elaborate further on the risks and downsides of proceeding without counsel, such as the risk that the defendant may have a viable defense of which he or she is unaware to a criminal charge.

When a defendant is represented by counsel, missteps of the attorney will, in some circumstances, lead to the invalidation of a guilty plea. A defendant represented by counsel is entitled, under the Sixth Amendment, to the effective assistance of counsel when deciding whether to enter a plea of guilty. That does not mean that the defendant is entitled to perfect advice when making this decision. Because of the many vagaries in a criminal case, it is not even realistic to expect such perfect advice from a defense attorney. A defense attorney, for example, often cannot predict with certainty whether a court would suppress certain evidence or which witnesses the judge or jury would find credible at trial.

Although a defendant is not entitled to perfect advice from his or her attorney when deciding whether to plead guilty, the defendant is entitled to "reasonably competent advice." *McMann v. Richardson* (S.Ct.1970). Defendants who contend that they did not receive such advice, however, must rebut a "strong presumption" that their attorneys acted within the "wide range of reasonable professional assistance." *Strickland v. Washington* (S.Ct. 1984).

Even if a defendant is successful in rebutting this presumption, that does not mean that the defendant's constitutional right to the effective assistance of counsel was violated and that the defendant's guilty plea will therefore be set aside. The defendant must in addition prove that he or she was prejudiced by counsel's deficient advice or performance. What this means in the guilty-plea context is that the defendant must prove that there is a "reasonable probability" that had the defendant received competent assistance from the defense attorney, the defendant would not have pled guilty and would instead have gone to trial. *Hill v. Lockhart* (S.Ct.1985).

When a defendant who entered a guilty plea received the effective assistance of counsel to which defendants are constitutionally entitled, the general rule applied in *Brady v. United States* and discussed earlier kicks in: the defendant cannot successfully challenge, on due-process grounds, the validity of the guilty plea simply because an independent violation of the defendant's constitutional rights occurred sometime before the guilty plea was entered. Thus, in *Tollett v. Henderson* (S.Ct.1973), the Supreme Court held that the defendant's guilty plea was not constitutionally defective just because the defendant was unaware, at the time the plea was entered, that the grand jury that had indicted him had been selected through an unconstitutional process that systematically excluded blacks. The Court noted that only if the failure of the defendant's attorney to apprise the defendant of this constitutional infirmity constituted ineffective assistance of counsel would the guilty plea be invalid.

The Supreme Court has carved out an exception to the general rule that a defendant has no constitutional right to raise independent constitutional claims after a guilty plea has been entered and accepted by a court. In *Menna v. New York* (S.Ct. 1975), a defendant was sentenced to jail for thirty days after a court held the defendant in criminal contempt for refusing to answer questions posed by a grand jury. Later, the defendant was prosecuted for this same failure to cooperate with the grand jury. The defendant claimed that this prosecution was barred by the constitutional prohibition of double jeopardy, but when he was unsuccessful in getting the criminal case dismissed, he pleaded guilty. On appeal, he resurrected his double-jeopardy claim.

The Supreme Court held that the defendant's entry of a guilty plea did not foreclose him from raising the double-jeopardy claim on appeal. The Court noted that *Tollett v. Henderson* and other related Supreme Court cases were not predicated on the premise that defendants waive their right to contest earlier constitutional violations when entering a plea of guilty. Those cases rather simply stand for the proposition that when a defendant pleads guilty, the defendant is admitting his or her guilt, which makes most earlier constitutional violations irrelevant. In *Menna*, however, the Supreme Court said that the constitutional violation of which the defendant complained was not rendered irrelevant simply because the defendant had pled guilty; the defendant was essentially claiming that no matter how clear his factual guilt, the government could not obtain a constitutional conviction.

The Court hastened to add in *Menna* that not all double-jeopardy claims can necessarily be raised following the entry of a guilty plea. The meaning of that caveat later became clear in *United States v. Broce* (S.Ct.1989). In that case, several defendants pled guilty to two separate counts of conspiracy. Later, they sought to set aside one of their sentences on the grounds that they had in fact been involved in only one conspiracy that overlapped both charges. Their dual convictions, they contended, therefore violated their right not to be twice placed in jeopardy for the same crime.

The Supreme Court, however, refused to consider their double-jeopardy claim, distinguishing *Menna v. New York* in the process. The Court noted that in *Menna*, the double-jeopardy violation was apparent from the record. By contrast, in *Broce*, to resolve the double-jeopardy issue, a court would have to delve outside the record to determine whether the defendants had committed only one or really two conspiracies. The exception to the general rule barring review of constitutional violations that preceded the entry of a guilty plea is thus a very narrow one; the exception only applies when "on the face of the record the court had no power to enter the conviction or impose the sentence."

While a defendant may not have a constitutional right to assert certain constitutional claims following the entry of a guilty plea, states and the federal government retain the prerogative to permit a defendant to later assert those claims on appeal. For example, a state statute may authorize a defendant who has pled guilty to challenge, on appeal, the denial of a motion to suppress evidence. If the appellate court rules that the lower court erred in refusing to suppress the evidence, the defendant may then be permitted to withdraw the guilty plea.

Conditional guilty pleas are another mechanism jurisdictions have employed that enable defendants to raise certain constitutional claims on appeal despite their entry of a guilty plea. A conditional guilty plea preserves the defendant's right to challenge on appeal a trial court's adverse ruling and withdraw the plea if that ruling is reversed. Rule 11(a)(2) of the Federal Rules of Criminal Procedure, for example, authorizes the entry of such a conditional plea provided that both the court and the prosecutor consent.

A defendant who enters a guilty plea may want to challenge the validity of that plea on appeal or assert one of the other few claims not relinquished through entry of the guilty plea. Consequently, defense counsel's failure to discuss with the defendant the pros and cons of filing an appeal and to determine whether the defendant wishes to do so usually constitutes unreasonable professional assistance. *Roe v. Flores–Ortega* (S.Ct.2000). As long as a "rational defendant" would have wanted to appeal, perhaps because there were nonfrivolous grounds for vacating the guilty plea, or the defendant, in any event, expressed an interest to counsel in appealing, this first precondition to a finding of ineffective assistance of counsel is met. In order to prevail on the Sixth Amendment ineffectiveness claim, thereby enabling the defendant to now file an appeal, the defendant must also establish that there is a "reasonable probability" that an appeal would have been filed if the defense attorney had discussed the subject with the defendant.

As mentioned earlier, in addition to the requirement that a guilty plea be rendered intelligently, a guilty plea must be voluntary to satisfy due process. In *Brady v. United States* (S.Ct.1970), the Supreme Court considered whether entering a guilty plea in order to avoid the death penalty automatically makes the plea involuntary. The Court concluded that it does not—that all of the circumstances surrounding the entry of a guilty plea must be examined in determining the plea's voluntariness. The Court noted that to hold otherwise—to hold that a guilty plea is invalid when entered in order to avoid a heavier penalty, in this case death—would conflict with the very underpinnings of the plea bargaining that is countenanced by the criminal-justice system. The Court then concluded that the defendant's guilty plea in the case before it was voluntary based on all of the circumstances, including the fact that he was represented by a competent attorney and that the state's case against him was quite strong.

Even when a defendant professes innocence at the time a guilty plea is entered, the plea may still be valid. In *North Carolina v. Alford* (S.Ct.1970), the Supreme Court upheld a guilty plea to second-degree murder entered by a defendant who insisted that he was innocent of the crime. The Court emphasized that there was "strong evidence" in the record that the defendant had indeed committed the murder. This strong factual basis helped to confirm that the defendant's guilty plea was "intelligently" made in the constitutional sense.

North Carolina v. Alford arguably seems to suggest that a factual basis, if not a strong factual basis, must exist for a guilty plea accompanied by a protestation of innocence to be valid. But in the absence of such an assertion of innocence, most courts have held that due process does not normally require that there be a factual basis for a guilty plea. *See, e.g., Meyers v. Gillis* (3d Cir.1996). Some lower courts have gone even further, holding that a factual basis is not constitutionally required even when a defendant insists that he or she is innocent of the crime for which a guilty plea is being entered. *See, e.g., Higgason v. Clark* (7th Cir.1993).

However, a factual basis may be, and often is, required by statutes or court rules governing the proceedings surrounding the entry of a guilty plea. *See, e.g.*, Fed. R. Crim. P. 11(b)(3). These statutes and rules often impose requirements that must be met for a guilty plea to be valid that go beyond the constitutional minima. For example, as discussed earlier, the right to due process generally does not entitle defendants to be apprised of the collateral consequences that may ensue from a conviction. Nonetheless, statutes or court rules may require court admonitions about some of these consequences, such as the possibility that the conviction may result in the defendant's deportation, before the court accepts a guilty plea.

While the Supreme Court in *North Carolina v. Alford* concluded that a guilty plea may be valid even though the defendant entering the plea insists that he or she is innocent, the Court at the same time emphasized that its decision did not mean that a trial court must accept the guilty plea of such a defendant. Whether to accept a defendant's plea of guilty generally falls within a court's discretion, and the refusal to accept the guilty plea of a defendant who professes innocence will not usually be considered an abuse of discretion. *France v. Artuz* (E.D.N.Y.1999).

If a federal court accepts a defendant's guilty plea, statements made by a defendant at a Rule 11 hearing may subsequently be considered by the court when sentencing the defendant, perhaps to augment the defendant's sentence. *Mitchell v. United States* (S.Ct.1999). But if the defendant invokes the Fifth Amendment privilege against self-incrimination at the hearing, the defendant runs the risk that the judge may refuse to accept the guilty plea because it may then lack the factual basis required by Rule 11(b)(3).

B. BREACHES OF PLEA AGREEMENTS

A plea bargain, as discussed earlier, is an agreement in which the defendant agrees to plead guilty in return for some concessions from the prosecutor. But what happens if one of the parties reneges on his or her part of the agreement?

Santobello v. New York (S.Ct.1971) addressed this question in a case involving a noncompliant prosecutor. In *Santobello*, a prosecutor had agreed to make no recommendation as to the sentence to be imposed for the gambling offense to which the defendant pled guilty. A different prosecutor, however, was assigned to handle the case at the sentencing hearing, and at that hearing, the prosecutor asked that the maximum prison sentence be imposed on the defendant. The sentencing judge ultimately imposed the maximum sentence, although he insisted that his decision was based on the defendant's criminal record and was not influenced at all by the prosecutor's sentencing recommendation.

Nonetheless, the Supreme Court concluded that the defendant had a right to relief because of the prosecution's failure to abide by the terms of the plea agreement. The Court left to the lower court the decision as to what remedy would be appropriate under the circumstances. The state court had two remedies from which to choose: require specific performance of the agreement, which would mean that the defendant would be resentenced by a different judge with no sentencing recommendation tendered by the prosecutor, or permit the defendant to withdraw his guilty plea. After withdrawing his guilty plea, the defendant could then decide whether to negotiate anew with the prosecutor or go to trial.

The Supreme Court's decision in *Santobello* is to be contrasted with its subsequent decision in *Unit-*

ed States v. Benchimol (S.Ct.1985). In *Benchimol*, the defendant pled guilty after the prosecutor agreed to recommend that the defendant be placed on probation. The prosecutor, however, apparently made a lackluster recommendation and also failed to explain why the government believed that a sentence to probation was appropriate. The court then sentenced the defendant to prison for six years.

The defendant argued that the government had failed to live up to the terms of its agreement, but the Supreme Court disagreed. Noting that the prosecutor had not promised to make the sentencing recommendation enthusiastically or to state reasons for the recommendation at the sentencing hearing, the Court was unwilling to read such terms into the agreement. Instead, the Court observed that if a defendant wants a prosecutor to make a sentencing recommendation in a certain way, the defendant must obtain an explicit commitment from the prosecutor to do so as part of the plea agreement.

The Supreme Court also distinguished *Santobello* in *Mabry v. Johnson* (S.Ct.1984). In *Mabry*, a prosecutor offered to recommend a 21–year prison sentence, to be served concurrently with two other prison sentences being served by the defendant, if the defendant agreed to plead guilty to the crime of being an accessory after a felony murder. The defendant, through his attorney, later accepted the offer, but the prosecutor then announced that he had made a mistake and that the offer was now a 21–year prison sentence to be served consecutively with the defendant's other prison sentences. The defendant eventually, though reluctantly, accepted this offer, and the court imposed the 21–year consecutive sentence.

Later, the defendant sought to hold the government to its original offer, arguing that the defendant's due-process rights were violated when the government withdrew an offer after its acceptance by the defendant. The Supreme Court concluded that the defendant's right to due process of law had not been abridged. The deciding fact for the Court was that at the time the defendant pled guilty, he knew that the prosecutor would only recommend a consecutive sentence. The defendant's guilty plea, therefore, unlike the plea in *Santobello*, did not rest on an "unfulfilled promise" of the prosecutor.

As is evident from the Supreme Court's decision in *Ricketts v. Adamson* (S.Ct.1987), defendants also have an enforceable obligation to abide by the terms of a plea agreement. In that case, a defendant charged with first-degree murder entered into a plea agreement under which he pled guilty to second-degree murder and received a prison sentence in return for testifying at the trials of two accomplices. The defendant did testify at their trials, but when his codefendants' convictions were reversed on appeal, the defendant refused to testify at their retrials unless the government agreed to release him from prison after he testified. The government responded by charging the defendant once again with first-degree murder. He was ultimately convicted of this crime and received a death sentence.

The defendant argued that his prosecution for first-degree murder was barred by the constitutional prohibition against double jeopardy. The Supreme Court responded that under the terms of the plea agreement, the agreement was null and void if the defendant refused to testify at the trials of his codefendants. By refusing to testify at the retrials of his codefendants, the defendant, according to the Court, assumed the risk that he would be found in breach of the plea agreement, thereby exposing himself to a prosecution for first-degree murder.

Defense attorneys can draw two important lessons from *Ricketts*, as well as *United States v. Benchimol.* First, counsel must take great care to ensure that a plea agreement specifically and clearly outlines the obligations of both the prosecutor and the defendant under the agreement. Second, should there still, for some reason, later be doubt regarding the scope of the defendant's obligations under a plea agreement, the defense attorney should seek clarification from the court as to the meaning of the plea agreement rather than rely on the defense attorney's own, and possibly erroneous, interpretation of the agreement.

C. CONSTRAINTS ON THE GOVERNMENT IN OFFERING INCENTIVES TO PLEAD GUILTY

A prosecutor can put a tremendous amount of pressure on a defendant to plead guilty without necessarily violating constitutional strictures. Of that there can be no doubt after the Supreme Court's decision in *Bordenkircher v. Hayes* (S.Ct. 1978).

Bordenkircher involved a defendant who had been charged with forging a check in the amount of $88.30, a crime for which he could be sent to prison for two to ten years. The prosecutor offered to recommend a five-year prison sentence if the defendant pled guilty. The prosecutor furthermore informed the defendant that if he refused to plead guilty, he would be prosecuted under the state's habitual-offender law because of his two prior felony convictions. Under this law, a person convicted of three felonies was subject to a mandatory life sentence in prison.

The defendant refused the prosecutor's offer and went to trial. After being convicted of the forgery offense and found to be a habitual offender, he was sentenced to life in prison.

The defendant argued that the prosecutor had unconstitutionally retaliated against him for having exercised his constitutional right to go to trial. In support of this argument, the defendant cited two Supreme Court cases—*North Carolina v. Pearce* (S.Ct.1969) and *Blackledge v. Perry* (S.Ct.1974). In *North Carolina v. Pearce*, the Supreme Court had held that when a judge imposes a higher sentence on a defendant following the successful appeal of a conviction in order to retaliate against the defendant for having taken an appeal, the defendant's right to due process of law is violated. And in

Blackledge, the Supreme Court had held that a defendant's due-process rights were violated when a prosecutor retaliated against him by charging him with felony assault after the defendant sought a new trial following his conviction of misdemeanor assault.

The Supreme Court repeated in *Bordenkircher* that it violates due process to punish a defendant for exercising his or her legal rights. The Court, however, then went on to say that such punishment does not occur when a prosecutor is exerting leverage on a defendant during the ''give-and-take'' of the plea-bargaining process, because the defendant is free to either accept or reject the prosecutor's plea offer. To hold otherwise, the Court noted, would lead to the invalidation of plea bargaining, because prosecutors often offer defendants strong inducements to plead guilty.

The dissenters in *Bordenkircher* responded that there was a way to retain plea bargaining while limiting the risk that the prosecutorial vindictiveness that offends due process has occurred: require prosecutors, if they wish to plea bargain, to bargain down from the charges initially filed. Charging decisions would then not hinge on defendants' willingness to forgo constitutional rights. The dissenters recognized that as a practical matter, this rule might simply lead some prosecutors to overcharge at the outset of a case. The dissenters still believed though that in order to detect and prevent abusive prosecutorial practices during plea bargaining, it was better to have the pressures that had been exerted on a defendant to plead guilty appear in the public record rather than be hidden in the form of undisclosed threats by a prosecutor.

Two assumptions underlay the Supreme Court's conclusion in *Bordenkircher* that the type of pressure exerted on the defendant to plead guilty in that case did not violate due process. First, the Court posited that when engaging in plea bargaining, the prosecutor and the defendant "arguably possess relatively equal bargaining power." This proposition seems dubious in light of the more direct and severe personal consequences that a defendant will suffer if convicted of a crime compared to the consequences that will befall a prosecutor who loses a case.

Second, the Court assumed that as long as a defendant is represented by a competent attorney and afforded the procedural safeguards that customarily surround the entry of a guilty plea, a defendant would be "unlikely to be driven to false self-condemnation" by the inducements to plead guilty offered by the prosecutor. One might equally argue, however, that a defendant facing, for example, a possible life sentence if the defendant does not plead guilty might agree to plead guilty in order to receive a vastly diminished prison sentence, even though the defendant is innocent and even though the defendant is represented by counsel.

Bordenkircher does not mean that there are no constitutional limits on the tactics that can be employed by a prosecutor when attempting to extract a guilty plea from a defendant. Even in *Bordenkirch-er*, the Court inserted some potentially important caveats into its opinion. The Court noted, for example, that the threatened filing of habitual-offender charges against the defendant was not unwarranted; in other words, the defendant could properly be charged as a habitual offender.

The Supreme Court also seemed to suggest in *Bordenkircher* that the result of the case might have been different if the prosecutor had tried to induce the defendant to plead guilty by promising to treat someone other than the defendant, such as a relative, more leniently if the defendant pled guilty or more severely if the defendant did not. Despite this intimation in the Court's opinion, most of the lower courts that have addressed this issue have concluded that an agreement to treat a third party more leniently does not automatically render a guilty plea involuntary. *See, e.g., Miles v. Dorsey* (10th Cir.1995).

Another point emphasized by the Court in *Bordenkircher* was that when the defendant rejected the prosecutor's offer, he was aware of the potential consequences ensuing from his decision to plead not guilty. This was not a case, the Court emphasized, where the prosecutor, without notice, sprang a more serious charge upon the defendant after plea negotiations had failed.

Despite that qualifying statement, the Supreme Court later concluded in *United States v. Goodwin* (S.Ct.1982) that a prosecutor can, before trial, bring more serious charges against a defendant after un-successful plea negotiations, even if the defendant was not made aware during the negotiations of the possibility of more serious charges being filed. The Court rejected the argument that in this type of situation there should be a presumption of prosecu-torial vindictiveness that the prosecutor has to re-but to avoid a finding of a due-process violation. The Court explained that there is much less basis for assuming, in the pretrial context, that additional charges have been filed for vindictive reasons than there is in the posttrial context, where a presump-tion of vindictiveness is warranted. *Blackledge v. Perry* (S.Ct.1974). In the pretrial setting, when the prosecutor is still putting the government's case together, it is to be expected that the prosecutor may discover information that indicates that more serious charges should be filed against the defen-dant.

Alabama v. Smith (S.Ct.1989) is another case where the Supreme Court refused to apply a pre-sumption of vindictiveness. In that case, a defen-dant received two concurrent 30–year prison sen-tences after pleading guilty to rape and burglary in return for dismissal of a sodomy charge. After se-curing the reversal of his convictions on appeal because his guilty pleas were invalid, he went to trial and was convicted on all three counts. In sentencing the defendant, the trial judge stated that the trial had revealed facts about the case of which the judge was previously unaware, such as that the defendant had raped the victim five times. The judge then sentenced the defendant to two concurrent life sentences in prison for the sodomy and burglary and imposed an additional 150–year sentence for the rape, to be served consecutively with the other two sentences.

The question for the Supreme Court was whether an increased sentence following the vacating of a guilty plea creates a presumption that the sentencing judge was retaliating against the defendant for exercising the right to contest the validity of the guilty plea. The Court said that for there to be such a presumption, there would have to be a "reasonable likelihood" that increased sentences following the setting aside of guilty pleas are due to judicial vindictiveness. The Court, however, was convinced that this "reasonable likelihood" of vindictiveness does not exist when a defendant was first sentenced following entry of a guilty plea and then resentenced following a trial. *Compare North Carolina v. Pearce* (S.Ct.1969) as it was construed in *Texas v. McCullough* (S.Ct.1986) (there is a presumption of vindictiveness when a conviction following a trial is reversed on appeal and a higher sentence is then imposed by the same judge who initially sentenced the defendant). The Court noted that during a trial, a judge usually will find out information about a crime and the defendant that was not revealed to the judge when earlier accepting the defendant's guilty plea—information that will often indicate that the defendant should receive a more severe sentence than that initially imposed.

The Supreme Court noted in *Alabama v. Smith* that if the defendant could prove that his enhanced sentences were actually imposed, not because of such new information, but because the judge was retaliating against the defendant for exercising the right to contest the validity of his guilty pleas, the defendant could still prevail on his due-process claim. But the point of the Supreme Court in *Alabama v. Smith* was that the defendant could not avail himself of a presumption of vindictiveness. Instead, to prevail on his due-process claim, the defendant had to assume the difficult task of proving the existence of actual vindictiveness.

The Supreme Court has not only condoned substantial prosecutorial inducements to plead guilty, but also substantial legislative inducements. In *Corbitt v. New Jersey* (S.Ct.1978), the Court upheld a statute that required imposition of a life sentence when a defendant convicted of first-degree murder had gone to trial but permitted imposition of either a 30–year prison sentence or a life sentence if the defendant pled *nolo contendere* to the murder charge. The defendant argued that this sentencing scheme unconstitutionally penalized him for exercising his constitutional right to go to trial. The Supreme Court responded that there is nothing inherently unconstitutional about offering a defendant an incentive to plead guilty, as demonstrated by the Court's decision in *Bordenkircher v. Hayes* (S.Ct.1978). In the Court's opinion, offering a defendant the possibility of more lenient treatment in return for a plea of guilty does not mean that the defendant is being punished if the defendant goes to trial and the opportunity for more lenient treatment is withheld.

The Supreme Court in *Corbitt* discussed its earlier decision in *United States v. Jackson* (S.Ct. 1968), a case that helps to clarify, at least somewhat, the distinction between constitutional and unconstitutional pressures that can be exerted on a defendant to plead guilty. In *Jackson*, the Supreme Court struck down a statute that authorized imposition of the death penalty for certain kidnappings if a defendant was convicted after a jury trial, but permitted imposition, at most, of a life sentence in prison if a defendant pled guilty or was convicted after a bench trial. According to the Court, the statute unconstitutionally impinged upon defendants' due-process right to plead not guilty and their Sixth Amendment right to a jury trial.

In *Corbitt v. New Jersey*, the Supreme Court noted two distinctions between the statute deemed unconstitutional in *Jackson* and the statute whose constitutionality was at issue in the case before it. First, the possible price of demanding a jury trial under the statute in *Jackson* was death, a penalty "unique in its severity and irrevocability." Second, a defendant, under the statute at issue in *Jackson*, could totally avoid the maximum penalty—death— by entering a plea of guilty. By contrast, under the statute upheld in *Corbitt*, the maximum sentence— life in prison—might still be imposed even if the defendant entered a no-contest plea.

In several cases, the Supreme Court has considered the validity of concessions extracted from a defendant during the plea-bargaining process. In *United States v. Mezzanatto* (S.Ct.1995), the Court held that a defendant can waive the protection that was then afforded by Rule 11 of the Federal Rules of Criminal Procedure and is now accorded by Federal Rule of Evidence 410(4). Under the federal rules, a defendant's statements made during plea negotiations generally are inadmissible at trial if the negotiations do not culminate in an agreement. Having received a green light from the Supreme Court in *Mezzanatto*, however, federal prosecutors now often refuse to enter into plea negotiations unless defendants agree that any statements they make during plea discussions can be used to impeach their contradictory testimony at trial.

A recurring question that the Supreme Court has yet to resolve is whether a prosecutor can condition a plea agreement on the defendant's waiver of the right to appeal. Most of the lower courts, thus far, have held that these waivers are enforceable except in narrowly defined situations, such as when the defendant contends on appeal that he did not receive the effective assistance of counsel to which he is constitutionally entitled, that the sentence exceeded the statutory maximum, or that the sentence was the by-product of racial discrimination. *See, e.g., United States v. Hahn* (10th Cir.2004). Other courts have proven more willing to delve into the validity of these kinds of waivers on a case-by-case basis. For example, in *United States v. Good-*

man (2d Cir.1999), the Second Circuit Court of Appeals held that a defendant cannot be forced, as a condition of entering into a plea agreement, to relinquish the right to appeal a sentence that fell below the statutory maximum but resulted from the judge's miscalculation of the sentence under the applicable sentencing guidelines.

Newton v. Rumery (S.Ct.1987) involved the validity of a different kind of agreement stemming from plea negotiations—an agreement by a defendant not to bring a civil suit against certain government officials in return for the dismissal of a felony criminal charge. The defendant in that case contended that such release-dismissal agreements are void because they are against public policy.

The Supreme Court agreed that such agreements pose many risks. Prosecutors may file frivolous criminal charges to induce individuals to abandon plans to sue government officials. In addition, prosecutions may be dropped when the interests of the public would be best served by pursuing a criminal conviction. And constitutional violations may go unremedied because of these agreements.

Nonetheless, the Supreme Court concluded that release-dismissal agreements are not *per se* invalid. Instead, each agreement must be examined on a case-by-case basis to determine its validity.

In a concurring opinion, Justice O'Connor provided some guidance as to what factors to consider when assessing a release-dismissal agreement's validity. Some of the relevant factors include: the defendant's knowledge and experience; the circumstances surrounding the making of the agreement, particularly whether the defendant was represented by counsel; the severity of the criminal charges pending against the defendant (because the more serious the charge, the more pressure the defendant will feel to enter into a release-dismissal agreement); whether a judge oversaw the execution of the release-dismissal agreement; and the extent to which the agreement was entered into to achieve some "legitimate criminal justice objective." This latter factor proved to be particularly important to the majority of the Supreme Court in upholding the release-dismissal agreement before it in *Newton*; there was evidence that the prosecutor entered into the agreement largely to spare a witness, whom the defendant had been charged with threatening, the trauma of testifying in the criminal and civil proceedings.

CHAPTER 3

THE SENTENCING PROCESS

A. RIGHTS DURING SENTENCING

Defendants in criminal trials have an array of constitutional rights. They have, for example, the right to call witnesses to testify on their behalf, the right to confront and cross-examine adverse witnesses, and the right to be found not guilty if the government fails to prove their guilt beyond a reasonable doubt. By contrast, convicted offenders have far fewer constitutional rights during sentencing proceedings.

1. The Right to Counsel

Defendants do have the right, under the Sixth Amendment, to have their attorneys assist them during sentencing hearings. *Mempa v. Rhay* (S.Ct. 1967). Many defendants, however, do not have the funds to hire their own attorneys and are unable to persuade an attorney to represent them free of charge, so the question of the scope of the right of indigent defendants under the Sixth Amendment to appointed counsel is an important one.

In *Scott v. Illinois* (S.Ct.1979), the Supreme Court, in a 5–4 decision, held that the right to appointed counsel at trial hinges on the actual penalty ultimately imposed on a defendant. If the penalty included some period of incarceration, then an indigent defendant had the right to appointed counsel at trial. Even if the court suspended the jail or prison sentence and placed the defendant on probation, the defendant had this right. *Alabama v. Shelton* (S.Ct.2002). But if the penalty did not include incarceration, then the defendant had no constitutional right to receive assistance from a court-appointed attorney at trial.

Although *Scott v. Illinois* involved a defendant convicted of a misdemeanor, the broad language of the Supreme Court's opinion seemed to suggest that the actual-incarceration standard is to be applied in all criminal cases, those involving felonies as well as misdemeanors. In a subsequent decision, however, the Court observed, though in *dicta*, that indigent defendants have the right to appointed counsel at trial in all felony cases. *Nichols v. United States* (S.Ct.1994).

The Supreme Court has yet to address the scope of the right to appointed counsel at a sentencing hearing. Unless the Court overrules *Scott v. Illinois*, it seems most likely that the Court will apply the actual-incarceration standard to sentencing proceedings in misdemeanor cases, because it is difficult to fathom the Court recognizing a broader right to appointed counsel at a sentencing hearing than exists at trial.

The Sixth Amendment right to counsel at sentencing hearings includes, logically, the right to the effective assistance of counsel. In determining whether that right has been abridged during a sentencing proceeding, courts apply a two-part test. *Strickland v. Washington* (S.Ct.1984).

Under this two-part test, the defense attorney first must have failed to render reasonable professional assistance during the sentencing stage of the criminal prosecution. The courts apply a "strong presumption" that an attorney acted reasonably, and it is incumbent on a defendant to rebut this presumption.

To prevail on an ineffectiveness claim, a defendant also must prove that he or she was prejudiced by the attorney's incompetent performance. To meet this burden, the defendant must prove that there is a "reasonable probability" that the defendant would have received a more lenient sentence had the attorney rendered reasonable professional assistance. In a capital case, for example, a defendant must prove that there is a reasonable probability that had the defense attorney performed competently, the defendant would not have received the death penalty. The burden of proof that must be met—reasonable probability—is not as high as a preponderance-of-the-evidence standard, which would require that it be more likely than not that the defendant was prejudiced by the errors made by defense counsel.

Any increase in the length of time a defendant will be incarcerated because of counsel's deficient performance can constitute the prejudice needed to establish ineffective assistance of counsel. *Glover v. United States* (S.Ct.2001). The Supreme Court has refused to require "substantial" prejudice as a predicate to finding a Sixth Amendment violation, in part because of the difficulty of differentiating between substantial and insubstantial prejudice.

The *Strickland* test applies to "virtually all" claims of ineffective assistance of counsel. *Williams v. Taylor* (S.Ct.2000). Only in "unusual" cases—when it would be "unjust" to treat the difference in outcome as "prejudice"—will the meeting of the two-part test not lead to a finding of unconstitutional ineffectiveness.

Lockhart v. Fretwell (S.Ct.1993) exemplifies such an unusual case. In that case, the defendant's attorney failed to make an objection that would have prevented imposition of the death penalty on the defendant based on the caselaw that then prevailed. The case upon which an objection could have been grounded was later overruled. Even though the defendant would not have received the death penalty if his attorney had made the appropriate objection, the Supreme Court concluded that the defendant was not unconstitutionally prejudiced. According to the Court, the existence of prejudice in that case depended not only on the effect that counsel's deficient performance had on the sentence imposed, but also on whether that sentence was "fundamentally unfair or unreliable." The Court concluded that there was no such unfairness or unreliability in the case before it because the defendant had only been deprived of the opportunity to have the sentencing court make a mistake.

The Sixth Amendment right to the assistance of counsel during sentencing proceedings includes the right, in at least some circumstances, to have the defense attorney notified before the defendant is interviewed about matters that may affect the sentence imposed. In *Estelle v. Smith* (S.Ct.1981), the defendant in a capital murder case was examined by a psychiatrist to determine whether he was competent to stand trial. To the defendant's surprise, the psychiatrist later testified for the prosecution at the defendant's sentencing hearing, describing the defendant as a sociopath. Holding that the defendant's Sixth Amendment right to counsel had been violated, the Supreme Court unanimously agreed that the defendant's attorney should have been notified that the psychiatrist's examination would encompass not only questions concerning the defendant's competency to stand trial, but also the subject of his future dangerousness.

2. The Rights to Have Access to and to Rebut the Presentence Investigation Report

While defendants have a Sixth Amendment right to the assistance of counsel during sentencing proceedings, most of the other procedural safeguards to which they are or may be entitled during those proceedings stem from the constitutional right to due process of law. The due-process guarantee in the Fifth Amendment applies in federal prosecutions, while its counterpart in the Fourteenth Amendment provides protection to defendants in state and local prosecutions.

Traditionally, the Supreme Court has balanced three factors when determining whether a particular procedural safeguard is required by due process. *Mathews v. Eldridge* (S.Ct.1976). The first is the private interest that is at stake. The more weighty the private interest, the more likely it is that the safeguard is an element of due process. The second factor looks at both the governmental interests that would be affected if the safeguard had to be provided and the way in which they would be affected. To the extent that an important governmental interest would be adversely affected by provision of the safeguard, it is less likely that the safeguard is constitutionally mandated. On the other hand, to the extent that a significant governmental interest would be furthered by incorporating a procedural safeguard into the process through which an individual is deprived of life, liberty, or property, it is more likely that the safeguard is required by due process. The final factor to be weighed when determining whether a procedural safeguard is constitutionally mandated is the value of the safeguard in terms of its ability to avert an erroneous deprivation of the private interest that is at stake. The higher the risk that individuals will be erroneously deprived of their life, liberty, or property without the safeguard, the more likely it is that the safeguard is a component of due process.

Gardner v. Florida (S.Ct.1977) illustrates how the Supreme Court has applied the three-part test, known as the *Mathews* balancing test, in the sentencing context. In *Gardner*, the defendant was sentenced to death based in part on confidential information in a presentence-investigation report that was not disclosed to either the defendant or his attorney. The state argued that disclosing such confidential information would adversely affect a number of important governmental interests. The state argued, for example, that without a promise of confidentiality, people would be less inclined to provide the information about a defendant upon which a sound sentencing decision is dependent. The Supreme Court responded that the interest in maximizing the quantity of information made available to the sentencer about the defendant and the defendant's crime was counterbalanced by the interest in ensuring that the information provided was true—an interest that would be furthered by affording the defendant the opportunity to be informed of, and respond to, the information submitted to the sentencer. In addition, the Supreme Court emphasized the centrality of the interest that was at stake in *Gardner*—the defendant's very life.

The state in *Gardner* also argued that the full disclosure of the contents of presentence-investigation reports would unduly delay sentencing proceedings because defendants would contest the contents of those reports. The Supreme Court was unconvinced by this argument. The Court was confident that presentence-investigation reports are generally reliable, so defendants will not usually challenge their contents. Even if they do, the Supreme Court noted that a sentencing judge can avoid a protracted hearing on the issue in dispute by refusing to consider the disputed material when sentencing a defendant. Finally, the Court observed that to the extent that some time must be expended to ensure that a sentencing decision is predicated only on reliable information, that time is well-spent when the defendant's life is at stake.

The state furthermore argued that fully disclosing the contents of a presentence-investigation report would at times impede a defendant's rehabilitation, because the reports sometimes include sensitive information concerning the results of a psychiatric or psychological evaluation of the defendant. The Supreme Court considered this argument to be specious in the case before it, where the state, by seeking the death penalty, had abandoned any pretense of pursuing a rehabilitative objective. In addition, the Court expressed doubt that the state's concern, even if legitimate, would justify refusing to disclose the sensitive information to the defendant's attorney.

According to the Supreme Court, the due-process violation in *Gardner* stemmed not only from the failure to permit either the defendant or his attorney to review portions of the presentence-investigation report, but also from the failure to afford the defendant the opportunity to "deny or explain" the information contained within the report. *See also Simmons v. South Carolina* (S.Ct.1994) (due process violated in capital sentencing hearing when the prosecutor argued that the defendant's future dangerousness warranted imposition of the death penalty, but the defendant was not permitted to inform the jury that if he was not sentenced to death, he would receive a life sentence with no chance of parole). The lower courts have concluded that this right to explain or rebut the hearsay statements considered by the sentencing judge extends to non-capital cases as well. *See, e.g., Ortiz v. Stewart* (9th Cir.1998).

A related due-process violation can occur, at least in some circumstances, when a defendant is provided no notice that the judge is contemplating imposing a sentence higher than the one sought by the prosecution or recommended in the presentence-investigation report. In *Lankford v. Idaho* (S.Ct. 1991), the Supreme Court held that a judge's decision to impose the death penalty, made after the government had announced its decision not to seek the death penalty, violated the defendant's right to due process of law. According to the Court, the defendant was entitled to notice that the judge was still considering imposing a death sentence. Still technically left open after *Lankford* is the question, described by the Supreme Court as a "serious" one, whether a defendant has a constitutional right to be notified that a judge is considering an upward departure from the sentence that normally would be imposed under sentencing guidelines. *Burns v. United States* (S.Ct.1991).

3. The Rights to Make a Statement to the Sentencer and to Present Evidence

While the Supreme Court held in *Gardner v. Florida* that defendants must be afforded the opportunity to "deny or explain" the information contained within a presentence-investigation report, the Court did not elaborate on what would be considered a constitutionally adequate opportunity to respond to the contents of the report. Is there only a right to have the defense attorney comment on the report's contents, or does the defendant also have the right to make a statement to the court? Does the defendant have the right to call witnesses to refute statements made in the presentence-investigation report, and does the defendant, in addition, have the right to confront and cross-examine adverse witnesses?

The Supreme Court has provided answers or partial answers to at least some of these questions. In *Hill v. United States* (S.Ct.1962), the Court considered whether defendants have a constitutional right of allocution at a sentencing hearing—the right to make a statement to the court before a sentence is imposed. The Court held in that case that there was no such right, but in the course of rendering this holding, noted that there were some special facts in the case before it. The defendant in *Hill* was represented by an attorney at the sentencing hearing, and the sentencing judge had not refused a request of the defendant to make a statement to the court. The court simply had failed to ask the defendant if there was anything he wanted to say to the court before he was sentenced. In addition, the defendant had not claimed that the sentencing judge misunderstood, or was unaware of, relevant facts when sentencing the defendant.

The question, of course, is whether any of these facts should make a difference to the issue of whether a defendant has a constitutional right of allocution. *Cf. Green v. United States* (S.Ct.1961), a case where the Supreme Court, in the course of discussing the right of allocution under Rule 32 of the Federal Rules of Criminal Procedure, said, "The most persuasive counsel may not be able to speak for a defendant as the defendant might, with halting eloquence, speak for himself." The lower courts currently are divided on the question whether defendants, outside the fact-specific context of the *Hill* case, have a constitutionally-based right of allocution. *See Boardman v. Estelle* (9th Cir. 1992) (listing cases).

In at least some instances, defendants have the right to call witnesses to testify on their behalf at a sentencing hearing. In *Green v. Georgia* (S.Ct. 1979), for example, the Supreme Court held that the defendant's right to due process of law was violated when he was not permitted to call a witness to testify at his capital sentencing hearing. The witness would have testified about a codefendant's admission that he had in fact killed the victim whom the defendant had been convicted of murdering. The Court, however, emphasized that the witness's testimony was "highly relevant" to a "critical" sentencing issue and that there were "substantial reasons" for crediting the witness's statement. It must also be remembered that *Green* was a capital case. The extent to which the right to call witnesses extends beyond the confines of the special facts of *Green* remains in doubt. *See also Ake v. Oklahoma* (S.Ct.1985) (indigent defendant who had raised an insanity defense in a capital case had a due-process right to receive the assistance of an appointed psychiatrist to testify on the subject of his future dangerousness, a ''significant factor'' at his sentencing hearing).

4. The Rights to Confrontation and Cross–Examination

Another question regarding the scope of defendants' procedural rights during sentencing proceedings is whether there is a right to confront and cross-examine adverse witnesses at a sentencing hearing. In *Williams v. New York* (S.Ct.1949), another capital case, the Supreme Court held that there is no such right. The Court's rationale rested in part on the tradition of maximizing the flow of information to the sentencer about the defendant and the defendant's crime. The Court was concerned that some individuals with information that would be helpful to the sentencing decision would refrain from providing that information if they then had to face the defendant and be subjected to questioning. The Court also expressed a concern that according defendants a right of confrontation and cross-examination would unduly prolong sentencing hearings.

The lower courts generally have concurred that defendants have no constitutional right to confront and cross-examine adverse witnesses at sentencing hearings. *See, e.g., United States v. Weekly* (8th

Cir.1997). These holdings have sparked some controversy. Under some sentencing systems, crimes with which the defendant was not charged but are related to the crime of which the defendant was convicted, can increase, often significantly, the defendant's sentence, though not above the maximum sentence authorized by statute. The commission of these uncharged crimes often is established through the statements of confidential government informants or other individuals that are then relayed through third persons at the sentencing hearing or in the presentence-investigation report. For example, in *United States v. Silverman* (6th Cir.1992), the defendant pled guilty to possession of a controlled substance with intent to distribute after selling a quarter of an ounce of cocaine to an informant. Hearsay statements mentioned in the presentence-investigation report and introduced at trial that the defendant had sold a kilogram of cocaine in the preceding year resulted in a five-year increase in the defendant's sentence. Nonetheless, the Sixth Circuit Court of Appeals held that the defendant had no constitutional right to confront and cross-examine the unnamed individuals whose statements had led to the sentence increase.

5. The Right to a Statement of Reasons for the Sentence Imposed

The lower courts have also held that, at least generally, due process does not require a sentencing judge to provide a defendant with a statement recounting the reasons why a particular sentence was imposed. *See, e.g., United States v. Golomb* (2d Cir.1985). Even if the lower courts are correct that there generally is no constitutional right to a statement of reasons for the sentence imposed, such a right, of course, may be accorded by statute or court rule, as can other rights that are not constitutionally mandated.

One notable exception to the general rule that due process does not require a statement of reasons for the sentence imposed is when a conviction obtained following a trial is reversed on appeal, the defendant is reconvicted, and the same judge who initially sentenced the defendant imposes a higher sentence the second time around. *See North Carolina v. Pearce* (S.Ct.1969) as construed by the Supreme Court in *Texas v. McCullough* (S.Ct.1986). In this situation, there is a presumption that the judge unconstitutionally imposed the increased sentence to retaliate against the defendant for having appealed the conviction. Unless this presumption is rebutted by legitimate reasons for the increased sentence that "affirmatively appear" on the record, the increased sentence will be vacated, and the defendant will be resentenced because of the violation of his or her right to due process of law.

On the other hand, there is no presumption of vindictiveness requiring a statement of reasons for an increased sentence when a "different sentencer" imposes the higher sentence after a second trial. *Texas v. McCullough* (S.Ct.1986). Nor is there a presumption of vindictiveness when the increased sentence is imposed by the same sentencer, but following the granting of a motion for a new trial. *Id.* According to the Supreme Court, when a trial judge has acknowledged the need for a new trial, the risk that the increased sentence was due to proscribed vindictiveness is sufficiently diminished that a presumption of vindictiveness is unwarranted. Finally, as was discussed in Chapter 2, no presumption of vindictiveness exists when a defendant's guilty plea was set aside on appeal and the increased sentence was imposed following the defendant's trial on the reinstated charges. *Alabama v. Smith* (S.Ct.1989).

6.   Standard of Proof/Jury Trial

During a sentencing hearing, a prosecutor will customarily point to aggravating factors that suggest that a more stringent sentence should be imposed on a defendant, while the defendant will cite mitigating factors that support imposition of a more lenient sentence. The Supreme Court has held that the burden of proving the existence of a mitigating circumstance can constitutionally be placed on a defendant, even in a capital case. *Walton v. Arizona* (S.Ct.1990). This conclusion makes sense when one remembers that defendants have readier access to much of the information commonly presented to mitigate a sentence, such as facts about the defendant's health, employment record, and educational background.

In *McMillan v. Pennsylvania* (S.Ct.1986), the Supreme Court answered some questions concerning the burden of proving aggravating factors. *McMil-*

lan involved a challenge to a state statute that required a sentencing judge to impose a minimum sentence of five years in prison on a defendant convicted of one of several crimes delineated in the statute if the judge found by a preponderance of the evidence (in other words, that it was more likely than not) that the defendant had "visibly possessed a firearm" at the time of the crime.

The defendants contended that this statute violated due process of law for two reasons. First, they argued that the visible possession of a firearm that triggered the mandatory five-year prison term constituted an element of the crimes with which they were charged, which meant that the requisite possession had to be proven beyond a reasonable doubt.

The Supreme Court disagreed. The Court noted that the Pennsylvania legislature specifically had said that visible possession of a firearm was not to be considered an element of the crime, but simply a sentencing factor. While the Court acknowledged that there were limits to the extent that a legislature could denominate a fact to be a sentencing factor rather than an element of the crime, the Court was convinced that those limits, whatever they might be, had not been exceeded in this case. The Court underscored, for example, that the state statute did not increase the maximum penalty that could be imposed on a person convicted of one of the crimes delineated in the statute. Instead, the statute simply defined, as the legislature had the prerogative to do, the weight to be given a particular sentencing factor when sentencing a defendant within the prescribed sentencing range. *See also Harris v. United States* (S.Ct.2002)(refusing to overrule *McMillan*).

The defendants in *McMillan* also argued that even if visible possession of a firearm could properly be considered a sentencing factor, the prosecution's burden of proving the existence of this factor under the statute—by a preponderance of the evidence—was too low. The defendants contended that due process required that a defendant's visible possession of a firearm at the time of the crime be established by at least clear and convincing evidence, a standard of proof higher than a preponderance, although not as high as proof beyond a reasonable doubt.

The Supreme Court summarily rejected this claim. Noting that defendants at sentencing hearings have already been found guilty beyond a reasonable doubt, the Court observed that traditionally there has been no required burden of proof at sentencing hearings. In the Court's opinion, the preponderance-of-the-evidence standard that had to be met under the statute therefore clearly satisfied, and may very well have exceeded, the requirements of the Constitution.

The Supreme Court in *McMillan* rejected one other claim concerning Pennsylvania's mandatory-minimum sentencing statute—one grounded on the Sixth Amendment right to a jury trial. The defendants contended that they had a right to have a jury, not a judge, make the determination whether they visibly possessed a firearm at the time of the crimes of which they were convicted. The Court simply responded that there is no right to have the question of one's sentence, as opposed to one's guilt or innocence, decided by a jury. Even in a capital case, there is no constitutional right to be sentenced by a jury. *Spaziano v. Florida* (S.Ct.1984) (death penalty imposed by judge upheld even though advisory jury recommended a life sentence in prison). As is discussed subsequently in this chapter, though, a defendant does have a Sixth Amendment right to have a jury make any factual findings regarding aggravating factors that are a prerequisite to imposition of a death sentence.

The Supreme Court distinguished *McMillan* in *Apprendi v. New Jersey* (S.Ct.2000). The sentencing statute whose constitutionality was at issue in *Apprendi* authorized a judge to increase a defendant's sentence by ten to twenty years above the maximum sentence for illegal possession of a firearm when the judge found, by a preponderance of the evidence, that the defendant had committed the crime with the intent to intimidate someone because of his or her race. In a 5–4 decision, the Supreme Court held that because the defendant's motive for committing the crime would extend his sentence beyond the statutory maximum, that fact was an element of the crime rather than a sentencing factor. Consequently, due process required that the prosecution prove the fact beyond a reasonable doubt. In addition, the defendant was constitutionally entitled to a jury determination of that fact.

The reasoning of *Apprendi* later led the Supreme Court to strike down the death-penalty structure in Arizona on Sixth Amendment grounds. *Ring v. Arizona* (S.Ct.2002). Under an Arizona statute, a judge determined whether defendants whom a jury had convicted of first-degree murder should be sentenced to death. Imposition of a death sentence was conditioned on the judge's finding of at least one aggravating circumstance set forth in the statute. Because the maximum sentence—death—could not be imposed without this factual finding, the Supreme Court held that capital defendants had a constitutional right to have a jury render this finding.

In *Blakely v. Washington* (S.Ct.2004), the Supreme Court further elaborated on the distinction between sentencing factors and elements of a crime. The defendant in that case pleaded guilty to second-degree kidnapping, a crime for which the statutory maximum sentence was ten years in prison. The state's sentencing guidelines under which the defendant was sentenced set the standard sentencing range for this crime at forty-nine to fifty-three months. However, the sentencing judge found that the defendant had committed the crime with "deliberate cruelty," an aggravating factor that, under the state's sentencing laws, provided grounds for departing upwards from the standard sentencing range. The judge then sentenced the defendant to prison for ninety months, a sentence about three years longer than the standard sentence prescribed by the guidelines but one that was below the statutory maximum sentence.

The Supreme Court, splitting 5–4, held that the defendant's sentence had been imposed in violation of his Sixth Amendment right to a jury trial. In demarcating the line where the right to a jury trial begins for *Apprendi* purposes, the Court said that the maximum sentence that a sentencing judge can impose cannot exceed "*the facts reflected in the jury verdict or admitted by the defendant.*" (emphasis in the original) Since the sentencing guidelines did not authorize a sentence higher than fifty-three months for the defendant's crime absent an additional factual finding—that an aggravating fact existed, the defendant had a constitutional right to have a jury determine whether the prosecution had proven this fact beyond a reasonable doubt.

The Court insisted in *Blakely* that its decision did not spell the end to determinate sentencing, including sentencing guidelines. Jurisdictions can, the Court said, take several different routes that will enable them to comply with the requirements of the Constitution while retaining their determinate-sentencing systems. They can, for example, hold bifurcated trials in which a jury first determines whether the defendant is guilty of the crime charged and then determines whether a fact not reflected in the initial verdict exists that warrants the imposition of an enhanced sentence. Alternatively, all of the facts needed to support imposition of the aggravated sentence can be established in a single jury trial.

The Court also reminded those who predicted that its decision would wreak havoc in determinate-sentencing systems across the country that defendants can waive their "*Apprendi* rights"; they can stipulate to the existence of an aggravating fact or facts or can agree to a judge, rather than a jury, conducting the factfinding that may lead to imposition of an enhanced sentence.

In *United States v. Booker* (S.Ct.2005), the Supreme Court concluded that the federal sentencing guidelines shared the same constitutional flaw as the guidelines that had been before the Court in *Blakely*: they provided for an increase in a defendant's sentence beyond the maximum authorized by the jury's verdict alone or the facts admitted by the defendant in a guilty plea. To remedy this constitutional problem, the Court held that the guidelines would remain in effect, but be advisory rather than mandatory. In other words, federal judges must continue to turn to the guidelines for guidance when sentencing a defendant but are not bound to follow them. If a sentencing decision later is challenged on appeal, the appellate court will then vacate the sentence only if it is "unreasonable."

If a fact is an element of a crime, a defendant in a federal prosecution also has a right under the Fifth Amendment to have that fact alleged in the criminal indictment. *Hamling v. United States* (S.Ct. 1974). Whether that latter right was abridged was the focus of *Almendarez-Torres v. United States* (S.Ct.1998), decided two years before *Apprendi*. The statute at issue in that case authorized an enhanced penalty of up to twenty years in prison, compared to a maximum sentence of two years, if a deported alien who illegally returned to the country previously had been convicted of an "aggravated felony." The Supreme Court, in another 5–4 decision, concluded that the previous conviction was a sentencing factor, not an element of the crime. The defendant's indictment, therefore, did not have to allege that fact.

In *Apprendi*, the Supreme Court described *Almendarez-Torres* as crafting a "narrow exception" to the general rule that a fact that enhances the statutory maximum sentence is an element of the crime. Recognizing such an exception might be defensible, according to the Court, because prior convictions used to elevate sentences were obtained during court proceedings replete with substantial procedural safeguards. But the Court in *Apprendi* acknowledged that it was "arguable" that *Almendarez-Torres* was wrongly decided, intimating that it might revisit the issue presented in that case in the future.

7. Double Jeopardy

Another constitutional provision that is implicated occasionally in sentencing proceedings is the Fifth Amendment's Double Jeopardy Clause. This provision, which prohibits the government from punishing a person twice for the same crime, bars the government from reprosecuting a person for a crime of which he or she was acquitted. *United States v. Ball* (S.Ct.1896). When a sentencing jury or judge refrains from imposing the death penalty in a capital case, the double-jeopardy ban also prohibits the government from once again pursuing the death penalty if the case is reversed on appeal and the defendant is reconvicted. *Bullington v. Missouri* (S.Ct.1981); *Arizona v. Rumsey* (S.Ct.1984).

On the other hand, double jeopardy does not preclude imposition of a higher sentence following a reconviction in a noncapital case. *Monge v. California* (S.Ct.1998). The Supreme Court has cited the uniqueness of the death penalty as the rationale for the Double Jeopardy Clause's differential treatment of capital and noncapital sentences. For double-jeopardy purposes, when a judge resentences a defendant in a noncapital case following an appellate reversal, the new sentence is imposed, with one exception, on a clean slate. That exception requires that the defendant be given credit for any time served on the original sentence. *North Carolina v. Pearce* (S.Ct.1969).

The defendant's right not to be subjected to double jeopardy is not violated when a court elevates a sentence because of uncharged criminal conduct and the defendant later is charged with a crime for that same conduct. In *Witte v. United States* (S.Ct. 1995), the judge who sentenced the defendant for a drug crime that had occurred in 1991 factored the defendant's involvement in other drug crimes that had occurred in 1990 into the sentence. Consideration of this uncharged conduct when computing the defendant's sentence led to a sixteen-year increase in his offense level under the federal sentencing guidelines. The Supreme Court, however, discerned no double-jeopardy problem when the defendant later was charged with, and convicted of, crimes stemming from the 1990 drug transactions. The Court explained that when the uncharged crimes had been used to calculate the defendant's sentence for the 1991 crime, the defendant was being punished, not for those uncharged crimes, but for the crime of which he had been convicted. The uncharged crimes, according to the Court, were simply an indicator of what would be an appropriate penalty for the offense of which the defendant had been convicted.

B. FACTORS CONSIDERED AT SENTENCING

Traditionally, courts have emphasized the breadth of information about an offender and the offender's crime that can be introduced at a sentencing hearing to ensure that the most appropriate penalty is imposed on an offender. The Supreme Court's decisions in *Blakely v. Washington* and *United States v. Booker*, on their face, did not narrow the broad range of facts that can be considered during the sentencing process. Those decisions simply held that before a particular fact can result in the imposition of a sentence outside the sentencing range established by the jury's verdict or facts admitted by the defendant when entering a guilty plea, the defendant has a constitutional right to have a jury determine whether the existence of the fact has been proven beyond a reasonable doubt.

Even without these procedural safeguards, the facts discussed below that the Supreme Court has held can be considered during the sentencing process can affect what sentence is selected from within the sentencing range delimited by the jury's verdict or the guilty plea. Assume, for example, that a jury's verdict could lead to the imposition of a sentence falling anywhere between two to five years in prison. Because, as is discussed below, a sentencing judge can consider a defendant's untruthfulness at trial when sentencing the defendant, the judge may decide to impose a sentence on the high end of that range—perhaps a sentence of five years—because of the defendant's perjurious testimony.

1.   Criminal Conduct and Convictions

Several Supreme Court cases illustrate the expansive scope of the information that can be considered by a sentencing judge. In *Williams v. New York* (S.Ct.1949), for example, the Court condoned consideration by a sentencing judge of a number of burglaries allegedly committed by the defendant, but of which the defendant had not been convicted. And in *United States v. Watts* (S.Ct.1997), the Court went even further, permitting consideration at sentencing hearings of crimes of which defendants have been acquitted. The Court pointed out that an acquittal simply means that the government was unable to prove guilt beyond a reasonable doubt. Because this high standard of proof does not apply at sentencing hearings, evidence about the criminal conduct may constitutionally be admitted at a sentencing hearing.

Williams v. New York laid the foundation for the Supreme Court's subsequent decision in *United States v. Grayson* (S.Ct.1978). In *Grayson*, the sentencing judge had imposed a more severe sentence on a defendant because the judge believed that the defendant had perjured himself when testifying at his trial. The defendant contended that for two reasons, consideration of his alleged perjury as an aggravating factor at the time of sentencing violated his right to due process of law. First, he argued that he was in effect being punished for a crime of which he had not even been convicted. The Supreme Court responded that a defendant's willingness to commit the crime of perjury is relevant to the question of what is the appropriate sentence for the crime of which he has been convicted, because a person who is willing to lie while under oath may be a less suitable candidate for rehabilitation.

The defendant in *Grayson* also argued that enhancing a sentence because of a defendant's suspected perjury at trial would unconstitutionally "chill" the exercise by defendants of their right to testify in their own behalf at trial. The Court responded that any right to testify at trial includes only the right to testify truthfully. So if consideration by sentencing judges of defendants' perjury when testifying at trial dissuades some defendants from taking the stand and testifying falsely, that chilling effect is constitutionally permissible. *See also United States v. Dunnigan* (S.Ct.1993) (constitutional to increase sentence under federal sentencing guidelines for "willfully obstructing or impeding proceedings" by committing perjury at trial).

A defendant's refusal to cooperate with authorities by providing information about the criminal activities of others can also, in some circumstances, properly be considered as an aggravating sentencing factor. In *Roberts v. United States* (S.Ct.1980), a defendant who had been charged with several drug offenses refused to name his drug suppliers. This refusal prompted the sentencing judge to impose a heavier sentence on the defendant.

The Supreme Court acknowledged that the defendant may have had legitimate reasons for refusing to cooperate with the authorities. By disclosing the requested information, he might have implicated himself in additional crimes, or he may have feared retaliation from his suppliers. The problem, from the Supreme Court's perspective, was that the defendant had failed to assert any of these reasons for refusing to cooperate at the time of sentencing. If he had, the judge could have assessed the legitimacy of the defendant's concerns about incriminating himself and his fears for his safety. Because the defendant had failed to explain to the sentencing judge why he was reluctant to cooperate with the authorities, he could not now complain of the court's consideration of his lack of cooperation when sentencing him.

Even when a defendant does not specifically invoke his or her privilege against self-incrimination at a sentencing hearing, the Fifth Amendment places at least some limits on the drawing of a negative inference from the defendant's failure to testify at that hearing. While a defendant, by entering a plea of guilty, forgoes the right to trial, including the protection afforded by the privilege against self-incrimination at the trial, that privilege still pertains to sentencing proceedings. Consequently, just as a judge or jury cannot infer a defendant's guilt from his or her failure to testify at trial, *Griffin v. California* (S.Ct.1965), neither can the sentencing judge infer certain facts about "the circumstances and details of the crime" because the defendant did not take the stand at the sentencing hearing to refute the prosecution's evidence, such as evidence about the amount of narcotics involved in a drug crime of which the defendant was convicted. *Mitchell v. United States* (S.Ct.1999).

A prior misdemeanor conviction, obtained when an indigent defendant was not represented by counsel but which did not result in incarceration, can constitutionally be considered as an aggravating factor when sentencing the defendant in a subsequent criminal case. *Nichols v. United States* (S.Ct. 1994) (reliance on uncounseled misdemeanor conviction when computing defendant's criminal-history score increased his prison sentence by over two years). Because of the actual-incarceration standard discussed earlier in this chapter, the uncounseled misdemeanor conviction was itself constitutional. Consequently, the conviction can be used to enhance the defendant's sentence, even when the defendant will be imprisoned for a lengthier period of time because of it. According to the Supreme Court, a conviction that was valid initially does not suddenly become invalid when used for enhancement purposes.

2. First Amendment Limitations

While the scope of the information about defendants and their crimes that may be introduced during sentencing hearings is quite vast, the Constitution does place some limits on the information that can be considered when sentencing a criminal defendant. For example, in *Dawson v. Delaware* (S.Ct.1992), the Supreme Court held that introducing evidence in a capital sentencing hearing that the defendant was a member of a prison gang comprised of white racists abridged his First Amendment right to freedom of association. At the same time, the Court intimated that if the evidence regarding the persons with whom the defendant associated reflected more than his abstract beliefs, it might be considered constitutionally at the time of sentencing. For example, evidence that the prison gang of which the defendant was a member had been involved in murders and violent prison escapes might have a bearing on the issue of the defendant's future dangerousness, an issue that may considered by a sentencing jury when deciding whether to impose the death penalty.

The First Amendment does not bar what are called hate-crime statutes, statutes that provide for an enhanced penalty when a victim was selected because of his or her race, gender, religion, or other statutorily specified attributes. *Wisconsin v. Mitchell* (S.Ct.1993). According to the Supreme Court, hate-crime statutes do not punish defendants because of their abstract beliefs or speech protected by the First Amendment. Those statutes instead inflict punishment because of the defendant's conduct, such as a battery or destruction of property, that is not protected by the First Amendment. Considering a defendant's motive for a crime when sentencing the defendant for this conduct does not somehow transform a constitutional sentence into an unconstitutional sentence; a defendant's motive for committing a crime traditionally has been a significant factor in sentencing decisions.

3. False Information

Townsend v. Burke (S.Ct.1948) is another case that illustrates that the Constitution places limits on the information that can be considered at the time of sentencing. *Townsend* involved a defendant who was sentenced to prison for a minimum of ten years and a maximum of twenty for burglary and robbery. The length of the sentence was due in large part to a string of prior convictions cited by the sentencing judge. In fact, however, the defendant had not been convicted in the cases to which the judge alluded. The criminal charges had been dismissed in one of those cases, and he had been acquitted in two others.

The Supreme Court held that the defendant's right to due process of law had been violated. *Town-*

send, however, does not stand for the proposition that a constitutional violation ensues whenever false information is introduced at a sentencing hearing. In *Townsend*, the Supreme Court emphasized that the information upon which the defendant's sentence was based was not only false, but "extensively and materially false." *Compare United States v. Addonizio* (S.Ct.1979) (judge's erroneous prediction of when the defendant would be released on parole was not "misinformation of constitutional magnitude," because the judge's expectations were unenforceable against the parole board). In addition, the sentencing judge must actually have relied on the material misinformation in order for a due-process violation to occur. It is for this reason that Rule 32(i)(3)(B) of the Federal Rules of Criminal Procedure directs judges faced with a defendant's challenge to the accuracy of information in a pre-sentence-investigation report or other information presented to the sentencing judge to either resolve the factual dispute or confirm that the disputed information was not taken into account when sentencing the defendant.

4. Unconstitutional Convictions

United States v. Tucker (S.Ct.1972) dealt with the validity of a sentence that was grounded on three prior convictions of the defendant, two of which were later determined to have been obtained unconstitutionally, in violation of the defendant's Sixth Amendment right to counsel. The Court held that the defendant, who had received the maximum sentence for his crime, was entitled to be resentenced because his sentence was based, at least in part, on "misinformation of constitutional magnitude." The Court observed that if the sentencing judge had been aware that the defendant had spent ten years of his life illegally confined in prison, the judge might very well have imposed a different sentence. *See also Johnson v. Mississippi* (S.Ct.1988) (death sentence based in part on a conviction that was later vacated violated Eighth Amendment's prohibition of cruel and unusual punishments).

United States v. Tucker was narrowly construed by the Supreme Court in *Custis v. United States* (S.Ct.1994). The defendant in *Custis* was sentenced under the Armed Career Criminal Act, a federal statute requiring imposition of a minimum prison sentence of fifteen years on a person with three prior convictions for a "violent felony" or a "serious drug offense" who was then convicted of possession of a firearm by a felon. The defendant contended that two of the prior convictions upon which his enhanced sentence was based had been obtained in violation of his constitutional rights. Specifically, he maintained that his convictions had been obtained in violation of due process of law and without the effective assistance of counsel to which he was constitutionally entitled. The federal judge who sentenced the defendant, however, refused to delve into the question of whether the prior state convictions upon which the defendant's enhanced sentence was based were in fact unconstitutional.

One of the questions before the Supreme Court in *Custis* was whether the defendant had a due-process right to challenge the constitutionality of his prior convictions when being sentenced under the Armed Career Criminal Act. The Supreme Court concluded that he did not. One of the Court's concerns was that requiring such collateral review of prior convictions would unduly delay and encumber sentencing proceedings under the Armed Career Criminal Act. Federal courts would be forced at the time of sentencing to sift through the records of state convictions, assuming that those records, many of which concerned convictions obtained many years earlier, still existed.

The Court was not convinced that *United States v. Tucker* required a contrary result. The defendant's prior convictions in *Tucker* upon which his sentence had been based had been unconstitutional due to the fact that he was not afforded the assistance of an attorney when those convictions were obtained. Describing this total failure to appoint counsel to represent an indigent defendant as a "unique constitutional defect," the Court in *Custis* concluded that a defendant being sentenced under the Armed Career Criminal Act has a due-process right to challenge a prior conviction only when the defendant has suffered such a total abridgment of the Sixth Amendment right to counsel.

The dissenting judges in *Custis*—Justices Souter, Blackmun, and Stevens—excoriated the majority opinion for the distinction it had erected between violations of the Sixth Amendment right to counsel due to a total failure to appoint counsel to represent a defendant and other constitutional violations. They pointed out, for example, that defendants who have not received effective assistance from their attorneys are in as dire straits as defendants who have received no assistance whatsoever.

The Court in *Custis* did emphasize that while the defendant had no constitutional right to challenge the constitutionality of his prior convictions when being sentenced under the Armed Career Criminal Act, he was not necessarily left remediless. According to the Court, the defendant could challenge the constitutionality of his prior convictions in a state postconviction proceeding or a federal habeas corpus action. If he was successful in getting any of these convictions set aside, he then could apply to the federal court to have his enhanced sentence under the Armed Career Criminal Act reduced.

While a prisoner may be able to challenge in a habeas corpus action or similar proceeding the constitutionality of a prior conviction that underlay an enhanced sentence, a prisoner generally has no constitutional right to challenge the enhanced sentence itself in a habeas corpus action on the grounds that it was founded on an unconstitutional prior conviction. *Daniels v. United States* (S.Ct.2001) (federal prisoners generally barred from bringing such collateral challenges under 28 U.S.C. § 2255); *Lackawanna County Dist. Attorney v. Coss* (S.Ct.2001) (state prisoners generally barred from bringing such collateral challenges under 28 U.S.C. § 2254). According to the Supreme Court, the same concerns that negate any constitutional right to challenge the constitutionality of prior convictions at a sentencing hearing apply when the enhanced sentence is challenged in a collateral proceeding. For example, pertinent records bearing on the validity of those convictions are just as difficult to locate and retrieve in habeas corpus actions.

As is true at sentencing hearings, there is an exception to the general rule barring the review in habeas corpus and similar proceedings of sentences that were predicated on allegedly unconstitutional prior convictions. That exception applies when a prior conviction was the end product of an alleged total failure to appoint counsel to represent an indigent defendant.

5. Illegally Obtained Evidence

One question that has yet to be resolved by the Supreme Court concerns the admissibility of illegally obtained evidence during a sentencing hearing. The brunt of the litigation on this question has concerned evidence seized in violation of the Fourth Amendment's proscription of unreasonable searches and seizures. Most of the lower courts have held that such evidence is admissible during a sentencing hearing, at least when the search's purpose was not to find evidence to enhance the defendant's sentence. *See, e.g., United States v. Acosta* (1st Cir.2002)(listing cases). In arriving at this conclusion, the courts have weighed the costs of applying the Fourth Amendment exclusionary rule against the benefits of applying the rule in the sentencing context. One of these costs is the withholding of probative and reliable evidence from sentencers, which can in turn lead to the imposition of inappropriate penalties on convicted offenders.

The lower courts have concluded that these costs generally outweigh any benefit that exclusion of the evidence might have in deterring violations of the Fourth Amendment by police officers. The courts reason that to the extent that the suppression of evidence has a deterrent effect on police officers, they generally will be dissuaded from violating the Fourth Amendment by the prospect that illegally seized evidence will be inadmissible at trial. The inadmissibility of the evidence at a sentencing hearing usually will not yield much, if any, additional benefit in terms of deterrence, unless the constitutional violation occurred for the express purpose of locating evidence to enhance the defendant's sentence.

6. Victim–Impact Statements

The Supreme Court has vacillated back and forth in recent years on the issue of the admissibility of victim-impact statements in sentencing proceedings in capital cases. The Court first confronted this issue in *Booth v. Maryland* (S.Ct.1987). In that case, a victim-impact statement was submitted to, and considered by, a jury which sentenced the defendant to death for murdering an elderly man and his wife. In that statement, the victims' relatives described what the victims were like and how traumatized the relatives were by the murders. In addition, the family members expressed their views about the crimes, reviling the defendant for having "butchered" the victims "like animals."

The Supreme Court in *Booth,* in a 5–4 decision, concluded that the introduction of this victim-impact evidence in a sentencing hearing in a capital case violated the defendant's right under the Eighth Amendment not to be subjected to cruel and unusual punishment. The Court gave several reasons why evidence about a victim's personal characteristics and the impact of a murder on the victim's survivors was inadmissible. First, the Court asserted that such evidence was simply irrelevant because it did not bear on the defendant's blameworthiness. The Court pointed out that defendants were often unaware, at the time they decided to murder the victims, of what their victims were like or whether they had families.

Second, the Court was concerned that the introduction of this type of victim-impact evidence would create a risk of unconstitutional dimensions that the death penalty would be imposed arbitrarily. The Court objected to having the decision to put a defendant to death hinge on whether the victim was portrayed as, and perceived to be, a "sterling member of the community." The Court was also concerned that some defendants might be sentenced to death simply because some family members were more articulate than others in describing their grief. In a dissenting opinion, Justice White spurned this latter argument, noting that variation in the persuasiveness of the testimony of witnesses and the arguments made by different prosecutors is the norm in criminal cases and is unavoidable.

Third, the Supreme Court was disturbed that victim-impact evidence would sidetrack sentencing juries from their primary, and critical, mission of determining whether defendants, in light of their personal attributes and the circumstances of their crimes, should be put to death. The Court also pointed to the difficulty that defendants often would have rebutting victim-impact evidence. For example, it usually would be strategically unwise for a defendant to cast aspersions on the character of a person that he or she had killed.

Turning to the issue of the admissibility of family members' opinions about the crime, the Court concluded, rather summarily, that such opinions were introduced for only one reason—to inflame the jury. Consequently, such opinions had no proper place in a capital sentencing hearing.

The Supreme Court partially overruled *Booth v. Maryland* only four years after its decision in that case. In *Payne v. Tennessee* (S.Ct.1991), the Court, in another 5–4 decision, concluded that it had erred in *Booth* when holding that it violates the Eighth Amendment to introduce in a capital sentencing hearing evidence about a victim's personal characteristics and the impact of a murder on family members. The Court observed that upon further reflection, it was convinced that this type of evidence did in fact bear on the defendant's blameworthiness, because defendants have always been held responsible for the harm caused by their criminal behavior. In addition, the Court was no longer concerned that introduction of victim-impact evidence would inappropriately shift the jury's attention away from the defendant. Instead, the Court noted that this evidence would appropriately expand the jury's focus, permitting the jury to see that just as the defendant is a unique individual, so was his or her victim. To do otherwise—to permit a defendant at a capital sentencing hearing to introduce any mitigating evidence whatsoever while treating the victim as a "faceless stranger"—in the Court's opinion "unfairly weighted the scales" in a capital sentencing hearing.

The Supreme Court also dismissed other concerns about victim-impact statements raised in *Booth.* The Court insisted that information about what a victim was like was not introduced to show that the victim was more worthy than others and that a defendant was therefore more deserving of death. This evidence was instead admitted to show the victim's "uniqueness as an individual human being" and the ensuing irremediable loss to the community caused by his or her death.

Nor was the Court concerned about the dilemma faced by defendants considering whether to rebut victim-impact evidence. The Court simply noted that this decision was no more difficult than other decisions that had to be made by a defendant during the litigation process.

The Supreme Court did observe in *Payne v. Tennessee* that while the introduction of victim-impact evidence normally would present no constitutional problem, sometimes such evidence might be "so unduly prejudicial" as to make the sentencing proceeding "fundamentally unfair," thereby violating the dictates of due process. The Court also noted that it was not overruling that portion of *Booth v. Maryland* that had held unconstitutional the admission of family members' descriptions and opinions of the defendant's crimes, because no such evidence had been presented during the sentencing hearing in the case before it.

CHAPTER 4

SENTENCING STATUTES AND GUIDELINES

There are two central decisions that must be made when sentencing a criminal defendant. The first is known as the in-out decision. Should the defendant be sentenced to prison or jail, or should the defendant instead be punished in the community? The second decision concerns the length, amount, and conditions of the defendant's sentence. If the defendant is to be incarcerated, how long should that incarceration last? Alternatively, if a community-based sanction is to be imposed on the defendant, how long should that sanction last (or, in the case of an economic sanction, how much should the defendant pay), and what conditions should accompany that sanction?

Sentencing systems vary as to how and where discretion in sentencing criminal defendants is allocated. The systems can be differentiated based on the roles played by legislatures, judges, sentencing commissions, and parole boards in determining the sentences imposed on and served by convicted offenders.

Sentencing systems can be divided into at least three general categories—those in which indeterminate sentencing statutes predominate; those in which determinate sentencing statutes are applied; and those in which sentencing guidelines further channel judges' sentencing discretion. Even within these broad categories, there is a great deal of variation in sentencing structures. There is also some overlap between the categories. For example, mandatory sentencing statutes, which are discussed later in this chapter, are considered a form of determinate sentencing, but they can often be found in jurisdictions with indeterminate sentencing statutes as well as in jurisdictions that employ sentencing guidelines.

A. INDETERMINATE SENTENCING STATUTES

In a jurisdiction with indeterminate sentencing, a judge sentences a person to prison for a range of time falling within parameters set by the legislature. A judge might, for example, sentence an armed robber to prison for a minimum of two and a maximum of fifteen years. A parole board then decides how much time the individual is actually confined in prison. The parole board might decide that the person is ready to be released from prison after two years. Alternatively, the parole board might decide that the person must remain in prison for the full fifteen years or might decide to release the prisoner from prison sometime in between the two-year minimum and the fifteen-year maximum period of incarceration.

One of the argued advantages of parole systems is that parole boards, drawing on the advice of correctional officials who have been able to closely observe prisoners during their confinement, can best determine when a prisoner is ready to be safely released back into the community. This argument is somewhat belied by the high recidivism rates of prisoners released on parole, although these high recidivism rates might also be due to other problems in correctional systems, including the lack of adequate plans and programs to facilitate inmates' successful reintegration into the community.

Another claimed benefit of parole systems is that they can help to relieve crowding in prisons. When a state's prisons become too crowded, the parole board can ease population pressures by releasing additional prisoners on parole. This touted benefit of parole, however, is often cited by critics as one of its chief drawbacks. The premature release of prisoners, they argue, jeopardizes the public's safety and undermines the other penological goals of incarceration.

There are two other major problems that stem from indeterminate sentencing structures. First, indeterminate sentences generate uncertainty regarding exactly how long inmates will be imprisoned, augmenting the stress and tension that inevitably attend incarceration. This stress and tension, in turn, can interfere with rehabilitation efforts and can compound the already difficult problem of safely managing prisoners. These adverse effects of indeterminate sentencing can be further aggravated by the resentment felt by prisoners as they observe other inmates whom they believe to be comparable to themselves being released on parole while they are left to languish in prison.

The other problem with indeterminate sentences is the enormous disparity in the length of confinement of comparable prisoners that can result when the discretion to determine how much time a person will spend in prison is remitted to a parole board. This disparity, as well as the psychological pressures mentioned earlier, can be mitigated somewhat by parole guidelines that guide parole boards in the exercise of their discretion and require them to justify release decisions that depart from the guidelines. Parole guidelines, however, cannot totally eliminate the disparity that accompanies indeterminate sentencing, because they only govern decisions concerning when prisoners will be released from prison. They have no application to the initial decision of judges to send or not send individuals to prison in the first place. Thus, a community-based sanction may be imposed on one person for a crime, while another person, who has committed a comparable crime and has a comparable criminal background, is sent to prison.

B.   DETERMINATE SENTENCING STATUTES

Determinate sentencing statutes avoid some of the problems of indeterminate sentences, but they have some of their own unique drawbacks. The nature and extent of those drawbacks depend on the type of determinate sentencing statute in question.

1. Determinate Discretionary Sentencing

Under a determinate-discretionary sentencing statute, a judge, when imprisoning an offender, selects a sentence from a range set by the legislature. The difference between a determinate-discretionary sentencing structure and an indeterminate sentencing system is that the judge, not a parole board, defines the amount of time that a person will be confined. For example, if the legislature authorizes a prison sentence of no less than one year and no more than fifteen years for an armed robbery, the sentencing judge picks a number within that range, such as four years, eight years, or ten years.

Two caveats must be added to this description of determinate-discretionary sentencing statutes. First, although such statutes delineate the range from which a judge will select a finite prison sentence for a particular crime, other statutes often authorize the judge to impose a community-based sanction if imprisonment is considered unnecessary. Second, while a judge under a determinate-discretionary statute imposes a finite prison term on an offender, the actual time that the offender remains behind bars may frequently be reduced by the earning of what are often called "good-time credits." With good-time credits, a prisoner's sentence is reduced by a prescribed amount of time for every day or month that the inmate refrains from violating prison rules or regulations. For example, a prisoner might have one day lopped off of his or her prison sentence for every day of good behavior.

In recent years, there has been a movement in some jurisdictions towards what is called "earned time." With earned time, inmates must do something more than just refrain from misconduct to earn credits that reduce their prison sentences; they must work, go to school, or participate in other programs that will make it more likely that they will refrain from committing crimes after their release from prison.

Convicted offenders are also often given credit for time they were incarcerated while awaiting trial or sentencing. For example, 18 U.S.C § 3585(b) provides that a federal offender sentenced to prison must be given credit for time spent in "official detention" before the prison sentence began. But in *Reno v. Koray* (S.Ct.1995), the Supreme Court held that 24–hour-a-day confinement in a community treatment center while awaiting sentencing did not constitute the "official detention" for which credit must be given under § 3585(b). Because the convicted offender in the case had been released on bail pending sentencing, although subject to the condition that he stay in the community treatment center all of the time, he was not, according to the Court, subject to "official detention" within the meaning of the statute.

Determinate-discretionary sentencing statutes offer the advantage of certainty. They avoid the tension felt by prisoners sentenced under indeterminate sentencing statutes who do not know how much time they will have to be confined in prison. But as is true with indeterminate sentencing systems, determinate-discretionary sentencing structures are characterized by sentencing disparity, and sometimes gross sentencing disparity, as judges pick and choose numbers within the imprisonment range defined by the legislature.

2. Presumptive Sentencing

One way to reduce the sentencing disparity mentioned above is through another type of determinate sentencing statute—a presumptive sentencing statute. A presumptive sentencing statute defines the presumptive sentence that the legislature wants imposed for a particular crime. If there are aggravating factors in a case, the statute often outlines how far above the presumptive sentence the judge may go in imposing a higher sentence. The judge's discretion is similarly circumscribed when a sentence more lenient than the presumptive sentence is imposed because of mitigating factors.

One of the problems with presumptive sentencing statutes is that they tend to fall prey to political pressures. Presumptive sentences are not selected after thoughtful and careful consideration, guided by research, as to what would be the most appropriate sentences from a penological standpoint. Instead, they are generally the reflexive response of legislators competing to demonstrate to the public how "tough" they are on crime. Over the years,

these legislatively prescribed presumptive sentences
tend to be continually ratcheted up as the out-
growth of this political posturing.

3. Mandatory Sentences

This same criticism about the politicization of
sentencing has been leveled against another category of determinate sentencing statutes—those prescribing mandatory-minimum sentences. As their
name suggests, mandatory-minimum sentencing
statutes require that offenders serve at least a specified amount of time in prison for particular crimes.
Many of these statutes are directed against drug
offenders and require prison sentences of five years,
ten years, fifteen years, and sometimes even life in
prison, depending on the amount of drugs involved.

The "three strikes and you're out" laws that
have been enacted in a number of states in recent
years are another type of mandatory-minimum sentencing statute. Under these laws, certain three-
time felons must be sent to prison for a very long,
statutorily-prescribed period of time—in some
states, to life in prison without the possibility of
parole.

The appeal of mandatory minimums to legislators is that by enacting them, the legislators can
appear, to an uninformed public, to be sending a
tough message to prospective criminals: "If you
commit this crime, you will spend this amount of
time in prison, no matter what." In practice, however, mandatory-minimum sentences are readily,
and very often, circumvented. A study conducted

by the United States Sentencing Commission in
1991, for example, revealed that about 40% of the
federal offenders whose crimes should have triggered mandatory-minimum sentences were able to
avoid these mandatory penalties. United States
Sentencing Commission, *Special Report to the Congress: Mandatory Minimum Penalties in the Federal Criminal Justice System* 89 (1991). What is particularly disconcerting about these statistics is that
the disparity in the enforcement of mandatory-minimum sentences has racial and ethnic overtones;
white defendants are much more likely to avoid
mandatory penalties than are African–American
and Hispanic defendants. Barbara S. Vincent &
Paul J. Hofer, *The Consequences of Mandatory
Minimum Prison Terms: A Summary of Recent
Findings* 23–24 (Federal Judicial Center 1994).

The reason why mandatory-minimum sentences
are so often circumvented is because their very
rigidity can lead to the imposition of what are
considered unjust sentences. While a particular penalty may generally be appropriate for most individuals who commit a particular kind of crime, there
will always be some individuals who don't fit the
prototype. For example, a mother who is arrested
for growing marijuana to be used to ease the suffering of her terminally ill son is unlike the typical
defendant who grows marijuana for personal use or
to make a profit. Even serious, violent offenders
cannot always be typecast into a single mold. A
woman who kills her husband several months after
finding pictures of him sexually molesting small

children, for example, is unlike a hired killer or a bloodthirsty sociopath.

Mandatory-minimum sentences can be circumvented in a variety of ways. Prosecutors can, for example, file charges that do not trigger a mandatory minimum, even though the defendant's actual crime falls within the scope of a mandatory-minimum sentencing provision. Alternatively, police may not arrest someone for a crime, or judges may dismiss charges or acquit someone of a crime, to avoid application of what is perceived to be an unjust mandatory penalty. The point is that there will always be discretion exercised in the imposition of criminal punishment. Mandatory-minimum sentencing provisions do not, as they purport to, eliminate sentencing discretion. They simply remove the exercise of that discretion from the public eye.

One of the by-products of this behind-the-scenes discretion is known as the "cooperation paradox." Prosecutors are typically much more willing to enter into a plea bargain under which a defendant avoids a mandatory-minimum sentence if the defendant provides the prosecutor with information that can help solve other crimes and secure other convictions. Low-level offenders involved, for example, in a drug conspiracy will often have little knowledge about the criminal enterprise of which they were a part that can be used as leverage to avoid a mandatory-minimum sentence. By contrast, high-level offenders, the ones most deeply involved in the criminal enterprise, have the most information to share with prosecutors and can often most readily evade a mandatory-minimum sentence. The end result is an upside-down sentencing system under which the least culpable offenders are punished more severely, and often much more severely, than the most culpable offenders.

C.   SENTENCING GUIDELINES

Sentencing guidelines, if structured properly, can avoid many of the pitfalls of determinate and indeterminate sentencing statutes. The Minnesota sentencing guidelines, the first presumptive guidelines drafted by a sentencing commission in this country, exemplify how sentencing guidelines can work. Sentences are calculated under these guidelines by employing a sentencing grid. This grid identifies what the presumptive sentence is for a person who has committed a crime of a certain severity level and who has a certain criminal-history score. A copy of the grid can be found on page 96. An offender's criminal-history score depends on: (1) the number of prior convictions as an adult; (2) the severity level of those earlier convictions; (3) the offender's juvenile record; and (4) whether the offender was awaiting sentencing for another crime, on probation or parole, or confined for a felony, gross misdemeanor, or one of certain specified juvenile offenses at the time the felony was committed for which the offender is now being sentenced.

A dark black line divides the Minnesota sentencing guidelines grid into two parts. There is a presumption that the sentences to the left of the black line will be stayed. A number of conditions can be attached to those stayed sentences, but as long as offenders abide by those conditions, they will not be sent to prison. On the other hand, there is a presumption that the sentences to the right of the black line will be executed—in other words, that the individuals who receive those sentences will actually be sent to prison.

MINNESOTA SENTENCING GUIDELINES GRID

Presumptive Sentence Lengths in Months

Italicized numbers within the grid denote the range within which a judge may sentence without the sentence being deemed a departure. Offenders with nonimprisonment felony sentences are subject to jail time according to law.

SEVERITY LEVEL OF CONVICTION OFFENSE (Common offenses listed in italics)		CRIMINAL HISTORY SCORE						
		0	1	2	3	4	5	6 or more
Murder, 2nd Degree *(intentional murder; drive-by-shootings)*	XI	306 *299-313*	326 *319-333*	346 *339-353*	366 *359-373*	386 *379-393*	406 *399-413*	426 *419-433*
Murder, 3rd Degree Murder, 2nd Degree *(unintentional murder)*	X	150 *144-156*	165 *159-171*	180 *174-186*	195 *189-201*	210 *204-216*	225 *219-231*	240 *234-246*
Criminal Sexual Conduct, 1st Degree Assault, 1st Degree	IX	86 *81-91*	98 *93-103*	110 *105-115*	122 *117-127*	134 *129-139*	146 *141-151*	158 *153-163*
Aggravated Robbery 1st Degree Criminal Sexual Conduct, *2nd Degree (c),(d),(e),(f),(h)*	VIII	48 *44-52*	58 *54-62*	68 *64-72*	78 *74-82*	88 *84-92*	98 *94-102*	108 *104-112*
Felony DWI	VII	36	42	48	54 *51-57*	60 *57-63*	66 *63-69*	72 *69-75*
Criminal Sexual Conduct, 2nd Degree (a) & (b)	VI	21	27	33	39 *37-41*	45 *43-47*	51 *49-53*	57 *55-59*
Residential Burglary Simple Robbery	V	18	23	28	33 *31-35*	38 *36-40*	43 *41-45*	48 *46-50*
Nonresidential Burglary	IV	12[1]	15	18	21	24 *23-25*	27 *26-28*	30 *29-31*
Theft Crimes (Over $2,500)	III	12[1]	13	15	17	19 *18-20*	21 *20-22*	23 *22-24*
Theft Crimes ($2,500 or less) Check Forgery ($200-$2,500)	II	12[1]	12[1]	13	15	17	19	21 *20-22*
Sale of Simulated Controlled Substance	I	12[1]	12[1]	12[1]	13	15	17	19 *18-20*

☐ Presumptive commitment to state imprisonment. First Degree Murder is excluded from the guidelines by law and continues to have a mandatory life sentence.

■ Presumptive stayed sentence; at the discretion of the judge, up to a year in jail and/or other non-jail sanctions can be imposed as conditions of probation. * * *

[1] One year and one day

Judges can impose a sentence other than the presumptive sentence under the Minnesota sentencing guidelines when there are "substantial and compelling" reasons for a departure. When a judge departs from the presumptive sentence, the judge must explain in writing the reasons for the departure.

There are two types of possible departures under the Minnesota sentencing guidelines—a dispositional departure and a durational departure. If a judge sends a person to prison when, under the guidelines, the presumption is that the sentence will be stayed, the departure is a dispositional one. Similarly, if a judge stays a sentence that presumptively should be executed, a dispositional departure has occurred. On the other hand, a judge's decision to impose a sentence that is either longer or shorter than the presumptive sentence set forth in the grid constitutes a durational departure. If the sentence imposed represents both a durational and a dispositional departure, the judge must separately explain the rationale for both departures.

While sentencing commissions, and sometimes judges, typically draft sentencing guidelines, legislatures still play a role in the sentencing process. Statutes outline the general range of sentences for a particular crime within which the guidelines must operate. In addition, legislatures generally are given the opportunity to approve or disapprove sentencing guidelines and revisions to those guidelines before they go into effect.

Sentencing guidelines, if drafted properly, offer a number of advantages to jurisdictions that adopt them. First, by identifying the penalty that generally should be imposed for a crime committed by an individual with a particular criminal background, the guidelines help to avert the sentencing disparity that plagues so many other types of sentencing systems. At the same time, by allowing departures from presumptive sentences, well-drafted sentencing guidelines offer judges the flexibility they need to ensure that appropriate sentences are imposed in atypical cases.

Another advantage of well-structured sentencing guidelines is that they can be calibrated to produce sentences that are more cost-effective and just. The comprehensive overview of sentences that occurs when sentencing guidelines are drafted can, for example, help to ensure that the sentencing system is characterized by proportionality, an integral component of any just sentencing system. When proportionality principles are incorporated into a sentencing system, more serious crimes are punished more severely, and individuals with more serious criminal histories are punished more severely than those with low criminal-history scores.

The Minnesota sentencing guidelines are a case in point. When the Minnesota Sentencing Guidelines Commission embarked on its mission to craft sentencing guidelines, the Commission stated that it recognized that prison space is a finite and very expensive resource and that therefore the guidelines should be selective as to whom is sent to prison. In establishing priorities for the use of prison space, the Commission came to two conclusions: first, that prison usually should be reserved for individuals who have committed serious, violent crimes or who have a lengthy history of criminal conduct; and second, that other offenders can be punished effectively, and if need be severely, in the community.

Another advantage of sentencing guidelines is that sentencing commissions continually monitor their implementation and can therefore finetune them, based on the information gathered, so that they better meet their objectives. Through this ongoing monitoring function, sentencing commissions can also avert crowding in a jurisdiction's prisons. But instead of taking crude measures like lopping the same amount of time off of all prisoners' sentences to alleviate crowding, sentencing commissions can carefully modulate the guidelines to ease crowding while taking care not to compromise the public's safety. If, for example, there is a rash of armed robberies in a state leading to an unexpected influx of these violent offenders into the state's prisons, the sentencing commission can modify somewhat the guidelines applicable to some less serious offenders to make room for the armed robbers.

Sentencing guidelines vary a great deal from jurisdiction to jurisdiction. The federal sentencing guidelines, for example, are much more complicated than the Minnesota guidelines. The federal guidelines contain forty-three offense levels compared to the eleven offense levels in Minnesota, and federal judges engage in complex numerical calculations before imposing a sentence under the federal guidelines.

Because of their differences, not all sentencing guidelines yield the advantages mentioned earlier. The federal sentencing guidelines, in particular, have been the subject of harsh criticism. One criticism leveled against them is that they are based on the incorrect premise that incarceration is the only form of tough punishment. As a result, the majority of federal prisoners are serving time for nonviolent crimes even though critics contend that many of these offenders could be punished effectively, and much more cheaply, in a comprehensive community-corrections system.

Another fundamental problem with the federal sentencing guidelines is that they were drafted without regard to available prison resources. The result has been an explosion in the number of federal offenders now sent to prison and a large financial burden on the taxpayers forced to pay the costs of building and operating the new prisons needed to accommodate this influx of prisoners.

Even those sentencing guidelines that were drafted with an eye towards available prison resources and that carefully establish priorities in the use of those resources are not problem-free. The Minnesota sentencing guidelines, for example, define when offenders should generally be imprisoned and for how long. They do not, however, guide judges in the exercise of their discretion when imposing community-based sanctions on offenders. The end result is disparity in the sentences of offenders serving their sentences in the community. One offender may, for example, receive a probation sentence of one length while another, almost identical offender is placed on probation for a much longer or shorter period of time.

One way to alleviate this problem is through the use of nonimprisonment guidelines that define the presumptive sentences for nonincarcerative penalties. North Carolina is an example of one state that has adopted such guidelines. Nonimprisonment guidelines are discussed in greater depth in the next chapter.

Another problem with sentencing guidelines is that if prosecutors do not agree with them, they often try to circumvent them. They may, for example, charge a defendant with a different crime than a defendant might normally be charged with in order to avoid a presumptive sentence that they believe is too high.

Some states have taken steps to limit prosecutors' ability to avoid the effects of sentencing guidelines. Prosecutorial guidelines, for example, are utilized in a few states to circumscribe prosecutors' discretion when they file charges and engage in plea bargaining.

Another way to curtail the circumvention of sentencing guidelines through the exercise of prosecutorial discretion is to base the presumptive sentence on the "real offense" rather than the offense of conviction. The federal sentencing guidelines reflect, to a certain extent, real-offense sentencing principles. The sentences for certain crimes under those guidelines are based not only on the crime of which the defendant was convicted, but also on other "relevant conduct."

Assume, for example, that a defendant is convicted under a federal statute of selling a small quantity of cocaine. The prosecutor then introduces evidence at the sentencing hearing that the defendant sold much larger quantities of cocaine in other related drug transactions. If the sentencing judge follows the federal guidelines, the defendant's offense level will be based on the cumulation of these drug amounts, perhaps adding years to the amount of time the defendant will have to spend in prison. The sentence imposed for the "real offense," however, cannot exceed the maximum sentence for the offense of conviction. In addition, after *United States v. Booker* (S.Ct.2005), which was discussed in the preceding chapter, the upwards sentencing adjustments prescribed in the federal guidelines to reflect the defendant's "real offense" are no longer mandatory, but advisory.

One criticism of real-offense sentencing concerns its practical effects: sentencing hearings can become bogged down as judges try to determine the crimes defendants actually committed. More fundamentally, critics have charged that real-offense sentencing denigrates the importance of criminal trials and generates perceptions of unfairness as defendants are sentenced based on criminal conduct with which they have not been charged and of which they may have even been acquitted.

The debate over real-offense sentencing is not likely to abate. After the Supreme Court's decisions in *Booker* and *Blakely v. Washington* (S.Ct.2004), a defendant's "real offense" can still affect the sentence imposed under advisory sentencing guidelines. In addition, in a jurisdiction with sentencing guidelines that judges are mandated, not just encouraged, to follow, the defendant's "real offense" may affect what sentence is selected from within the sentencing range stemming from the jury's verdict or the facts admitted in the defendant's guilty plea. And in a state with an indeterminate sentencing structure, judges may be vested with the broad discretion to impose a sentence that reflects the severity of the defendant's "real offense" provided that the sentence does not exceed the maximum penalty for the offense of which the defendant was convicted.

D.   *EX POST FACTO* LAWS

When modifying sentencing guidelines as well as sentencing laws, care must be taken to avoid violating the constitutional provisions that prohibit *ex post facto* laws. Article I, § 9 of the United States Constitution prohibits Congress from enacting *ex post facto* laws, while Article I, § 10 prohibits the states from enacting such laws. A sentencing law or guideline that increases the punishment for a crime after the crime has been committed violates the *ex post facto* prohibition. *See, e.g., Miller v. Florida*

(S.Ct.1987) (unconstitutional to impose a presumptive sentence under sentencing guidelines that was higher than the presumptive sentence in effect at the time of the crime). To avoid *ex post facto* problems, a law or guideline increasing the penalty for a crime must apply prospectively only—to crimes committed after the adoption of the modified statute or guideline.

Legislatures must also take care not to violate the prohibition on *ex post facto* laws when enacting statutes changing the rate at which prisoners accumulate early-release credits while they are incarcerated. In *Weaver v. Graham* (S.Ct.1981), the Supreme Court struck down, on *ex post facto* grounds, a statute enacted after the date of the prisoner's crime that decreased the rate with which good-time credits can accumulate. The effect of this statute would have been to extend the length of time the prisoner would have been confined compared to the amount of time he would have been confined under the law in effect at the time of his crime. And in *Lynce v. Mathis* (S.Ct.1997), the Court held that a state could not constitutionally revoke another kind of sentencing credits to which the prisoner in question was entitled under a statute in effect at the time of his crime—credits that reduced the length of confinement because of crowding in the state's prison system.

On the other hand, in *California Dep't of Corrections v. Morales* (S.Ct.1995), the Supreme Court held that a state statute that increased the length of time between parole-suitability hearings for certain offenders did not constitute an *ex post facto* law. The statute in question authorized the parole board to defer the parole-suitability hearing of a prisoner with two or more homicide convictions for up to three years if the board both found that it was "not reasonable to expect" that parole would be granted during the intervening years and explained the reasons for this conclusion. The statute in effect at the time of the murder for which the prisoner in the case was imprisoned, by contrast, had provided for annual parole-suitability hearings.

The prisoner argued that the new statute unconstitutionally increased the punishment for his crime, because it eliminated the possibility that he might be released on parole during the three-year period between his parole-suitability hearings. The Supreme Court, however, concluded that the risk that the statute had enhanced the prisoner's punishment was too remote and speculative to give rise to a constitutional violation. The Court emphasized both that the statute applied to a category of prisoners whose release on parole was extremely unlikely and that the board had to follow certain procedures to ensure that parole-suitability hearings were deferred only in appropriate cases.

In *Garner v. Jones* (S.Ct.2000), the Supreme Court also upheld, in the face of an *ex post facto* challenge, modified rules promulgated by a parole board that lengthened the time lapse between parole hearings—from three to eight years—for prisoners serving life sentences. The Court held that the rules, on their face, did not violate the prohibition on *ex post facto* laws. Underscoring that the rules provided for expedited reconsideration of a prisoner for parole release when there had been a "change in circumstances," the Court concluded that the altered rules did not create a "significant risk" that prisoners with life sentences would, in general, spend more time in prison than they would have under the board's previous rules. At the same time, the Court left open the possibility that the new rules, as actually applied to a particular prisoner, might enhance that prisoner's punishment in contravention of the *Ex Post Facto* Clause.

CHAPTER 5

COMMUNITY–BASED SANCTIONS

As was mentioned in Chapter 1, one of the central problems with many of the sentencing systems in this country is that they offer judges too few sentencing options. The end result is that inappropriate penalties are imposed on criminal offenders—penalties that are either too lax or overly stringent. If corrections and sentencing systems are to be efficacious, just, and cost-effective, a broad spectrum of sanctions must be incorporated into them so that judges can impose, in each case, the most appropriate sanction under the circumstances.

Community-based sanctions, if properly structured, offer many advantages—to victims, to the public, and to offenders and their families. Some of these advantages include the following: (1) Such sanctions are generally cheaper, and often substantially cheaper, than incarceration in either prison or jail. (2) By punishing offenders in the community, family ties can be preserved, which in turn will enhance the likelihood that rehabilitative endeavors will be successful. In addition, the severe emotional trauma that ensues, particularly in children, when a close family member is incarcerated can be avoided. (3) If offenders are punished within the community, they can, if they are employed, continue to work, enhancing their rehabilitation prospects and the likelihood that they will be able to pay restitution to the victims of their crimes. (4) The economic burden on taxpayers that stems from the punishment of criminal offenders can be diminished further as offenders working within the community pay taxes and support their families instead of having the public support them through welfare payments. (5) By serving their sentences in the community, offenders can avoid the criminogenic influences that prevail in prisons and jails as well as the dependency that incarceration fosters. (6) By imposing community-based sanctions on those offenders who can be punished safely and effectively in the community, crowding in prisons and jails can be alleviated, thereby making the correctional facilities safer and easier to manage and less likely to be embroiled in litigation. In addition, the efficacy of prison and jail educational, training, work, and treatment programs can be enhanced as the number of inmates who have needs to be met by such programs is reduced.

Community-based sanctions can be punishing, as research on the responses of offenders offered the choice between going to prison or being subjected to a community-based sanction have confirmed. Some studies have revealed that once informed of the rigorous conditions of intensive-supervision programs in the community, up to one third of offenders have opted instead to go to prison. Multiple surveys of prisoners asked to rank the severity of certain community sanctions compared to incarceration have corroborated that incarceration is not, in the eyes of prisoners, inevitably the most punitive sanction. *See* Joan Petersilia, *Reforming Probation and Parole in the 21st Century* 71 (2002).

A. COMMUNITY–BASED SENTENCING OPTIONS

Some of the sanctions to be found in a comprehensive community-corrections system include: unsupervised probation, standard supervised probation, intensive-supervision probation, community service, home confinement without electronic monitoring, electronically-monitored home confinement and other forms of electronic monitoring, outpatient treatment programs, inpatient treatment programs, day fines, restitution, and day reporting centers. In addition, a comprehensive community-corrections system would generally include a pretrial-services program and a restorative-justice program, including victim-offender mediation. The purpose of a pretrial-services program is to ensure that only those individuals who pose a substantial risk of not appearing at trial or of endangering the public are confined in jail while awaiting trial. Some of the community-based sanctions mentioned above are briefly described below.

1. Probation

Probation is one of the most frequently imposed criminal sanctions. When offenders are placed on probation, they are required to abide by certain conditions of their probation. If they violate any of these conditions, the terms of their probation may be modified to increase the level of supervision or the amount of restrictions to which they are subject. Alternatively, their probation sentences may be revoked and prison sentences imposed in their stead.

Probation is not a monolithic sanction. Probation sentences can vary tremendously in terms of the constraints that are imposed on probationers. Probation often entails only perfunctory supervision, if any, of a probationer. A probationer may, for example, only be required to meet with a probation officer once a month or talk on the telephone with the probation officer once a week.

A form of probation known as intensive-supervision probation has been utilized increasingly for offenders needing a greater level of supervision within the community. Offenders sentenced to intensive-supervision probation are generally required to meet with their probation officers a number of times each week, and they may be subjected to unannounced home visits and random drug urinalysis tests. Intensive-supervision probationers are also frequently required to undergo substance-abuse treatment and to work or go to school.

Sentencing courts have traditionally been accorded broad discretion when defining the conditions of a probation sentence. As long as those conditions are reasonably related to the penological goals of probation, courts have generally been deemed to have the statutory authority to impose them. Some states apply variations of this reasonable-relationship test, requiring, for example, that the condition be reasonably related to the crime of which the offender was convicted.

Probation sentences can be combined in a variety of ways with incarcerative sentences. One common combination is what is known as a "split sentence"—a sentence to prison or jail followed by a period of probation.

"Shock incarceration" is another example of a hybrid sanction. Offenders placed in shock-incarceration programs, more commonly known as boot camps, are confined for usually three to six months in a military-type setting. During this time period, they are subjected to strict discipline, physical exercise, and hard labor, and they participate in drills and ceremonies. If they successfully complete the program, they are resentenced to probation, avoiding confinement in prison. Researchers have found that boot camps do not result in lower recidivism rates when compared to either community penalties or incarceration. One reason cited for the failure of boot camps to have significant crime-reduction benefits is the lack of follow-up with boot-camp participants upon their return to their communities to assist them in their efforts to adopt a crime-free lifestyle.

2. Day Reporting Centers

Day reporting centers provide another way of intensively supervising offenders in the community.

These centers vary in the way in which they are operated. A common pattern is for offenders to report to a center each day, where they must then write down their itineraries for the day—where they will be at all times. Throughout the day, staff members then confirm, through telephone calls and visits, that the offenders are where they are supposed to be. Offenders may be required to spend a great deal of time at the day reporting center itself, participating in mandated educational, treatment, or counseling programs. When not at the center or at work, they can also be required to do community service.

3. Home Confinement and Electronic Monitoring

Another community-based sanction that is being used with increasing frequency across the country is home confinement. Home confinement is another sanction notable for its diversity. Offenders can be required to stay at home for a few hours each day, or they may be confined to their homes for up to twenty-four hours a day. In addition, home confinement may or may not be monitored electronically.

If home confinement is electronically monitored, a variety of devices can be used to enforce the home-confinement sanction. Offenders may, for example, be required to wear a radio transmitter that constantly sends a signal confirming their presence in their homes to a central computer. If the offenders leave their homes, the computer alerts officials, who can then track them down. In addition, the computer can be programmed to alert officials if offenders attempt to remove the radio transmitter.

Another monitoring system uses a computer to call offenders' homes at random intervals. Offenders then confirm their presence in the home by inserting a wristlet they are required to wear into a verifier box attached to the phone, through a voice-verification process, or through other means. Measures can be employed with this type of monitoring system as well to prevent or detect offenders' attempts to foil monitoring by removing their wristlets or otherwise tampering with the monitoring equipment.

The technology for electronically monitoring offenders in the community is continually evolving and improving. For example, Global Positioning System satellite monitoring can be used to pinpoint an offender's exact whereabouts, and authorities can be alerted when an offender enters into a prohibited area. In addition, electronic-monitoring devices can be used for purposes other than to confirm that an offender is home or at another location. For example, some devices can analyze an offender's breath to determine whether the offender has consumed any alcohol, in violation of the terms of the home-confinement sentence. If a positive reading for alcohol is recorded and then verified by the monitoring computer, a probation officer can be sent to the offender's home to administer a breathalyzer test.

4. Economic Sanctions

One way to punish criminal offenders is to impose a financial burden on them for their transgressions. A common means of doing this is through a fine.

In Europe, it has been widely recognized that fines can be a tough and effective form of punishment. The use of fines is also advantageous because it frees up resources that can be used for the supervision or incarceration of offenders for whom such supervision or incarceration is necessary.

In this country, the potential of fines as meaningful and effective punishments has not been realized. Fines have been underutilized, in part because of the way in which fine systems are structured in this country. Generally, judges in the United States adopt one of two approaches when imposing a fine. One approach is a tariff system under which a set fine is imposed for a certain offense. Since the amount of the fine is the same regardless of an offender's financial means, the tariff system often results in fines that are either too high or too low. Poor offenders may be unable to pay the designated amount, while the fine may be so low as to constitute almost no punishment at all for wealthier offenders.

The other approach commonly taken when imposing a fine is an *ad hoc* approach under which a judge imposes a fine based on what is often a guesstimate of what an offender is able to pay. Having obtained information about, for example, where the offender lives, whether or not the offender is employed, and how many dependents the offender must support, the judge then selects the fine amount. The problem with this gut-feeling approach to the imposition of fines is that, as with a tariff system, it often leads to the imposition of fines that are too high or too low to meet their penological objectives. In addition, this approach leads to a great deal of disparity in the amount of the fines imposed on similarly situated offenders.

To avoid these problems of sentencing disparity and fines that are too high or too low to meet their penological objectives, many European countries and a few jurisdictions in this country have adopted day-fine systems, thereby greatly expanding the utility and effectiveness of fines as criminal sanctions. For example, in West Germany in 1968, just before a day-fine system was implemented, 113,000 custodial sentences of less than six months were imposed. By 1976, the number of such sentences had declined to less than 11,000. During this same time period, the proportion of criminal offenders in West Germany who were fined increased from 63% to 83%. Sally Hillsman et al., U.S. Dep't. of Justice, *Fines in Sentencing: A Study of the Use of the Fine as a Criminal Sanction—Executive Summary* 17 (1984).

Fines continue today to be the preferred criminal sanction in Germany. In other countries as well, a fine is the presumptively appropriate penalty for criminal conduct, and a judge must provide a written explanation if some sentence other than a fine is imposed.

The computation of a day fine is a two-step process. First, the sentencing judge determines how many units of punishment should be imposed on a particular offender. One unit in a particular jurisdiction may, for example, be the equivalent of a day's worth of income or a certain fraction of that income. This part of the sentencing decision is made without regard to the offender's financial means. A judge may, for example, decide that the number of units that equals one week's worth of income should be imposed on a particular offender for a particular crime.

The judge must then translate this unit number into a financial figure based on information about an offender's financial means. Thus, if the sentence is the one mentioned above—one week's worth of income, the judge must determine the offender's weekly income and then set that amount as the fine. Because the units of punishment in a day-fine system are selected without regard to an offender's financial means, the end result is a rough, though clearly not exact, equivalency in the fines imposed on criminal offenders. At the same time, since the punishment units are then translated into terms which reflect offenders' actual financial situation, it is less likely that fines that are unrealistically high or palpably low for particular offenders will be imposed.

If fines are not closely calibrated to offenders' ability to pay them, the end result will frequently be nonpayment of the fines. The question arises as to whether the Constitution places any limits on what governmental officials can do in response to such nonpayment.

In *Williams v. Illinois* (S.Ct.1970), the Supreme Court answered this question in the affirmative. In *Williams*, the defendant, who was convicted of petty theft, was sentenced to jail for one year, the statutory maximum, and ordered to pay a $500 fine and $5 in court costs. The defendant, however, was unable to pay the fine and court costs. He was indigent and, due to his incarceration, unemployed. He was therefore required to stay in jail an extra 101 days under a state statute that authorized fines to be "worked off" at the rate of $5 for every one day in jail.

The Supreme Court concluded that the incarceration of the defendant because of his indigence beyond the maximum period of time that a nonindigent person could be confined in jail for theft violated the defendant's Fourteenth Amendment right to be afforded the equal protection of the law. The Supreme Court reached the same conclusion the next year in *Tate v. Short* (S.Ct.1971). In that case, an indigent defendant, who had failed to pay fines imposed for traffic offenses that were not even punishable by incarceration, was then incarcerated "solely because of his indigence."

Williams and *Tate* set the stage for *Bearden v. Georgia* (S.Ct.1983), a case in which the Supreme Court addressed the constitutional constraints on the revocation of probation for failure to pay a fine. The Supreme Court sidestepped the equal-protection issue raised by the revocation of probation in such circumstances and instead focused on the requirements of due process of law. The Court began by noting that the automatic revocation of probation for failure to pay a fine is fundamentally unfair and therefore violates due process. The Court added that pragmatic considerations also counsel against such automatic revocation, because indigent probationers facing the prospect of incarceration if they fail to pay their fines might commit crimes to obtain the funds needed to pay them.

The Supreme Court held in *Bearden* that before probation can be revoked for failure to pay a fine, a court must determine the answers to a series of questions. First, did the probationer deliberately refuse to pay the fine despite having the means to do so? If so, the probation sentence can constitutionally be revoked. If not, the court must turn to the next question: Did the probationer make adequate *bona fide* efforts—attempting, for example, to secure employment or borrow money—to obtain the funds to pay the fine? If the probationer failed to make such *bona fide* efforts, the revocation of probation is again constitutionally permissible. If the probationer, however, made such *bona fide* efforts but still failed to procure the necessary funds, then the court must determine whether there are any adequate ways, other than incarceration, of punishing the probationer. If there are such viable alternatives, then the incarceration of the probationer for failure to pay a fine violates due process. If there are no such alternatives available though, incarceration for failure to pay a fine is constitutionally permissible because, as the Court said in *Bearden*, "[a] defendant's poverty in no way immunizes him from punishment." Of course, in a well-structured, comprehensive, community-corrections system, adequate alternative means of punishing an offender who was initially fined will usually exist.

Another economic sanction commonly imposed on criminal offenders is restitution. Restitution differs from a fine in that it is paid to the victim of the crime rather than the government. Its primary purpose is to compensate the victim for certain injuries caused by the crime. The offender may, for example, be required to pay for the victim's medical expenses stemming from the crime, for income lost while recuperating from injuries caused by the crime, or for the value of property stolen or destroyed during the crime's commission.

While one of the purposes of restitution is compensation, it is still considered a criminal penalty rather than a civil remedy. The ordering of restitution by a judge therefore does not abridge the constitutional right under the Seventh Amendment to a jury trial in a common-law suit where the amount in controversy exceeds twenty dollars. *United States v. Dubose* (9th Cir.1998).

As is true with other economic sanctions, the challenge for a court that wishes to order the payment of restitution is to craft a restitution order that does not impede the offender's rehabilitation. If the restitution amount exceeds the defendant's ability to pay that amount, there is a very real risk that the order will literally induce the offender to "rob Peter to pay Paul."

Mindful of this problem, many restitution statutes direct judges to consider the defendant's financial resources and needs when calculating the amount of restitution. Other restitution statutes, on the other hand, direct convicted offenders who commit certain types of crimes to pay full restitution to their victims, regardless of the offenders' economic circumstances. For example, the Mandatory Victims Restitution Act, 18 U.S.C. § 3663A, provides for the payment of mandatory restitution by persons convicted in federal court of a violent crime. The defendant's financial resources, income, and financial obligations can, however, affect the payment schedule outlined in the restitution order.

Another tack is for judges to enter restitution orders that fully cover the victim's losses. Payment of part or all of the restitution award can then be stayed because of the defendant's present financial situation. If the defendant's financial status changes for the better in the future, the stay can be lifted, and the defendant will then have to pay the remaining sum due.

Some more economic sanctions have been added to the sanctions menu in recent years. One is to deny individuals convicted of specified crimes of certain government benefits, such as student loans, as part of their sentence. *See, e.g.*, 21 U.S.C. § 862. Under other statutes, a person convicted of a partic-

ular crime can lose certain government benefits
even when the sentence does not include such a
forfeiture of benefits. Chapter 9 discusses this and
other "collateral consequences" of a conviction.

Another type of financial penalty or assessment is
to require offenders to defray the costs of processing
their cases through the criminal-justice system and
the costs of the sanctions imposed on them. Some
examples of the fees that are now assessed on
criminal offenders include: residential fees for offenders staying in work-release centers or other
correctional residential facilities in the community;
restitution-collection fees; substance-abuse assessment fees for the evaluation of offenders for drug or
alcohol problems; substance-abuse treatment fees;
counseling fees; probation-supervision fees; community-service fees; home-confinement fees; and court
costs.

Because of the danger mentioned earlier that
offenders may be overwhelmed by unrealistic economic demands placed upon them, to both their,
their families', and the public's detriment, it is
imperative that these fees and assessments, as well
as all other economic sanctions, be coordinated and
integrated. In addition, the American Bar Association has advocated that costs and fees, unlike fines
and restitution, not be considered part of the criminal sentence. *ABA Standards for Criminal Justice,
Sentencing Alternatives and Procedures and Appellate Review of Sentences*, Standard 18–3.22(a) (3d
ed. 1993). Failure to pay such costs or fees could not
then lead to the revocation of probation. Instead,

the government would recoup the money through the means typically employed to enforce a civil judgment, such as the garnishment of wages.

5. Community Service

Community service is a sanction through which offenders pay back the community for the harm caused by their criminal behavior by doing work that benefits the public. The range of tasks that offenders can be ordered to perform is almost endless. Offenders can be required, for example, to plant trees, pick up litter, refurbish buildings in low-income areas that are particularly ravaged by crime, and assist charitable and other nonprofit organizations.

The advantages that the public can reap from community-service sentences are great. This sanction, however, like many other community-based sanctions, is not widely used and even when utilized in a jurisdiction, is often used only sporadically. One of the chief roadblocks to the widespread imposition of this sanction is the lack of a central agency in many jurisdictions that is responsible for coordinating the imposition and implementation of community-service sentences. In addition, community-service sentences face union opposition. Finally, concerns about governmental liability for injuries incurred when offenders are performing community-service work may inhibit the widespread use of community service as a sentencing option.

B. COMPREHENSIVE AND INTEGRATED CORRECTIONS SYSTEMS

While it is important that judges have an array of sanctions from which to choose when sentencing criminal offenders so that the most appropriate penalty is imposed in each case, it is equally important that a structure be put in place to ensure that these sanctions are achieving their objectives and that community-corrections systems are operating as cost-effectively as possible. In recent years, a number of states have adopted community-corrections acts to put this structure in place.

In 1992, the American Bar Association adopted a resolution calling on each state and United States territory to adopt a comprehensive community-corrections act. At the same time, the ABA promulgated a Model Adult Community Corrections Act to provide guidance to states enacting or revising their own community-corrections acts. While the ABA Model Act contemplates that its provisions may have to be modified to fit the contours of a particular state's sentencing and corrections systems, there are certain key provisions in the Model Act that are considered central to the goal of making sentencing and corrections systems more integrated and cost-effective. Some of these key ingredients include the following:

1. provision for a wide array of community-based sanctions that includes, but is not limited to: unsupervised probation, standard supervised probation, intensive-supervision probation, com-

munity service, home confinement with and without electronic monitoring, electronic surveillance, outpatient treatment programs, inpatient treatment programs, day reporting centers, day fines, and restitution;

2.   establishment of a rebuttable presumption that a community-based sanction is the most appropriate penalty for the following types of offenders: those convicted of misdemeanors; those convicted of nonviolent felonies, including drug offenses; and those who violate a condition of their probation, parole, or other community sanction and whose violation is either noncriminal or, if charged as a crime, would be a misdemeanor or a nonviolent felony;

3.   the development of a statewide community-corrections plan by a broad-based group comprised of individuals from key constituencies within the criminal-justice system, such as law enforcement, prosecution, defense, judges, community corrections, and institutional corrections, as well as members of the public;

4.   implementation of the community-corrections act at the local level by a similarly broad-based community-corrections board;

5.   technical assistance and training to facilitate the achievement of the Act's goals and to avoid unnecessary and costly duplication of efforts when community-corrections programs are being established and revamped;

6. monitoring of the Act's implementation at both the state and local level;

7. provision for the adequate funding of community sanctions; and

8. provision for the education of the public about community-based sanctions—about how punishing they can be, about how they can be structured to reduce, although not eliminate, risks to the public's safety, and about their costs relative to the costs of incarceration.

This latter requirement is particularly critical if community-corrections programs are to reach their potential. Studies have shown that what an informed public wants, in terms of the punishment of criminals, varies greatly from the desires of an uninformed public. For example, over four hundred adults in Alabama were asked during a survey conducted in 1988 about the penalty they would impose in twenty-three hypothetical cases. Initially, when given the choice between only prison and probation, the respondents opted for incarceration in eighteen of the cases. When later given five other sentencing options from which to choose and about which they had been informed, the respondents chose imprisonment in only four of the cases. Intermediate sanctions were preferred for even very serious crimes, such as a third drug-dealing conviction, embezzlement of $250,000, and the commission of an unarmed burglary for the second time. *See* John Doble & Josh Klein, *Punishing Criminals: The Public's View—An Alabama Survey* (1989). These findings have been replicated in surveys conducted in other states.

With the aid of a comprehensive community-corrections act, a sentencing system can be structured that provides offenders with incentives to work towards rehabilitating themselves. In a thought-provoking article, Pierre du Pont, a former governor of Delaware, proposed that multi-tiered sentencing systems be created under which offenders are assigned to one of ten different levels that vary in terms of the amount of supervision to which an offender is subjected and the number of privileges the offender is accorded. Offenders who conform to the requirements of their sentences can work their way down the tiers, gradually enjoying greater freedom and more privileges, while the level of supervision can be increased and more privileges withheld if offenders do not abide by the requirements that have been imposed on them. *See* Pierre S. du Pont IV, U.S. Dep't. of Justice, *Expanding Sentencing Options: A Governor's Perspective* (1985). A grid that reflects how such a multi-tiered sentencing system would work can be found on the next page.

Restrictions	Level I	Level II	Level III	Level IV	Level V	Level VI	Level VII	Level VIII	Level IX	Level X
Mobility in the community [1]	100 percent (unrestricted)	100 percent (unrestricted)	90 percent (restricted 0-10 hours/week)	80 percent (restricted 10-30 hours/week)	60 percent (restricted 40 hours/week)	30 percent (restricted 50-100 hours/week)	20 percent (restricted 100-140 hours/week)	10 percent (90 percent of time incarcerated)	Incarcerated	Incarcerated
Amount of supervision	None	Monthly written report	1-2 face-to-face/month; phone contact	3-6 face-to-face/month; weekly phone contact	2-6 face-to-face/week; daily phone contact; weekly written reports	Daily phone contact; daily face-to-face; weekly written reports	Daily onsite supervision 8-16 hours/day	Daily onsite supervision 24 hours/day	Daily onsite supervision 24 hours/day	Daily onsite supervision 24 hours/day
Privileges withheld or special [2] conditions	100 percent (same as prior conviction)	100 percent (same as prior conviction)	1-2 privileges withheld	1-4 privileges withheld	1-7 privileges withheld	1-10 privileges withheld	1-12 privileges withheld	5-15 privileges withheld	15-19 privileges withheld	20 or more privileges withheld
Financial obligations [3]	Fine, court costs may be applied (0- to 2-day fine)	Fine, court costs, restitution; probation (supervisory fee may be applied; 1- to 3-day fine)	Same (increase probation fee by $5-10/month; 2- to 4-day fine)	Same (increase probation fee by $5-$10/month; 3- to 5-day fine)	Same (pay partial cost of food/lodging/supervision fee; 4- to 7-day fine)	Same as Level V (8- to 10-day fine)	Same as Level V (11- to 12-day fine)	Fine, court costs, restitution payable upon release to Level VII or lower (12- to 15-day fine)	Same as Level VIII	Same as Level VIII
Examples (Note: many other scenario could be constructed meeting the requirements at each level)	$50 fine, court costs; 6 months unsupervised probation	$50 fine, court costs, restitution; 6 months supervised probation; $10 monthly fee; written report	Fine, court costs, restitution; 1 year weekend community service; no drinking	Weekend community service or mandatory treatment 5 hours/day; $30 month probation fee; no out-of-State trips	Mandatory rehabilitation skills program 8 hours/day; restitution; $40/month probation fee; no drinking; curfew	Work release; pay portion of food/lodging; restitution; no privileges outside mealtimes; no drinking; no sex; weekends home	Residential treatment program; pay portion of program costs; limited privileges	Minimum-security prison	Medium-security prison	Maximum-security prison

1. Restrictions on freedom structure an offender's time, controlling his or her schedule, whereabouts, and activities for a designated period. To the extent that monitoring is not standard or consistent or to the extent that no sanctions accrue for failure on the part of the offender, the time is not structured. It could consist of residential, part-time residential, community service, or other specific methods for meeting the designated hours. The judge could order that the hours be met daily (e.g., 2 hours/day) or in one period (e.g., weekend in jail.

2. Privileges/conditions: choice of job, choice of residence, mobility within setting, driving, drinking (possible use of Antabuse), out-of-State trips, phone calls, curfew, mail, urinalysis, associates, areas off limits.

3. As a more equitable guide to appropriate fines, the amount would be measured in units of equivalent daily income, such as 1 day's salary = "1-day fine."

Source: Pierre S. du Pont, *Expanding Sentencing Options: A Governor's Perspective* (National Institute of Justice 1985).

Drug courts exemplify another means through which courts can tailor their responses to violations by some offenders of the conditions of a community sanction. Drug courts are utilized in some jurisdictions for certain kinds of drug offenders. An offender processed through a drug court is subject to intensive treatment requirements and frequent urinalysis tests. The offender must appear often in court where the drug-court judge reviews the offender's progress and modifies the constraints to which the offender is subject based on the offender's progress or lack thereof. In many jurisdictions in which drug courts have been established, the criminal charges are dismissed upon an offender's successful completion of the program.

Drug courts have served as the template for the establishment of other specialized courts that have a treatment and problem-solving orientation to criminal cases. Mental-health courts, which handle certain categories of cases involving offenders with mental illnesses, are one notable example of these specialized courts.

Nonimprisonment guidelines that employ what are called sanctioning units are still another mechanism for contouring sentences to meet the variant circumstances of offenders. Kay Knapp, the former director of the Minnesota Sentencing Guidelines Commission, has described how sanctioning units could be incorporated into sentencing systems:

> Such an approach rests on the development of two concepts: (1) sanctioning levels; and (2) exchange rates. The first concept, sanctioning level, is substituted in the guidelines system for the more traditional sanction. Thus, instead of defining six months imprisonment as the proper pre-

sumptive sentence for a particular category of offenders, the policy would prescribe a sanctioning level of six units (or eight or ten or twelve). The concept of exchange rates would be used to translate units into specific sanctions, such that one unit translates into 40 community service hours, or a month in jail, or two months on probation, or two weeks in residential treatment. Essentially the court would be provided with a menu of sanctions from which to fashion a sentence to meet the sanctioning level prescribed by policy.

Kay A. Knapp, "Next Step: Non–Imprisonment Guidelines," *Perspectives* 10 (American Probation and Parole Association; Winter, 1988).

The use of sanctioning units and exchange rates would help to avert disparity in the imposition of community-based sanctions. Incorporating a broad range of sanctions into a sentencing system with sanctioning units and exchange rates would also help to ensure that judges have the flexibility they need to impose the most appropriate type of penalty on a criminal offender.

CHAPTER 6

THE DEATH PENALTY

Few areas of criminal justice have prompted as much controversy and debate as the death penalty. Is the death penalty constitutional and if so, in what circumstances? And even if it is constitutional, when, if ever, should society ever resort to the imposition of this penalty?

In 1972, the Supreme Court in *Furman v. Georgia* (S.Ct.1972) struck down Georgia's death-penalty statute. The Court held that the statute violated the Eighth Amendment's prohibition of cruel and unusual punishments because it left the decision whether to impose the death penalty within the unconfined discretion of the sentencing judge or jury. The end result was such arbitrary imposition of the death penalty that those individuals who received the death penalty could not readily be distinguished from those who did not.

After *Furman*, states across the country, including Georgia, scrambled to enact death-penalty statutes that would pass constitutional muster. In *Gregg v. Georgia* (S.Ct.1976), the Supreme Court was asked to decide whether Georgia had succeeded in achieving this objective. The Court first, however, addressed the threshold question whether the death penalty can ever be constitutional for the crime of murder.

In answering this question, the Supreme Court said that it must begin with the presumption that a penalty selected by the legislature is constitutional. A "heavy burden," the Court observed, rests on those who seek to rebut this presumption. Ultimately, the Court concluded that this burden had not been met in this case. In other words, the death penalty is not *per se* unconstitutional.

In the course of arriving at this conclusion, the Court first examined whether the death penalty contravenes society's "evolving standards of decency." The Court concluded that it does not, citing several reasons for this conclusion.

First, it is evident from the text of the Constitution that the framers of the Constitution had contemplated that death would be imposed as a penalty for some crimes. The Due Process Clauses in the Fifth and Fourteenth Amendments, for example, require that due process be afforded individuals deprived of "*life*, liberty, or property." In addition, the Fifth Amendment's double-jeopardy prohibition refers to persons being twice placed in jeopardy of "*life* or limb," and the same amendment requires that indictments be obtained in "capital" cases.

Second, the Supreme Court cited the history of the death penalty—its long acceptance, up through the present, as a penalty for murder. In fact, under the common law, death was the mandatory penalty for murder.

Third, the Court noted the response of state legislatures to *Furman*. When it became apparent from *Furman* that death-penalty statutes throughout the country were unconstitutional, a wave of new death-penalty laws were enacted. At least thirty-five states enacted such laws, a strong indicator, in the Court's mind, that the death penalty, in some circumstances, comports with societal standards of decency.

Fourth, the Court cited the results of public-opinion surveys that revealed that a majority of Americans favored the death penalty at the time of the Court's decision. In a dissenting opinion, Justice Marshall rejoined that support for the death penalty diminishes substantially when the public is fully informed about the penalty and its consequences. In other words, the views of an informed public vary greatly from those of an uninformed public.

Finally, the Court relied on the willingness of juries to sometimes return verdicts of death as another indicator that the death penalty does not inherently conflict with societal standards of decency.

Concluding that the death penalty for murder does not conflict with societal standards of decency did not end the Supreme Court's analysis under the Eighth Amendment. The Court noted that even if the death penalty comported with societal standards of decency, as reflected by such objective indicators as the statutes enacted by legislatures and the sentencing practices of juries, the death penalty would still be unconstitutional if it was "excessive." The Court was essentially saying that while the opinions of legislatures would be given great weight when assessing the constitutionality of a penalty, their opinions would not, and could not, be conclusive. Otherwise, the Cruel and Unusual Punishment Clause would have no meaning, because its very purpose is to guard against the penchant of legislatures to overreact sometimes to the problem of crime in a way that flouts the respect for human dignity that the Court says lies at the heart of the Eighth Amendment.

According to the Supreme Court in *Gregg v. Georgia*, the death penalty would be unconstitutionally excessive if it resulted in the "unnecessary and wanton infliction of pain" or was a grossly disproportionate penalty for the crime committed. The dissenters argued that the death penalty in fact constituted the unnecessary and wanton infliction of pain since there was a viable and less drastic way of punishing murderers other than killing them—confining them for the rest of their lives in prison. The majority responded that there is no least-drastic-alternative requirement subsumed within the Eighth Amendment. The death penalty would therefore only be considered the unnecessary and wanton infliction of pain if it was so devoid of any penological justification as to constitute the "gratuitous infliction of suffering."

According to the Supreme Court, this requirement was not met because three penological objectives are furthered or arguably furthered by the death penalty. The first is retribution. Some people, the Court observed, might legitimately feel that death is the only appropriate penalty for certain particularly opprobrious crimes.

The second penological objective served by the death penalty to which the Court alluded is incapacitation. Simply put, once people are dead, they can and will commit no further crimes.

Finally, the Court noted the argued deterrent function of the death penalty—using the prospect of death as a punishment to dissuade people from committing murders. The Court acknowledged that the empirical evidence regarding the death penalty's claimed deterrent effects is inconclusive. But the Court refused to discount this penological objective as a reason for upholding the death penalty, saying that it was up to legislatures to resolve the questions concerning the efficacy of the death penalty as a deterrent.

The Supreme Court ended its Eighth Amendment analysis of the generic question—can the death penalty ever be constitutionally imposed for the crime of murder?—by concluding that the penalty is not grossly disproportionate in every case involving the deliberate taking of a life. The Court then turned to the question whether the death-penalty statute before it was constitutional.

The Supreme Court answered this question in the affirmative. The Court held that this statute, unlike the statute that the Court struck down in *Furman v. Georgia*, contained safeguards that, in the

Court's view, were adequate to prevent the arbitrary and capricious imposition of death as a penalty for the crime of murder. Particularly significant to the Court was the way in which the statute limited the discretion of the sentencing jury or judge; the sentencer had to find, beyond a reasonable doubt, that at least one of ten aggravating factors delineated in the statute existed before the death penalty could be imposed. The Court also highlighted another procedural safeguard designed to avert the arbitrary imposition of the death penalty—automatic review by the Georgia Supreme Court of all death sentences.

Although the Supreme Court in *Gregg v. Georgia* seemed confident that Georgia's death-penalty statute was crafted, on its face, in a way to avoid the arbitrary and capricious imposition of death sentences, statistics presented to the Court in a subsequent case revealed that there is racial disparity in the implementation of that statute. In *McCleskey v. Kemp* (S.Ct.1987), the Supreme Court considered the constitutional implications of a study that found that African–American defendants convicted of murder in Georgia were more likely to receive the death penalty than defendants who were white. The study also found that the race of the victim had a bearing on the likelihood of receiving a death sentence; defendants whose victims were white were much more likely to receive the death penalty than defendants whose victims were black. The death penalty was imposed in 22% of the murder cases involving a black defendant and a white victim, 8%

of the cases involving a white defendant and a white victim, 3% of the cases involving a white defendant and a black victim, and only 1% of the cases in which both the defendant and the victim were black.

The defendant in *McCleskey*, an African–American man sentenced to death for killing a white police officer, argued that the above statistics confirmed that racial discrimination permeated the capital-punishment system in Georgia, in violation of the Fourteenth Amendment's guarantee of equal protection of the law and the Eighth Amendment's prohibition of cruel and unusual punishments. The Supreme Court, however, in a 5–4 decision, concluded that the defendant's right to be accorded the equal protection of the law had not been violated, since there was no evidence that the jury in this particular case had imposed the death penalty because of the defendant's race or the race of his victim. Nor was there any evidence that the Georgia legislature had acted with the intent to discriminate against African Americans when enacting the death-penalty statute.

The absence of proof that race had been a factor in the jury's decision in this particular case to return a death sentence was also cited by the Court in rejecting the defendant's claim that his sentence constituted cruel and unusual punishment. The Court was unconvinced that there was unconstitutional arbitrariness in the imposition of death sentences in Georgia simply because of the demonstrated risk that racial bias plays a role in juries' decisions to sentence a defendant to death. The Court emphasized that Georgia's capital-punishment system contained many procedural safeguards to avert arbitrariness in the imposition of the death penalty. Refusing to "assume that what is unexplained is insidious," the Court concluded that the statistical risk that the death penalty was imposed because of the defendant's or the victim's race was not "constitutionally significant."

This observation of the Court drew a sharp rebuke from Justice Brennan. In his dissenting opinion in which Justices Marshall, Blackmun, and Stevens joined, Justice Brennan noted that for every eleven defendants in Georgia sentenced to death for killing a white person, only five would have received the death penalty if their victims had been black. He argued: "Surely we would not be willing to take a person's life if the risk that his death was irrationally imposed is *more* likely than not."

Concerns about the arbitrary imposition of the death penalty have prompted the Supreme Court to strike down death-penalty statutes whose language is unconstitutionally vague. *See, e.g., Maynard v. Cartwright* (S.Ct.1988) (statute treating the fact that a murder was committed in an "especially heinous, atrocious, or cruel manner" as an aggravating factor was unconstitutionally vague). Similar concerns have led the Court to hold death-penalty statutes that mandate the imposition of the death penalty for certain crimes to be unconstitutional. In *Woodson v. North Carolina* (S.Ct.1976), the Supreme Court cited three reasons why a mandatory death-penalty statute for first-degree murder was unconstitutional under the Eighth Amendment. First, the mandatory death-penalty statute, according to the Court, conflicted with societal standards of decency. Although the Court acknowledged that at common law the mandatory penalty for murder was death, the Court essentially said that times have changed. As an indicator of current societal values, the Court pointed to the frequent decisions of juries in jurisdictions with mandatory death-penalty statutes to acquit murderers in order to avoid having them subjected to a penalty that, under the circumstances, is too harsh. The Court also underscored that in jurisdictions with discretionary death-penalty statutes, juries decide that the death penalty is not appropriate in the vast majority of capital murder cases.

The Supreme Court cited the movement away from mandatory death-penalty statutes as a further indicator of societal standards of decency. By 1963, no state mandated death for the crime of murder. While it was true that some states had resurrected the practice of mandating death for certain crimes after the Supreme Court decided *Furman v. Georgia* in 1972, the Supreme Court viewed these legislative enactments as rather frantic attempts by the states to comport with the dictates of *Furman* rather than as a newfound endorsement of mandatory death sentences.

The Supreme Court's second reason for holding that the mandatory death-penalty statute in *Woodson* violated the Eighth Amendment was that the statute, despite its mandatory character, as a practical matter left the decision whether to impose the death penalty within the unbridled discretion of the jury. This problem of unchanneled jury discretion stemmed from the phenomenon mentioned earlier of juries acquitting some defendants, but not others, to avoid imposition of the death penalty. The end result was arbitrariness in the selection of those defendants who would be put to death for their crimes.

The third constitutional defect identified in the mandatory death-penalty statute in *Woodson* was that it abridged the right of defendants under the Eighth Amendment to an individualized sentencing determination in a capital case. The mandatory death-penalty statute lumped all first-degree murderers into an amorphous mass, treating all of them as deserving a death sentence. The Supreme Court said in *Woodson* that the "fundamental respect for humanity" that undergirds the Eighth Amendment instead requires that juries be permitted to consider the individuality of defendants in capital cases— their personal attributes, their backgrounds, and any circumstances of their crimes that counsel against imposing the death penalty.

Since *Woodson*, the Supreme Court has struck down other mandatory death-penalty statutes. *See, e.g., Sumner v. Shuman* (S.Ct.1987) (mandatory death sentence for a murder committed when serving a life sentence without possibility of parole is unconstitutional); *Roberts v. Louisiana* (S.Ct.1977) (mandatory death sentence for murdering a police officer violates the Eighth Amendment). Having some type of mandatory component in a death-penalty statute does not always, however, contravene the Eighth Amendment. For example, in *Blystone v. Pennsylvania* (S.Ct.1990), the Supreme Court upheld a death-penalty statute that required the imposition of the death penalty when a sentencing jury found that the aggravating circumstances in a case outweighed any mitigating circumstances.

In each of the cases in which the Supreme Court has held a mandatory death-penalty statute unconstitutional, the Court has emphasized the right of defendants to bring to the attention of the sentencer any mitigating circumstances that might demonstrate that imposition of a death sentence is unwarranted. *See also Hitchcock v. Dugger* (S.Ct.1987) (defendant has the right to introduce evidence of mitigating circumstances not listed in the death-penalty statute). Some Supreme Court Justices have contended that there is an irreconcilable conflict between the Eighth Amendment requirement that sentencing discretion in capital cases be circumscribed to prevent the arbitrary imposition of the death penalty and the requirement that sentencing be individualized, with expansive consideration by the sentencer of mitigating circumstances, to ensure that only those individuals who deserve to die for their crimes receive the death penalty. These Justices, however, have disagreed on how the Court should respond to this conflict. After many years of supporting the death penalty, Justice Blackmun, shortly before retiring from the Court, called on the

Court to declare the death penalty *per se* unconstitutional and to end what he considered its futile quest to reconcile the competing goals of avoiding arbitrariness while at the same time providing for individual fairness in the imposition of the death penalty. *Callins v. Collins* (S.Ct.1994) (Blackmun, J., dissenting). Justice Scalia, on the other hand, has urged the Court to simply abandon the requirement that sentencers be permitted to consider an unlimited array of mitigating circumstances in capital cases. *Walton v. Arizona* (S.Ct.1990) (Scalia, J., concurring).

Precluding a defendant from presenting information to the sentencer in a capital sentencing trial may, at times, violate a constitutional provision other than, or in addition to, the Eighth Amendment. For example, when the defendant's future dangerousness has a bearing on the imposition of the death penalty, the defendant has a due-process right to inform a jury when a life sentence, under state law, forecloses any possibility of release on parole. *Shafer v. South Carolina* (S.Ct.2001). A prosecutor, however, can constitutionally respond to the presentation of this information to the jury by requesting an instruction apprising the jury that the exercise of executive clemency powers might still lead to the defendant's release from prison. *California v. Ramos* (S.Ct.1983).

While the Supreme Court has held that the Eighth Amendment prohibits legislatures from requiring imposition of the death penalty for certain crimes, the Court has also identified certain instances when the death penalty can never be imposed. One of those instances is when an individual has been convicted of raping, but not murdering, an adult. In *Coker v. Georgia* (S.Ct.1977), the Supreme Court held that no matter how vicious and injurious a rape, the death penalty for rape is disproportionate to the severity of the crime because it does not involve the taking of a human life. The Court added that its conclusion that the death penalty was an unconstitutionally disproportionate penalty for raping an adult was buttressed by the following facts: only one state authorized the death penalty for raping an adult (two others authorized the death penalty for raping a child), juries in the state of Georgia rarely sentenced rapists to death, and very few countries in the world authorized the death penalty for rape.

Although the Supreme Court has ruled that the death penalty for rape, at least for rape of an adult, is unconstitutional because the victim is not killed, a defendant need not actually be the person who killed a victim in order for imposition of the death penalty to be constitutional. In *Tison v. Arizona* (S.Ct.1987), the Supreme Court considered the constitutionality of the death sentences imposed on two brothers who had smuggled guns into a prison and then used them to help their father and another prisoner escape. The father and the other prisoner later shot and killed four people who had stopped to help them when their car broke down. The two brothers, who were present during the murders and did nothing to stop them, were convicted of capital

murder under both the state's felony-murder statute and a statute that held certain felons responsible for crimes committed by their accomplices.

The Supreme Court, in a 5–4 decision, upheld
these death sentences, noting that the brothers'
participation in "the felony" was "major" and that
they had acted with "reckless indifference to human life" by helping to effectuate a prison escape
that they knew posed "a grave risk of death." The
Court distinguished the case before it from *Enmund
v. Florida* (S.Ct.1982). In that case, the Court had
struck down the death sentence imposed on a defendant who had driven the getaway car in an armed
robbery but had not killed the two murder victims.
The defendant in *Enmund*, according to the Court,
had played only a minor role in the armed robbery
and murders, and there was no finding that he had
acted with the intent that the victims be killed or
with reckless disregard that such loss of life might
ensue.

The Supreme Court has addressed the constitutional significance of a number of other factors in
the death-penalty context. The Court has flip-
flopped on the question whether the Eighth Amendment permits the imposition of the death penalty on
persons who are mentally retarded. In *Penry v.
Lynaugh* (S.Ct.1989), the Court held that while a
defendant's mental retardation is a mitigating circumstance that may counsel against imposition of
the death penalty, executing a mentally retarded
defendant is not *per se* unconstitutional. Thirteen
years later, in *Atkins v. Virginia* (S.Ct.2002), the

Supreme Court reversed its position. In concluding that executing a person who is mentally retarded conflicts with the "evolving standards of decency that mark the progress of a maturing society," the Court emphasized that eighteen states prohibited the execution of the mentally retarded, up from only two at the time *Penry* was decided. To the Court, the significance of this policy shift lay not in the exact number of states that prohibited the execution of the mentally retarded, but in the "consistency of the direction of change."

In *Atkins*, the Supreme Court cited another reason why the Eighth Amendment barred the execution of the mentally retarded: the fact that they are at "special risk of wrongful execution." Because of their limited mental faculties, mentally retarded defendants are, according to the Court, more likely to confess to a crime of which they are innocent. For the same reason, they are typically inept witnesses, and their mental deficiencies impede their ability to assist their lawyers in preparing and presenting their defense.

The Supreme Court also has vacillated on the question whether the Eighth Amendment bars imposition of the death penalty on defendants who were under eighteen when they committed their crimes. In *Stanford v. Kentucky* (S.Ct.1989), the Court held that the Constitution permits defendants who were sixteen or seventeen at the time of their crimes to be sentenced to death. Sixteen years later, in a closely divided 5–4 decision, the Supreme Court retracted this holding. In *Roper v. Simmons*

(S.Ct.2005), the Court opined that a "national consensus" against the execution of juveniles had emerged since *Stanford* was decided. Thirty states now banned the juvenile death penalty, five more than when the Court rendered its decision in *Stanford*. In addition, over the past decade, executions of defendants who were under eighteen when they committed their crimes were carried out in only three states.

The Supreme Court considered these "objective indicia of consensus" as confirmation that society views juveniles as less culpable than adult criminals. The Court concurred with this assessment, though adding that it still had to decide for itself whether the death penalty was a disproportionate and therefore unconstitutional punishment for juveniles. The Court then said that the death penalty's retributive aim did not support the application of the death penalty to juveniles, since juveniles, due to their immaturity, are less blameworthy than adults for their crimes. The Court also concluded that the death penalty would be less likely to accomplish its deterrent objective in this context, because juveniles are prone to acting impulsively and rashly.

As final support for its decision, the Court in *Roper* noted that the United States was the only country in the world that officially condones the execution of defendants who were under eighteen at the time of their crimes. While the Court emphasized that it was not bound to follow international laws and practices when interpreting the meaning of the Eighth Amendment, it also said that those laws and practices are "instructive" when deciphering what is and is not a cruel and unusual punishment.

Even when it is constitutional to impose the death penalty on a defendant, circumstances may develop that preclude, for constitutional reasons, the execution of that sentence. In *Ford v. Wainwright* (S.Ct.1986), the Supreme Court held that executing an insane person would constitute cruel and unusual punishment. In discussing why the states universally prohibit the execution of insane prisoners, the Court noted that there are doubts about whether the death penalty can serve its retributive aim when the individuals being executed are so mentally deranged that they cannot understand why they are being killed. In addition, the Court acknowledged the religious roots of the opposition to the execution of the insane—the belief that people should only be executed after they have had a chance to ask God to forgive them for their sins. Still unresolved by the Court is the question whether a prisoner constitutionally can be forced to take medication that will make the inmate competent for execution.

While the Supreme Court has held that a death sentence can, in certain circumstances, be constitutionally imposed and executed, the policy debate regarding the propriety and advisability of retaining the death penalty has intensified in this country in recent years. Part of this debate has been fueled by evidence of large-scale errors in the imposition of the death penalty. *See, e.g.*, James S. Liebman et al., *A Broken System: Error Rates in Capital Cases, 1973–1995* 5 (2000) (reporting reversals in 68% of over 4,500 capital cases resulting in death sentences). Some of these errors have led to innocent persons being sentenced to death. Among the endemic problems contributing to this high error rate is the failure of some defense attorneys in capital cases to provide their clients with the effective assistance of counsel to which they are constitutionally entitled. *See* Stephen B. Bright, *Neither Equal Nor Just: The Rationing and Denial of Legal Services to the Poor When Life and Liberty Are at Stake*, 1997 Ann. Surv. Am. L. 783 (1999).

CHAPTER 7

CRUEL AND UNUSUAL PUNISHMENT AND NONCAPITAL CASES

A. DISPROPORTIONALITY CLAIMS

In the noncapital context, cruel and unusual punishment claims generally have focused on the alleged gross disproportionality of a penalty to the severity of the crime of which a defendant was convicted. In *Rummel v. Estelle* (S.Ct.1980), the Supreme Court confronted such a claim. The defendant in that case was sentenced to life in prison under a Texas recidivist statute that mandated a life sentence upon conviction of a third felony. The defendant's first felony conviction was for obtaining $80 worth of goods or services through the fraudulent use of a credit card. His second felony conviction was for forging a check worth $28.36, and his third was for obtaining $120.75 by false pretenses.

Rebuffing the defendant's claim that his life sentence constituted cruel and unusual punishment, the Supreme Court, in a 5–4 decision, dismissed the significance of an array of factors to which the defendant pointed in support of his claim. First, the defendant underscored that all of his crimes were nonviolent. The Court responded that society can have a strong interest in deterring or punishing crimes that are nonviolent in nature. As examples of serious, but nonviolent, crimes, the Court cited bribery, antitrust violations, and the violation of clean-air or water standards by the head of a large corporation.

Second, the defendant reminded the Court that his crimes had involved only a "small" amount of money. The Supreme Court responded that what is a small or a large amount of money is a question which is best remitted to the legislature. In addition, the Court noted that there was another state interest at stake here other than the interest in punishing those who unlawfully acquire the property of others—the interest in punishing more severely those individuals who repeatedly flout the law.

Third, the defendant pointed to the unusual severity of his penalty compared to the way in which other states punish three-time felons. The Supreme Court did not consider this factor of any import either. The Court noted that many states only varied slightly from Texas in the way in which they punished repeat offenders. The Court also cited the difficulty of comparing sentencing statutes in different states, because the states vary widely in their parole practices and the granting of good-time credits. In other words, comparing the sentences imposed in different jurisdictions can be misleading because there are often substantial differences between the sentences imposed on individuals and the sentences actually served. For example, while the defendant in *Rummel* had received a life sentence, he would become eligible for parole after serving twelve years in prison.

The Supreme Court's principal response to the defendant's referral to the sentencing practices of other states, however, was that even if a state punishes a crime more severely than any other state, that fact does not mean that the punishment is cruel and unusual. A state has the prerogative, observed the Court, to view the severity of a crime differently than other states. In the Court's words, "[a]bsent a constitutionally imposed uniformity inimical to traditional notions of federalism," there will almost always be one state that punishes a particular crime more severely than any other state.

The Supreme Court also dismissed the defendant's argument that a comparison of how Texas punished criminals who have committed other crimes is relevant to the question whether a grossly disproportionate penalty had been imposed on him. The Court said that comparing the penalties for different crimes is a fruitless exercise, because different crimes can implicate quite different societal interests.

In *Hutto v. Davis* (S.Ct.1982), the Supreme Court followed *Rummel's* lead and cursorily rejected the defendant's Eighth Amendment disproportionality claim. The defendant in *Hutto* had been sentenced to prison for a total of forty years for the possession and distribution of about nine ounces of marijuana. The Supreme Court, however, reiterated that it was reluctant, except in an "exceedingly rare" case, to usurp the legislative prerogative to define the penal sanction to be imposed for a crime.

The Supreme Court's handling of the disproportionality claims in *Rummel v. Estelle* and *Hutto v. Davis* is to be contrasted with the result and analysis in *Solem v. Helm* (S.Ct.1983). The defendant in *Solem* had also, like the defendant in *Rummel*, received a life sentence under a recidivist statute, although the life sentence was without the possibility of parole. The defendant in *Solem*, however, had been convicted of many more felonies than the defendant in *Rummel*—seven, and his convictions were for seemingly more serious crimes—three third-degree burglaries, a third-offense drunk driving, grand larceny, obtaining money under false pretenses, and writing a bad check for one hundred dollars. The Supreme Court in *Solem* nonetheless concluded, in another 5–4 decision, that the defendant's life sentence constituted cruel and unusual punishment.

Solem and *Rummel* can be reconciled on their facts, because, as mentioned earlier, the life sentence in *Solem*, unlike the life sentence in *Rummel*, was without the possibility of parole. What is more difficult to square is the Supreme Court's analysis in *Solem* of the factors that the Court said bear on the resolution of an Eighth Amendment disproportionality claim and its dismissal of these same factors in *Rummel* as irrelevant.

In *Solem*, the Supreme Court set forth a three-part analysis to be undertaken by courts considering Eighth Amendment disproportionality claims. First, a court should consider the severity of the crime and the harshness of the penalty that was imposed for the crime. In assessing the severity of the crime, the Supreme Court in *Solem*, in seeming contradiction with what it had said earlier in *Rummel*, counselled courts to consider the "absolute magnitude" of the crime—how much money, for example, a defendant had stolen—and whether the crime involved violence or the threat of violence. The Court mentioned other factors that bear either on the harm caused or threatened by the defendant or the defendant's culpability, including whether a crime was a lesser-included offense or the greater offense, whether the defendant had attempted or completed the crime, what the defendant's state of mind was when committing the crime—whether negligent, reckless, knowing, intentional, or malicious, and what the defendant's motive was.

The second and third components identified by the Supreme Court in *Solem* as relevant to an Eighth Amendment disproportionality analysis had likewise been discounted by the Court in *Rummel*— the sentences imposed within the state for other crimes and the sentences imposed in other jurisdictions for the crime of which the defendant had been convicted. Yet despite the conflict between the Court's analysis in *Solem* and its analysis in *Rummel*, the Court in *Solem* did not overrule its decision in *Rummel*.

In *Harmelin v. Michigan* (S.Ct.1991), the Supreme Court was presented with the opportunity to eliminate the confusion engendered by its opinions in *Rummel* and *Solem*. Instead, the Court rendered, once again, another 5–4 decision, with no view on what is the appropriate Eighth Amendment disproportionality analysis commanding the support of a majority of the Justices on the Court.

The defendant in *Harmelin* had received a life sentence after being convicted of possessing 672 grams of cocaine. The defendant's conviction was his first, but the statute under which he was sentenced mandated life imprisonment without parole for possession of more than 650 grams of cocaine.

A majority of the Court rejected the defendant's claim that his sentence was unconstitutionally disproportionate to the severity of the crime of which he was found guilty, but the Justices split as to their reasoning. Two of the Justices—Justice Scalia, joined by Chief Justice Rehnquist—insisted that there is no proportionality principle in the Eighth Amendment that governs prison sentences. Based on Justice Scalia's interpretation of the history of the Eighth Amendment, he argued that the Eighth Amendment is concerned with the kinds of penalties imposed for crimes rather than with the extent to which those penalties, or at least prison sentences, have been calibrated with the crimes for which they are imposed. In addition, Justice Scalia cited the text of the Eighth Amendment as support for his position that there is no disproportionality principle subsumed within it that encompasses prison sentences. The Eighth Amendment, he pointed out, specifically proscribes "excessive fines," but says nothing about excessive prison sentences. Justice Scalia conceded that despite this silence, there is still a proportionality requirement in the Eighth Amendment that has to be met in a capital case. "Death is different" than any other criminal sanctions, he explained.

In a dissenting opinion joined by Justices Blackmun, Stevens, and Marshall, Justice White chastised Justice Scalia for what Justice White considered his skewed reading of the Eighth Amendment. Justice White wondered how the same words, "cruel and unusual," could mean one thing in the capital context and another thing in the noncapital context; grossly disproportionate sentences, he argued, were either unconstitutional or they were not.

Justice White also ridiculed the notion that the proscription in the Eighth Amendment of "excessive" fines somehow implied that excessive prison sentences were constitutional. Not only was this reading of the Constitution, in Justice White's opinion, illogical, but it demanded a level of clarity and specificity in the language of the Constitution that was not the norm. As examples of the vague language that permeates the Constitution, Justice White cited the requirements of "due process of law" and the Fourth Amendment's prohibition of "unreasonable searches and seizures."

Justice Kennedy, joined by Justices O'Connor and Souter, upheld the defendant's sentence in *Solem* for a different reason than that propounded by Justice Scalia. Unlike Justice Scalia, Justice Kennedy believed that the Eighth Amendment contains a proportionality requirement, though a "narrow" one, that applies to prison sentences. Justice Kennedy simply felt that in this case, that requirement had been met; in other words, the defendant's sentence was not "grossly disproportionate" to the crime of which he was convicted.

What was most significant about Justice Kennedy's opinion was the way in which he said the *Solem* balancing test should be applied. In his opinion, the second and third factors of that test—intra- and interjurisdictional sentencing practices—should be examined by a court only in the unusual case when the first factor supports an inference of "gross disproportionality." Citing the tremendous harm to society caused by drug use, including drug-related violence, Justice Kennedy then concluded that a comparison of the gravity of the crime with the harshness of the penalty imposed did not create such an inference in this case.

In his dissenting opinion, Justice White strongly objected to Justice Kennedy's description of the severity of the defendant's crime. Justice White argued that the defendant was no more responsible for all of the adverse consequences that stem from drug use than those who sell alcohol are responsible for all of the adverse effects that attend the abuse of alcohol. Justice White furthermore underscored that the defendant was a first-time offender and that he had only been convicted of possession of the cocaine, not possession with the intent to distribute.

More fundamentally, Justice White disagreed with the twist given by Justice Kennedy to the *Solem* balancing test. How, Justice White queried, is a court supposed to assess objectively how grave a crime is compared to the harshness of the penalty imposed without looking at sentencing practices both within and outside the jurisdiction?

When Justice White applied the full *Solem* balancing test to the facts of the case before the Court, he concluded that the defendant's life sentence without the possibility of parole was unconstitutionally disproportionate. In addition to his observation mentioned earlier about the gravity of the defendant's crime, Justice White cited the following factors as support for his conclusion: the fact that the defendant's sentence was the harshest that could be imposed in the state because Michigan has no death penalty; the fact that not even second-degree murderers, rapists, or armed robbers had to be sent to prison for life in Michigan; and the fact that no other state punished a crime like the defendant's as harshly.

Interestingly, while the defendant in *Harmelin* failed to prevail in the Supreme Court on his federal constitutional claim based on the alleged disproportionality of his sentence, the statute under which he was convicted was later stricken down by the Michigan Supreme Court as violative of the state constitution. *People v. Bullock* (Mich.1992). The Michigan Supreme Court explained that the ban under the state constitution of "cruel *or* unusual" punishments was broader than the proscription of "cruel *and* unusual" punishments in the Eighth Amendment.

There was another issue before the Supreme Court in *Harmelin v. Michigan* that managed to command a majority view on the Court. The defendant in *Harmelin* had argued that the mandatory nature of his sentence made his sentence unconstitutional. He contended that, as in the death-penalty context, he had the right to individualized sentencing. The issue raised by the defendant had significant national implications because of the large number of mandatory-minimum sentencing statutes that have been enacted in recent years as part of the drive to "get tough" on crime. A majority of the Court—Justice Scalia and Chief Justice Rehnquist in one opinion, and Justices Kennedy, O'Connor, and Souter in another—noted that death is different from other criminal sanctions and that therefore a mandatory prison sentence is not inherently unconstitutional.

The Supreme Court has acknowledged that its decisions adjudicating claims that a prison sentence, due to its length, was unconstitutional have created a "thicket of Eighth Amendment jurisprudence." Yet the division within the Court regarding the appropriate analytical framework for resolving such claims persists, with no single test commanding the support of a majority of the Court. In *Ewing v. California* (S.Ct.2003), for example, Justices Scalia and Thomas continued to maintain that the Eighth Amendment simply does not forbid the imposition of what some people might consider grossly disproportionate prison sentences. Three Justices—Justices O'Connor, Rehnquist, and Kennedy—said that the approach outlined by Justice Kennedy in *Harmelin* should be followed. In other words, a court should engage in an intrajurisdictional and interjurisdictional comparison of criminal penalties only in the "rare case" when the prison sentence, compared to the crime for which it was imposed, creates an inference of gross disproportionality. Four Justices—Justices Stevens, Souter, Ginsburg, and Breyer—countered that the three-part *Solem* test seemed to be the most appropriate one for the Court to apply. Under this test, as mentioned earlier, the intra- and interjurisdictional comparisons are a central and mandatory component of the Eighth Amendment analysis.

The Supreme Court was also closely divided on the merits of the defendant's Eighth Amendment claim in *Ewing*. The defendant in that case had been sentenced to prison for twenty-five years to life under California's three-strikes law, with no possibility of parole before he had served the minimum twenty-five year sentence. While the defendant had a long criminal record, having been convicted of such crimes as battery, multiple thefts, possession of drug paraphernalia, possession of a firearm, four burglaries, and robbery, the crime that triggered application of the three-strikes law was his theft of three golf clubs worth about twelve hundred dollars. The Supreme Court split 5–4 in holding that the defendant's sentence did not abridge the Eighth Amendment.

In addition to prohibiting cruel and unusual punishments, the Eighth Amendment bars the imposition of "excessive fines." In determining whether a fine is unconstitutionally "excessive," courts apply the same test they apply when determining whether a penalty is unconstitutionally "cruel and unusual." *United States v. Bajakajian* (S.Ct.1998). In other words, a fine is "excessive" within the meaning of the Eighth Amendment when it is "grossly disproportional to the gravity of a defendant's offense."

Even when a sentence is not unconstitutionally disproportionate within the meaning of the Eighth Amendment, a defendant may argue that the sentencing judge erred in imposing such a long prison sentence or high fine. Although defendants occasionally prevail on such claims, appellate courts have traditionally been extremely reluctant to vacate a sentence because of its length or amount. A standard commonly applied when determining whether to set aside a sentence is whether it reflects a "clear abuse of discretion." *Manes v. State* (Wyo.2004).

B. CHALLENGES REGARDING THE NATURE OF A CRIMINAL SANCTION

Some Eighth Amendment challenges to sentences in the noncapital context have contested the constitutionality of the kind, rather than the length or amount, of the penalty imposed. These types of claims typically have involved two kinds of sentences—what are called "shame sentences" and sentences involving medical interventions.

1. Shame Sentences

Shame sentences have at least one common component—the public degradation of the offender. Shame sentences date back in this country to colonial times. The letter "A" sewn on the clothing of a person who had committed adultery is the most well-known example of a shame punishment imposed in the colonial era.

Today, shame sentences can take many forms. Some judges, for example, have required defendants convicted of drunk driving to publicize their convictions on a license plate or bumper sticker. Others have required defendants to erect signs on their property publicizing their crimes, most often when the defendant was guilty of a violent crime or sex offense.

Often courts have skirted the question whether a particular shame punishment violates the Eighth Amendment by holding that the jurisdiction's sentencing laws do not authorize the kind of penalty the judge imposed. But some shaming punishments have surmounted this statutory hurdle. For example, in *United States v. Gementera* (9th Cir.2004), the Ninth Circuit Court of Appeals held that the Sentencing Reform Act, 18 U.S.C. § 3583(d), permitted the sentencing judge to require a defendant convicted of mail theft to wear or carry a two-sided placard announcing, "I stole mail. This is my punishment," in front of a post office for eight hours.

The court found this condition of the defendant's supervised release to be "reasonably related" to at least one of the penological objectives outlined in the statute—rehabilitation—and therefore within the statute's scope.

When a shaming punishment falls within the boundaries of the court's statutory sentencing authority, the court may then have to address head-on the question whether the sentence inflicts cruel and unusual punishment on the defendant. Thus far, most, though not all, Eighth Amendment challenges to shame sentences have been rejected by the courts. For example, in *United States v. Gementera*, the case mentioned above, the court of appeals upheld the constitutionality of the supervised-release condition requiring the defendant, in a most public way, to acknowledge his guilt of mail theft; the court found no evidence that this shaming sanction departed from societal standards of decency. But the cases adjudicating the constitutionality of shame sentences are very fact-specific, so the outcome of these cases might vary if the facts were somewhat modified. In *Gementera*, for example, the signboard condition was combined with other requirements that, according to the court of appeals, would enable the defendant to make amends for his wrongdoing and reintegrate into society. These requirements included the writing of letters of apology to his victims and the delivery of lectures to high-school students about how his criminal misdeeds had hurt him and his future.

2. Medical Interventions

Medical interventions also are beginning to be incorporated into defendant's sentences in ways that may give rise to Eighth Amendment claims. Some state statutes, for example, permit or require the administration of medication to certain sex offenders to "chemically castrate" them. These medicines decrease men's libido and sexual activity, but they also have adverse side effects. Common side effects include high blood pressure, fatigue, weight gain, and smaller testes, although more serious complications can ensue, such as blood clots, breathing problems, and depression. At this point, the caselaw on chemical castration is sparse, and its constitutionality has not been resolved definitively. But the practice of chemically castrating some sex offenders has incited a debate in the academic and policymaking realms about the soundness and propriety, from a policy perspective, of this practice.

CHAPTER 8

PAROLE RELEASE AND PROBATION AND PAROLE REVOCATION

In a jurisdiction that has a parole system, a parole board determines how much of an individual's prison sentence will actually be served behind bars. The parole board's decision on when to release someone from prison is based in part on its prediction of the likelihood that a prisoner will successfully reintegrate himself or herself into society and refrain from future criminal activity. When a person is released on parole, however, that person typically remains under the control of correctional authorities until the expiration of the maximum sentence imposed by the sentencing judge.

In recent years, the concept of parole has sparked criticism. Four major objections have been asserted against incorporating parole into a sentencing system. First, parole systems can lead to disparity in sentences. Although that disparity can be mitigated somewhat by the adoption of parole guidelines that channel and circumscribe the parole board's exercise of its discretion, disparity remains in the initial decision whether to send a person to prison. Second, the uncertainty parole systems spawn regarding when inmates will actually be released from prison can cause tension, frustration, and even despair in inmates, making them more difficult to manage and interfering with attempts to help them rehabilitate or habilitate themselves while they are incarcerated. Third, parole systems, which often enable inmates to be released from prison years before they have served their maximum prison sentences, can foster disrespect and even contempt for the legal system. And fourth, the concern about crowding in a jurisdiction's prisons that often drives many parole-release decisions leads to the premature release of many prisoners and consequently the endangerment of the public.

The problems caused by parole have led many states and the federal government to abandon their parole systems and move towards more determinate sentencing systems. (Some of the different types of determinate sentencing systems are discussed in Chapter 4.) Fueling this systemic change has been the demand for what is called "truth in sentencing."

Some of the jurisdictions that have abolished parole have instituted what is known as "supervised release" in its stead. Supervised release, like parole, follows a period of incarceration. One of the distinctions between parole and supervised release is that a judge imposes the supervised-release term as part of a defendant's sentence. A defendant, for example, might be sentenced to prison for four years to be followed by one year of supervised release.

Another distinguishing feature of supervised release is that a judge, rather than an administrative body, may define the conditions to which an individual will be subject during the supervised-release period. Some jurisdictions also vest judges with the authority to determine whether a supervisee has violated a release condition and, if so, whether that violation warrants the return of the supervisee to prison or some augmentation of the supervised-release conditions. Other jurisdictions charge administrative bodies with the task of making these decisions.

Parole systems still exist in many states, and even in jurisdictions that have abolished parole, parole boards continue to operate, deciding when inmates who were sentenced under earlier sentencing statutes providing for parole release will be released from prison and when they should be returned to prison for violating the terms and conditions of their parole. It is therefore important to understand the constraints the Constitution places on parole-release and revocation decisions and on somewhat similar decisions concerning the revocation of probation.

A. PROBATION AND PAROLE REVOCATION

1. Due Process

It behooves us to begin with a discussion of the constitutional requirements that govern parole and probation revocation, since the Supreme Court's analysis of the constitutional implications of parole release was, in part, an offshoot of its analysis of parole revocation. In *Morrissey v. Brewer* (S.Ct. 1972), the Supreme Court addressed the question whether the Due Process Clause of the Fourteenth Amendment provides any protection to individuals facing the prospect of having their parole revoked. The Court had to first resolve the threshold question whether the revocation of parole deprives a person of "liberty" within the meaning of the Due Process Clause. The Court answered this question in the affirmative, noting the "grievous loss" that attends the revocation of parole. While the Court acknowledged that the freedom that a parolee has is conditional and limited, it at the same time recognized that parolees enjoy many of the freedoms of an ordinary citizen and may spend many more years in prison if their parole is revoked.

The Court in *Morrissey* then turned to the question of what process is "due" a parolee facing the possible revocation of his or her parole. The Court began by noting that parole revocation is different from a criminal prosecution, even though the end result may be the same—incarceration in prison. A criminal prosecution may result in the loss of what the Court described as "absolute liberty," while parole revocation affects only the conditional liberty of a parolee. Therefore, according to the Court, a parolee is not entitled during a parole-revocation proceeding to "the full panoply of rights" that attend a criminal prosecution.

The Court also noted that the state has an "overwhelming interest" in being able to send parolees who have violated the conditions of their parole release back to prison without having to undergo the burdens of a formal trial. At the same time, the Court pointed to two other state interests that supported extending a significant measure of procedural protection to parolees during parole-revocation proceedings—the government's interest in avoiding erroneous parole revocations and the government's interest in treating parolees fairly, at least in part to avoid the resentment of parolees, and the ensuing adverse effects on their rehabilitation, caused by the perception of unfair treatment.

The Supreme Court's assessment of the interests at stake during parole-revocation proceedings led it to conclude that parolees are entitled to the following procedural safeguards before final revocation of their parole: First, when parolees are arrested and detained for suspected violations of the conditions of their parole, they must be afforded a preliminary hearing to determine whether there is probable cause to believe that they violated the terms or conditions of their parole. This preliminary hearing must be held at a place "reasonably near" the place where the arrest or the alleged parole violation occurred and as "promptly as convenient" after the arrest.

Second, parolees must be provided with notice of their impending preliminary hearing, of the parole violations with which they are charged, and of the hearing's purpose—to determine whether there is probable cause to believe a violation has occurred. Third, parolees have the right to attend their preliminary hearing and to make a statement in their own behalf. Fourth, the parolees can submit documents at the hearing and call witnesses to testify about relevant issues. Fifth, the parolees can, upon request, confront and cross-examine adverse witnesses who have provided information supporting the revocation of parole, unless such confrontation and cross-examination would jeopardize an informant's safety.

Sixth, the probable-cause determination must be made by someone who is not "directly involved" in the case. In other words, any parole officer who investigated or reported the alleged parole violation cannot serve as the hearing officer responsible for making the probable-cause assessment. It is not necessary though for a judge to make the probable-cause assessment. Even another parole officer can perform this function as long as the officer has had no direct involvement in the case.

Finally, the hearing officer must summarize the evidence adduced at the hearing, outline which of this evidence was relied on by the hearing officer, and state the reasons for finding that the detention of the parolee pending a final revocation hearing is warranted.

In another case, the Supreme Court clarified that the preliminary hearing, the first step in the parole-revocation process, can be skipped if the reason for the contemplated revocation is the commission, while on parole, of a crime of which the parolee has already been convicted. *Moody v. Daggett* (S.Ct. 1976). With the high standard of proof that applies in criminal proceedings—beyond a reasonable doubt, a conviction, by definition, establishes probable cause to believe a parolee has violated the standard parole condition to refrain from criminal activity.

Once it has been determined that there is probable cause to believe a parolee has violated the terms or conditions of his or her parole, the parolee can be sent back to prison to await a final revocation hearing, if the parolee wants a hearing. That hearing must be held within a "reasonable time" after the parolee has been taken into custody for the parole violation, but according to the Supreme Court in *Morrissey v. Brewer*, two months is not an excessive amount of time for the parolee to have to wait for the final hearing.

Morrissey outlined a number of procedural safeguards that must attend the final revocation hearing. Those safeguards include: (1) written notice of the alleged violation or violations of parole; (2) the opportunity to attend the hearing and explain why the revocation of parole is unwarranted; (3) the right to present witnesses and documentary evidence in the parolee's defense; (4) the right to be apprised of evidence that supports the revocation of parole; (5) the right to confront and cross-examine adverse witnesses unless there is "good cause" for not according the parolee these rights; (6) the right to have the final revocation decision made by a "neutral and detached" decisionmaker; and (7) the right to receive a written statement outlining the evidence relied on by this decisionmaker and the reasons for revoking the individual's parole.

In *Young v. Harper* (S.Ct.1997), the Supreme Court held that a "preparole conditional supervision program" was sufficiently like parole to give rise to a liberty interest. Consequently, a participant in the program, which was implemented to alleviate prison crowding, could not be sent back to prison unless afforded the protection of the procedural safeguards set forth in *Morrissey v. Brewer.*

In *Gagnon v. Scarpelli* (S.Ct.1973), the Supreme Court held that probationers are also entitled to the procedural protections outlined in *Morrissey* before their probation is revoked. *Gagnon* also answered a question left unresolved in *Morrissey*—whether indigent individuals facing the revocation of their probation or parole have the right to have counsel appointed to assist them during the revocation proceedings.

The Court began by discussing some of the drawbacks of affording appointed counsel in revocation proceedings involving indigent probationers or parolees. If attorneys were appointed to represent indigent probationers and parolees, the government would, in turn, most likely hire attorneys to represent the government. Revocation proceedings would then be transformed, according to the Court, into adversarial proceedings that are less focused on the rehabilitative needs of probationers and parolees.

The proceedings would drag on much longer, and the financial costs to the government, for appointed counsel as well as counsel for the government, would be great.

The Court then refused to adopt an across-the-board rule that indigent probationers and parolees either have, or do not have, the right to appointed counsel during revocation proceedings. Instead, the Court held that whether there is a right to the assistance of appointed counsel during a revocation proceeding has to be decided on a case-by-case basis. The Court noted that in most cases, due process does not require the provision of such assistance. The individuals confronting revocation have either been convicted of, or admitted committing, a crime, and any mitigating circumstances that might counsel against the revocation of probation or parole are straightforward enough not to require an attorney for their explication.

At the same time, the Supreme Court recognized that the fundamental fairness commanded by due process sometimes requires the provision of appointed counsel to indigents involved in revocation proceedings. The Court in *Gagnon* mentioned two instances when the provision of counsel is presumptively necessary: one, when the probationer or parolee makes a "timely and colorable claim" that he or she has not committed the alleged probation or parole violation; and two, when the violation is clear or undisputed, but there are substantial mitigating factors which suggest that revocation is unwarranted and those factors are difficult to explain because of their complexity or for other reasons. The Court in *Gagnon* added that if a request for appointed counsel is denied, the reason for that denial must be set forth in the record.

Left unresolved by the Supreme Court in *Gagnon* was the question of the scope of the right to retained counsel during probation- and parole-revocation proceedings. Specifically, the question that remains is: Does the right to be represented by a retained attorney extend beyond those instances when indigents have a right to appointed counsel? In other words, is a parolee entitled to the assistance of an attorney during a parole-revocation proceeding as long as the parolee pays for that assistance?

There is Supreme Court precedent that arguably points both ways in answering this question—towards holding that the right to retained counsel is broader than the right to appointed counsel and towards holding that the two rights correspond in their scope. In criminal trials, defendants have the right to the services of retained attorneys, even in cases where there is no right to appointed counsel. On the other hand, in *Wolff v. McDonnell* (S.Ct. 1974), a case discussed subsequently in Chapter 13, the Supreme Court held that prisoners have no right to be represented by an attorney, whether retained or appointed, in prison disciplinary hearings. What is potentially significant about *Wolff* is that many of the reasons given by the Court in that case for not recognizing a right to counsel during disciplinary proceedings were the same as those asserted by the Court in *Gagnon v. Scarpelli* for limiting the right to appointed counsel during probation- and parole-revocation proceedings.

Another question that has not been resolved definitively by the Supreme Court concerns the burden of proof that the government must meet in establishing a probation or parole violation. Most courts have held that a violation must be proven by a preponderance of the evidence—in other words, by proof that it is more likely than not that the violation occurred—or by an even lower standard of proof. *See, e.g., Johnson v. United States* (D.C.App. 2000). The standard of proof applied in revocation proceedings explains why an acquittal of a criminal charge does not bar the revocation of a person's probation or parole for the conduct upon which the charge was based. Just because the government could not meet its burden of proving the individual's guilt beyond a reasonable doubt does not mean that the government cannot meet the lower standard of proof that applies in a revocation proceeding.

Revocation of probation or parole for criminal conduct of which a person has already been acquitted or convicted also does not violate the double-jeopardy prohibition found in the Fifth Amendment and applicable to the states through the Due Process Clause of the Fourteenth Amendment. When individuals' probation or parole is revoked and they are sent to prison, they are technically being punished and sent to prison for the original crime of which they were convicted, not their more recent criminal conduct.

Sometimes a revocation hearing will precede a trial for the alleged crime that triggered the revocation proceeding. Because the standard of proof applied at revocation hearings is lower than the standard of proof governing criminal trials, the question arises whether a decision not to revoke a person's probation or parole after a revocation hearing forecloses a subsequent criminal prosecution for the same conduct that was at issue in the revocation proceeding. In other words, is the government estopped from pursuing the criminal prosecution?

Most courts have answered this question in the negative, in large part because of their concern that a contrary holding would frustrate the government's interest in responding quickly to probation and parole violations. *See, e.g., State v. Brunet* (Vt. 2002). In order to avoid the collateral-estoppel effects of an adverse decision at a revocation hearing, the government would delay pursuing revocation until it had fully amassed the evidence supporting the revocation of probation or parole.

2. The Fifth Amendment Privilege Against Self–Incrimination

When persons on probation or parole meet with their probation or parole officers, matters may be discussed that lead to the making of incriminating statements by the probationer or parolee. In *Minnesota v. Murphy* (S.Ct.1984), the Supreme Court considered the admissibility of such incriminating statements in a criminal trial. The case involved a defendant who was on probation for the crime of false imprisonment. One of the conditions of his probation sentence was that he "be truthful" with his probation officer "in all matters." During a meeting between the defendant and his probation officer, the probation officer questioned him about his reported involvement in the rape and murder of a woman. The defendant admitted committing the crimes, and he was then charged with, and convicted of, murder.

The defendant argued before the Supreme Court that the incriminating statements he made in response to questions posed by his probation officer should have been suppressed because the probation officer failed to give him *Miranda* warnings before questioning him. The probation officer did not, for example, tell him that he had the right to remain silent. The Court, however, rejected this argument because the defendant was not "in custody" when he met with his probation officer in her office. Consequently, the requirements set forth in *Miranda* v. *Arizona* (S.Ct.1966) did not apply.

The defendant also argued that his statements should have been suppressed because an unconstitutional burden was placed on his Fifth Amendment privilege against self-incrimination when he was questioned by the probation officer. He contended that he was placed between the proverbial rock and a hard place when he was questioned: if he refused to answer his probation officer's questions, he risked having his probation revoked because of his failure to comply with the terms and conditions of his probation. But if he did answer her questions truthfully, he would make incriminating statements that could be (and were) used against him in a criminal prosecution for murder.

The Supreme Court agreed that if the state in this case had, in effect, threatened to revoke the defendant's probation unless he gave a statement that might be used to incriminate him in a criminal prosecution, the state would have placed an unconstitutional burden on the defendant's exercise of his Fifth Amendment privilege. His statements would then have to have been suppressed. And if he had refused to answer the questions, his probation could not have been revoked because of that refusal. The Court, however, simply did not interpret the probation condition to which the defendant was subject as requiring the defendant to respond to questions when his answers might be used against him in a criminal prosecution. In other words, all that the defendant in this case had to do when confronted with the probation officer's questions about the rape and murder was invoke his privilege against self-incrimination.

In a footnote in *Minnesota v. Murphy*, the Supreme Court observed that a person's probation can lawfully be revoked for refusing to answer questions bearing on his or her criminal activities if the state has granted the probationer immunity from criminal prosecution. In addition, the Court noted that threatening to revoke a person's probation unless he or she answers questions about noncriminal activity that may lead to the revocation of probation is different, from a constitutional perspective, from threatening to revoke probation unless the probationer answers questions that pose a "realistic threat of incrimination" in a criminal prosecution. Requiring a probationer to answer questions that may be used to revoke probation, but which do not involve criminal conduct, is permissible because the Fifth Amendment privilege only prevents the government from compelling a person to make statements that may be used in a criminal prosecution. And a probation-revocation proceeding, according to the Court, is not a "criminal proceeding."

Thus, if a probation condition restricts where a probationer can travel, a probationer can be required to answer questions about his suspected violation of that condition. If he refuses to answer the questions, his probation may be revoked. But his probation may also be revoked if he answers the questions and admits violating the condition. Because the privilege against self-incrimination does not extend to statements about noncriminal activities, probationers may therefore sometimes find themselves faced with a catch–22 when being questioned by a probation officer.

Sometimes convicted sex offenders are required to participate in sex-offender treatment programs as a condition of their probation. As part of the treatment process, participants often have to admit their culpability of the crimes of which they were convicted and discuss the circumstances surrounding those offenses. Some participants have balked at making those disclosures, because they were challenging the legality of their convictions on appeal or in postconviction proceedings or because of their professed fear that they might be prosecuted for perjury once their inculpatory admissions confirmed that they had lied at their trials.

Courts are divided on the question whether the revocation of probation because of a probationer's refusal to disclose and discuss the information that is a requisite for participation in a sex-offender treatment program abridges the Fifth Amendment privilege against compelled self-incrimination. The Supreme Court has yet to address this question, although it did rule in *McKune v. Lile* (S.Ct.2002) that a prisoner who refuses to make such mandated admissions and disclosures as part of a treatment program conducted in a medium-security unit of a prison can be transferred to a maximum-security unit without violating his Fifth Amendment privilege. This case is discussed in greater depth in chapter 14.

3.   The Fourth Amendment

The rights of probationers and parolees are not only limited because of the probation and parole conditions to which they are subject but also because the Constitution applies differently to them than it does to ordinary citizens. In *Griffin v. Wisconsin* (S.Ct.1987), the Supreme Court upheld a search of a probationer's apartment that was effected without a warrant and without probable cause. The search was conducted by probation officers, but several police officers were also present while the search was being conducted.

In determining whether the warrantless search of the probationer's apartment without probable cause violated the Fourth Amendment, the Supreme Court applied the Fourth Amendment balancing test under which the nature of the intrusion is balanced against the need for the intrusion—in this case, the need for a warrantless search and one predicated on something less than probable cause. In analyzing the nature of the intrusion, the Court opined that the intrusion caused by searches involving probationers is dissipated because probation officers are not probationers' complete adversaries but act with their best interests in mind.

Turning to the need for the intrusion, the Court concluded that warrant and probable-cause requirements would unduly encumber the effective supervision of probationers. The Court stated that requiring probation officers to first obtain a warrant before searching a probationer's home would interfere with the functioning of probation systems because judges, rather than probation officers, would be determining how closely probationers should be supervised. In addition, a warrant requirement would cause delay in the search of probationers' homes, impeding the ability of probation officers to act quickly in response to concerns that probationers are not abiding by the conditions of their probation. Warrant and probable-cause requirements would also, in the Court's view, undermine the ability of probation systems to deter probationers from violating the conditions of their probation, because probationers would know that significant limitations have been placed on the authority of probation officers to enter into their homes and conduct a search.

In *United States v. Knights* (S.Ct.2001), the Supreme Court even more narrowly construed the scope of probationers' Fourth Amendment rights, upholding a warrantless search of a probationer's apartment conducted, not by a probation officer, but by a detective from the sheriff's office who had a reasonable suspicion that the apartment contained evidence of several crimes. In balancing the intrusiveness of searches conducted by law-enforcement officials for evidence of a crime against the need for such searches, the Court emphasized that their intrusiveness is diminished because probationers' liberty is already restricted. Whatever intrusion does ensue is counterbalanced, according to the Court, by the significant need to permit law-enforcement officials to conduct warrantless searches of probationers' residences, a need that stems in part from probationers' high rate of recidivism.

Since the search at issue in *United States v. Knights* was grounded on reasonable suspicion, the Supreme Court in that case specifically left two questions unresolved. The first is whether a search of a probationer's residence is constitutional if it is not based on even a reasonable suspicion that the residence harbors evidence of a crime. The second question is whether such a suspicionless search would, in any event, comport with the Fourth

Amendment when a probationer has agreed, as a condition of the probation sentence, that his or her residence will be subject to searches even in the absence of reasonable suspicion.

Another significant Fourth Amendment question that has yet to reach the Supreme Court is if and when the compulsory DNA testing of individuals convicted of certain crimes is constitutional. Thus far, the majority of the lower courts have upheld the constitutionality of laws mandating that DNA samples be obtained from prisoners and persons placed on probation, parole, or supervised release. *See, e.g., United States v. Kincade* (9th Cir.2004). Statutes vary regarding the convicted individuals subject to mandatory DNA testing, and legislatures have been moving to expand the scope of DNA-testing requirements. The pertinent federal statute, for example, now extends to persons convicted of any federal felony or several other kinds of crimes. 42 U.S.C. § 14135a(d).

When the Fourth Amendment rights of a probationer or parolee are violated, any illegally seized evidence cannot, as a general rule, be admitted in a criminal trial. In *Pennsylvania Bd. of Probation and Parole v. Scott* (S.Ct.1998), the Supreme Court considered whether illegally obtained evidence must also be excluded from a parole-revocation hearing. To resolve this issue, the Court applied the balancing test it typically utilizes when assessing the scope of the Fourth Amendment exclusionary rule. Under this test, the Court weighs the costs of applying the exclusionary rule in a particular context—in this case, parole-revocation proceedings–against the benefits of applying the exclusionary rule in that context.

The Supreme Court first found that barring the consideration of probative evidence during a parole-revocation process would exact a "costly toll," interfering with the truthfinding function of that process. The exclusion of this evidence would then permit some parolees to violate the conditions of their parole with impunity, undermining the government's "overwhelming interest" in ensuring that parolees, persons who have demonstrated a propensity to commit crimes, abide by the terms of their release from prison. The Court was also concerned that applying the exclusionary rule in revocation proceedings would prolong them, making them more costly, and transform them into an adversarial process that might make parole boards less inclined to grant parole in the first place.

The Supreme Court then concluded that the benefits of applying the exclusionary rule in parole-revocation proceedings, in terms of deterring violations of the Fourth Amendment, would not outweigh the costs. The Court was unconcerned that admitting illegally obtained evidence at parole-revocation hearings would induce parole officers to violate the Fourth Amendment. The Court characterized parole officers as "neutral" supervisors less prone to violating constitutional rights than police officers "engaged in the often competitive enterprise of ferreting out crime." In addition, the Court stated that alternatives other than excluding evidence from revocation hearings, including disciplinary sanctions and civil liability, would adequately deter parole officers from violating the Fourth Amendment. Interestingly, the Supreme Court has found these same alternatives to be ineffectual deterrents for police officers. *Mapp v. Ohio* (S.Ct. 1961).

The Supreme Court in *Pennsylvania Bd. of Probation and Parole v. Scott* also rejected the argument that allowing illegally obtained evidence to be considered during revocation hearings would offer a substantial incentive for police officers to ignore Fourth Amendment restrictions. The Court opined that most police officers would continue to abide by the requirements of the Fourth Amendment, because their primary objective when investigating crimes is to obtain evidence that can be admitted at a criminal trial. The four dissenting Justices—Justices Souter, Ginsburg, Breyer, and Stevens— strongly disagreed with this supposition. Citing the relative ease of revoking parole compared to obtaining a criminal conviction, the dissenters contended that revocation proceedings will often be the focal concern of law-enforcement officials. In other words, the revocation hearing will be, in their minds, "the principal, not the secondary, forum" in which evidence of a crime will be introduced. In the dissenters' view, exempting revocation proceedings from application of the exclusionary rule would therefore substantially erode its deterrent effects.

4. Policy Issues

Apart from the constitutional questions concerning the revocation of probation or parole, there are a number of policy questions concerning not only the procedural aspects of revocation proceedings, but the substantive standards that should have to be met for revocation to occur. Questions regarding the most appropriate way in which to respond to various types of probation and parole violations have become of particularly pressing importance as the nation's already crowded prisons and jails have become increasingly filled with individuals incarcerated following the revocation of their probation or parole. The American Bar Association's Model Adult Community Corrections Act, which was discussed in Chapter 5 on page 123, prescribes the taking of a different tack towards probation and parole violations than either ignoring the violations or automatically incarcerating individuals for them. The Act instead establishes a presumption, though a rebuttable one, that imposition of a community-based sanction is the appropriate response to a violation that involves either noncriminal conduct, such as failing to report to a probation officer, or criminal conduct that, if charged, would be either a misdemeanor or a nonviolent felony.

B. PAROLE RELEASE

For a prisoner, a parole board's decision whether to release the prisoner on parole is a momentous one. The decision, like the decision whether to revoke a person's parole, will determine whether a person is free to live in the community or must instead be isolated and confined in prison, perhaps for many more years. Yet from a constitutional standpoint, parole-release decisions and parole-revocation decisions are, according to the Supreme Court, very different.

In *Greenholtz v. Inmates of Nebraska Penal and Correctional Complex* (S.Ct.1979), the Supreme Court held that just because a jurisdiction establishes a parole system and offers a prisoner the possibility of being released on parole does not mean that a "liberty" interest that triggers due-process protections is implicated when a parole board is making its release decision. The Court cited two reasons for distinguishing parole release from parole revocation. First, the Court said that there is an enormous difference between losing the liberty that one has and not being given the liberty that one wants. Second, the Court stated that the nature of the decisions made during the parole-release and revocation processes is, in the Court's opinion, very different. The Court acknowledged that both processes require the resolution of factual questions and the making of subjective assessments about a person's suitability to live in the community. The Court noted, however, that the question addressed during the first step of the parole-revocation process is purely factual: Did the parolee violate the terms or conditions of his or her parole? A negative answer to this question requires a finding in the parolee's favor and obviates the need to turn to the second step of the two-stage process, where the parolee's suitability to remain in the community, despite the violation of parole conditions, is considered. The Court noted in *Greenholtz* that by contrast, when a parole board is making a parole-release decision, no set of facts mandates a prisoner's release from prison on parole. Consequently, because of the more amorphous nature of the parole-release decision, the Supreme Court believed that a prisoner's hope of being released on parole is too tenuous to give rise to a liberty interest.

The Supreme Court in *Greenholtz* recognized that there are protectible liberty interests beyond those inherent in the Constitution. A state, through its own laws or regulations, can create a liberty interest encompassed by the protections of due process. The Court in *Greenholtz* in fact found that the state's parole statute created a protectible liberty interest in being released on parole. The statute in question provided that a prisoner "shall" be released on parole "unless" certain delineated circumstances existed, such as a "substantial risk" that the prisoner would not abide by the conditions of his or her parole.

While the Supreme Court in *Greenholtz* emphasized that the state statute before it had a "unique structure," in a subsequent case, the Court found that a statute with even more general language than the statute in *Greenholtz* created a liberty interest triggering due-process protections. In that case, *Board of Pardons v. Allen* (S.Ct.1987), the statute in question stated that a prisoner "shall" be released on parole "when ... there is a reasonable probability that the prisoner can be released without detriment to the prisoner or to the community" and "only for the best interests of society." According to the Court, the expectation that this statute created that a prisoner would be paroled in certain circumstances generated constitutional protections.

By contrast, a general practice or custom of releasing inmates in certain circumstances from prison will not, by itself, create a liberty interest in such release. In *Connecticut Board of Pardons v. Dumschat* (S.Ct.1981), a prisoner claimed that he was deprived of his liberty without due process of law when his application for the commutation of his life sentence for murder was denied. The prisoner contended that he had a justifiable expectation that his sentence would be commuted, one that amounted to a liberty interest, because the vast majority of inmates with life sentences in the state had their sentences commuted. The Supreme Court disagreed. Emphasizing that the decision whether to commute a prisoner's sentence fell within the unconfined discretion of the Connecticut Board of Pardons, the Court observed that a liberty interest was not created just because the Board had been generous towards prisoners in the past when exercising that discretion. According to the Court, for a liberty interest to exist, the Board's discretion would actually have to be circumscribed by some statute or governmental rule.

The Supreme Court distinguished *Dumschat* in *Ohio Adult Parole Authority v. Woodard* (S.Ct.

1998). In *Woodard*, the prisoner was seeking commutation of his death sentence. In a 5–4 decision, the Court held that since his life was at stake, he was entitled to the protections of due process during the clemency proceedings, although the scope of those protections was not fully defined in the Court's splintered decision.

The dissenters in *Woodard*—Justices Rehnquist, Scalia, Kennedy, and Thomas—asserted that the clemency proceedings did not even implicate a constitutionally protected interest. According to them, the prisoner had already been deprived of his interest in life during the trial and sentencing—proceedings replete with procedural safeguards—that had culminated in his conviction and death sentence.

As will be discussed in Chapter 14, the Supreme Court in *Sandin v. Conner* (S.Ct.1995) substantially modified the test to be applied when determining whether a state has created a liberty interest, at least in the prison context. No longer are courts supposed to scan statutes in search of the combination of "substantive predicates" and mandatory language that used to lead to a finding that a prisoner had a liberty interest. It is now somewhat unclear what circumstances will give rise to a liberty interest in parole release. As was mentioned earlier, the Supreme Court in *Greenholtz* held, though in a 5–4 decision, that just setting up a parole system does not create a liberty interest in parole. In addition, the Court has now abandoned the kind of statutory analysis that led to a finding of a liberty interest in both *Greenholtz* and *Board of Pardons v. Allen*.

Compounding the confusion though, the Court in *Sandin* cited *Board of Pardons v. Allen*, seemingly with approval, as an example of a case involving a state-created liberty interest.

When a prisoner has a liberty interest derived from state law in being granted parole release, the prisoner, of course, can only be deprived of that interest in accordance with the requirements of due process of law. What due process means in the parole-release context is very different from what it means in the parole-revocation process, in part because of the differences that exist, according to the Supreme Court, between the interests that are at stake in the two processes.

Greenholtz answered only some of the questions about the procedural safeguards that must attend the parole-release decisionmaking process. The Supreme Court first said in that case that inmates who are eligible for parole, but whose chances of being released on parole are slim, have no constitutional right to a formal parole hearing. When the chances of being released on parole are remote, inmates would benefit little from such formal hearings, while the burden to the government of providing such hearings would be great. At the same time, the Court emphasized that in Nebraska, the state in which the case arose, all inmates who were eligible for parole had the right to an informal parole-review hearing where they could state why they believed they should be released on parole. The existence of this alternative review mechanism for inmates unlikely to be released on parole was relevant because, as Justice Marshall recognized in his opinion partially dissenting from the majority's opinion, the procedures that are constitutionally due in a particular situation may depend on what other procedural safeguards are already in place.

The Supreme Court in *Greenholtz* also rejected the argument that an inmate denied parole is entitled to be informed of the evidence supporting the parole board's decision. The Court believed that requiring such a summation of the evidence relied upon would transform parole-release hearings into adversary proceedings, fostering ill will between inmates and correctional officials and thereby undermining the long-range rehabilitative objectives of parole. What is a bit curious about this conclusion is that in *Wolff v. McDonnell* (S.Ct.1974), a case dealing with the procedural safeguards that must attend prison disciplinary hearings, the Supreme Court had noted that one of the principal purposes of such hearings is to aid inmates' rehabilitation. Yet in *Wolff*, the Court required a disciplinary decisionmaker to provide an inmate with a written statement recounting both the evidence relied on and the reasons for the disciplinary action taken.

Although the Supreme Court concluded in *Greenholtz* that inmates denied parole have no right to a statement outlining the evidence upon which the parole board based its decision to deny parole release, the Court at the same time emphasized, as it had when discussing the inmates' claim concerning the need for formal hearings, that an alternative procedural safeguard was afforded inmates denied parole in Nebraska. Inmates were apprised, although very generally, of the reason or reasons why the parole board had decided not to release them from prison.

In a dissenting opinion, Justice Marshall vehemently disagreed that these statements satisfied the requirements of due process, particularly because they were so general and recited in such a rote fashion as to be almost meaningless. The majority of the Nebraska inmates denied parole were simply told that continuing their treatment, education, or work assignment in prison would significantly increase the likelihood that they would abide by the law upon their release from prison. Justice Marshall believed that the inmates were entitled to a "meaningful explanation" of the reasons why they were denied parole. Requiring such an explanation would not impose an undue burden on the parole board, he argued, because it is not "burdensome to give reasons when reasons exist."

Justice Marshall also believed that the inmates had a right to be apprised of the evidence upon which the denial of parole was predicated. This statement of the evidence and reasons would, in his opinion, promote care on the parole board's part when rendering its release decision, and it would help to ensure that the decision was not grounded on erroneous information. The statement would have the added benefit of apprising a prisoner of the steps that he or she needs to take to increase the prospects of being released on parole. Finally, Justice Marshall argued that the written statement of evidence, along with other procedural safeguards, would aid, rather than impede, inmates' rehabilitation by providing them with the assurance that the proceedings in which they had been involved had been conducted fairly.

Perhaps the clearest indicator of the contracted scope of prisoners' due-process rights in the parole-release context was the Court's summary treatment in *Greenholtz* of the inmates' claim that the notice they received of impending parole-release hearings was constitutionally deficient. While the inmates were told the month before their hearing that their parole hearing would be scheduled sometime during the following month, they were not apprised of the date of the hearing until the day on which it was to be held. In addition, they were not apprised of the factors upon which the parole board would be resting its parole-release decisions. While four dissenting Justices argued that the way in which the inmates were notified of the parole hearings nullified their statutory rights to call witnesses to testify on their behalf and to receive the assistance of an attorney at the hearings, the Court in a footnote cursorily, and in the dissenters' view erroneously, responded that the inmates had not claimed that the present system of notifying them of their upcoming parole hearings seriously prejudiced their ability to prepare for them.

Greenholtz is significant, not only for the procedural safeguards to which it said inmates do not have a right during parole-release proceedings, but for the safeguards about whose constitutional necessity it expressed no view. Some of the questions that remain after *Greenholtz* include the following: Do inmates have the right to present documentary evidence to the parole board during parole-release hearings? Do they have the right to present witnesses to testify on their behalf before the parole board? Do they have the right to confront and cross-examine adverse witnesses or the right to check their files to ensure that the information upon which the parole board is basing its decision is accurate? Do the inmates, at least in some circumstances, have the right to be represented by an attorney at the parole hearing or to receive some alternative form of assistance? *Cf. Wolff v. McDonnell* (S.Ct.1974) (recognizing that when an inmate charged with disciplinary misconduct is illiterate or the case is so complex that assistance is needed to ensure that any defense is adequately prepared and presented, the inmate has a due-process right to assistance from another inmate, a staff member, or a "sufficiently competent" inmate assigned by the staff to provide such assistance). Finally, do inmates have the right to have a "neutral and detached" decisionmaker make the parole decision?

In answering these questions, the balancing test enunciated in *Mathews v. Eldridge* (S.Ct.1976) will be applied. Under this three-pronged test, which is discussed more fully elsewhere in this book (*see* Chapter 3 on page 50 and Chapter 14 on page 298), the following three factors, you will recall, are weighed when determining whether a particular procedural safeguard is required by due process: the private interest at stake; the way in which, and extent to which, a governmental interest or interests would be affected if the procedural safeguard were put in place; and the safeguard's value in terms of reducing the risk of an erroneous deprivation of the private interest at stake in the proceeding.

CHAPTER 9

COLLATERAL SANCTIONS AND CONSEQUENCES

A. THE REINTEGRATION OF RELEASED PRISONERS INTO SOCIETY: PRACTICAL OBSTACLES

Each year, over 600,000 prisoners are released from prison. Eventually, almost all prisoners return to society. The hope, of course, is that these individuals have learned a lesson from their incarceration and will now become productive and law-abiding members of society. The reality is often otherwise.

Individuals who enter prison uneducated and with few job skills generally leave prison in the same condition. Added to these obstacles impeding released prisoners' successful reintegration into the community is the stigma that accompanies the label "ex-con," a stigma that makes it difficult for released prisoners to find jobs. Perhaps not surprisingly, a high percentage of ex-prisoners remain unemployed even a year after their release from prison. This fact is a particular concern because studies have confirmed that individuals who are unemployed following their release from prison are much more likely to resume committing crimes.

See Joan Petersilia, *When Prisoners Come Home* 112 (2003).

Prisoners usually leave prison with other problems that contributed to their criminal behavior unresolved, such as substance-abuse problems or the lack of coping skills, including the ability to control anger, needed when facing the inevitable frustrations of life. Incarceration itself can affect prisoners' psyche in a way that further exacerbates the difficulty they face in adapting to life outside prison. During what is known as the "prisonization process," prisoners, for example, become highly dependent on others to make choices for them, leaving them ill-equipped to initiate the steps that will help them turn their lives around when they return to their communities. Released prisoners are further disadvantaged because the neighborhoods and communities to which most of them return are ravaged by crime and poverty and do not offer the family and other support systems that will help them return to society successfully.

With no jobs awaiting them and few job prospects, little money, and serious unaddressed and unresolved personal problems, it is little wonder that prison gates have become nothing more than revolving doors for thousands of released prisoners. One study conducted by the Bureau of Justice Statistics revealed, for example, that almost 60% of the inmates in state prisons had been incarcerated previously. Bureau of Justice Statistics, U.S. Dep't of Justice, *Prisons and Prisoners in the United States* 15 (1992).

B.   THE REINTEGRATION OF RELEASED PRISONERS INTO SOCIETY: LEGAL OBSTACLES

The practical obstacles discussed above are not the only ones impeding released inmates' reintegration into society. Released prisoners, as well as others convicted of crimes, face legal obstacles that serve as constant reminders that they must continue to pay a price for their criminal misdeeds. *See* Office of the Pardon Attorney, U.S. Dep't of Justice, *Civil Disabilities of Convicted Felons: A State-by-State Survey* (1996). Some of these legal impediments arise automatically upon a conviction, though they are not part of the defendant's sentence. These legal penalties are known as "collateral sanctions." A classic example of a collateral sanction is the denial of voting privileges because of a felony conviction.

The other principal kind of legal disability that may ensue from a criminal conviction but is not encompassed within the sentence is known as a "discretionary disqualification." One of the distinguishing features of a discretionary disqualification, as its name suggests, is that its imposition falls within the discretion of a governmental official or entity. A drug offender's loss of public-housing benefits is an example of a discretionary disqualification; the drug-related activity that culminates in a conviction for a drug crime may, but does not have to, lead to the denial of public housing to the convicted offender.

Very often, the distinction between collateral sanctions and discretionary disqualifications is overlooked, with both concepts subsumed within the more general term, "collateral consequences." Some of the more prevalent collateral consequences of a conviction are discussed below.

1.   Employment Restrictions and Restrictions on Government Benefits

Some statutes bar ex-felons from certain jobs. A conviction for a crime involving official misconduct, for example, may foreclose future government employment. The nation's armed services are also forbidden from hiring convicted felons, although exceptions can be made in "meritorious cases." 10 U.S.C. § 504.

Other statutes make convicted felons ineligible for certain government benefits. For example, individuals convicted of a felony drug crime cannot receive Temporary Assistance for Needy Family benefits or food stamps unless states opt out of the eligibility ban or limit the length of the ineligibility period. 21 U.S.C. § 862a(a), (d)(1)(A), (B). In addition, persons involved in drug-related activity can be evicted from or denied public housing, and a drug-related conviction can provide the requisite evidence of this activity. 42 U.S.C. § 1437d(l)(6). Individuals convicted of certain drug offenses also forfeit their eligibility for federal student financial aid, including student loans, for a period of time that varies depending on the type and number of their drug convictions. 20 U.S.C. § 1091(r)(1).

2. Restrictions on Political Rights

Ex-felons frequently are prohibited by statute from serving on juries. Another civil penalty that often attends a felony conviction is a restriction on the right to vote. Almost all states disallow prisoners from voting, and most extend the voting ban to probationers and parolees. A number of states also disenfranchise convicted felons who have completed serving their sentences. Out of the almost five million people barred from voting in 2004 because of a felony conviction, a third had fully served their sentences. The Sentencing Project, *Felony Disenfranchisement Laws in the United States* 1, 3 (2004).

In *Richardson v. Ramirez* (S.Ct. 1974), the Supreme Court considered the constitutionality of a restriction on voting privileges due to a felony conviction. In that case, three individuals who were denied the right to vote in California because of felonies of which they were convicted years earlier filed a lawsuit in which they contended that the abridgment of their voting rights violated their Fourteenth Amendment right to the equal protection of the law. They contended that the curtailment of their right to vote would be constitutional only if the curtailment was necessary to the promotion of a compelling governmental interest. They argued that such a compelling interest did not exist and that, in fact, the government's interest in reintegrating ex-offenders into society pointed in the opposite direction—towards extending the right to vote to former felons.

The Supreme Court disagreed that a compelling interest has to be furthered to justify a restriction on the voting rights of ex-felons. The Court pointed out that another provision in the Fourteenth Amendment specifically contemplates and condones the disenfranchisement of individuals convicted of crimes. That provision, section 2 of the Fourteenth Amendment, provides for reduced representation in Congress when a state denies certain individuals the right to vote. Section 2 carves out an exception, though, when individuals are disenfranchised because of their participation in a rebellion "or other crime."

In *Hunter v. Underwood* (S.Ct.1985), the Supreme Court distinguished its decision in *Richardson v. Ramirez* and struck down a provision of the Alabama Constitution that prohibited persons convicted of crimes involving "moral turpitude" from voting. The Court found that the constitutional provision had been enacted in order to disenfranchise African Americans and in fact had had a disproportionately adverse effect on their voting privileges. Because of the voting ban's discriminatory intent and its disparate impact on African Americans, the Court concluded that the ban violated the Equal Protection Clause of the Fourteenth Amendment.

Separate and apart from the question of the constitutionality of laws disenfranchising convicted felons is the question of their soundness from a policy perspective. This latter question has political implications. Researchers have concluded that the disenfranchisement of convicted felons has affected the outcome of past elections, including the 2000 presidential election. Christopher Uggen & Jeff Manza, Democratic Contraction? Political Consequences of Felon Disenfranchisement in the United States, 67 Am. Soc. Rev. 777, 792 (2002). In addition, electoral districts are based on population size, and prisoners currently are counted as residents of the places where they are incarcerated. With most prisons located far from the inner-city areas from where most prisoners come and prisoners barred from voting, the end result is a shifting of political power from urban areas with heavy concentrations of minorities to rural areas largely populated by whites.

3. Restrictions on Sex Offenders: Notification, Registration, and Civil-Commitment Laws

In recent years, some of the most significant restrictions imposed on ex-felons have been directed towards sex offenders. These restrictions fall into three categories: (1) registration requirements; (2) community-notification requirements; and (3) civil confinement.

What has come to be known as "Megan's Law" illustrates the first two kinds of restrictions imposed on certain convicted sex offenders. "Megan's Law" was enacted in 1994 by the New Jersey legislature after a seven-year-old girl was raped and murdered by a man who had two previous convictions for sexually assaulting children. N.J. Rev. Stat. §§ 2C:7–1 to –19. The law has two primary

components. The first part requires certain convicted sex offenders to register with the local police
department. Failure to comply with this requirement is a crime.

The second part of "Megan's Law" requires law-
enforcement officials to notify certain individuals
and entities of a sex offender's presence in the
community. Who must be notified depends on the
sex offender's risk of reoffense, which is determined
by the prosecutor in the county where the offender
was convicted, the prosecutor in the county where
the offender lives, and law-enforcement officials
asked to participate in the assessment process. If
the reoffense risk is low, only law-enforcement
agencies likely to encounter the offender have to be
notified. If the sex offender poses a moderate risk of
reoffense, agencies, such as schools, that supervise
or provide care to children or women must be
notified. And if the reoffense risk is high, members
of the public "likely to encounter" the sex offender
must be notified, including people living in the
offender's neighborhood.

Other states have followed New Jersey's lead and
enacted registration and community-notification
laws for sex offenders. The enactment of these laws
has been encouraged by a federal statute that requires states to adopt sex-offender registration laws
with community-notification provisions in order to
be eligible for certain federal funding. *See* 42 U.S.C.
§ 14071.

Sex-offender registries are now commonly posted on Internet websites. In *Connecticut Dep't of Public Safety v. Doe* (S.Ct.2003), the Supreme Court considered whether convicted sex offenders living in Connecticut have a constitutional right to a hearing at which a determination would be made as to whether they are "currently dangerous" before their names and other personal information, including a photograph, are posted in the sex-offender registry available for public viewing in certain state offices and on-line. The Court noted that the state's public-notification law did not make the inclusion in the registry of information about a sex offender contingent on a finding of dangerousness. The Court therefore unanimously held that due process did not accord convicted sex offenders in the state the right to a hearing to determine whether a fact existed that was irrelevant under the state's registration and public-notification provisions. By contrast, according to the New Jersey Supreme Court, a convicted sex offender has a due-process right to a judicial hearing before being subject to the community notification in New Jersey that attends classification as a moderate or high risk. *Doe v. Poritz* (N.J.1995).

In *Smith v. Doe* (S.Ct.2003), the Supreme Court addressed a different question about a sex-offender registration and public-notification law: whether the application of the Alaskan law to sex offenders whose convictions preceded the law's enactment violated the constitutional prohibition on *ex post facto* laws. As was discussed in Chapter 4, an *ex post facto* law is one that augments the punishment for a crime after its commission.

The registration provisions at issue in *Smith* required convicted sex offenders to provide the Alaska Department of Public Safety with updated information about themselves, including their place of employment and physical description, for fifteen years or, in some cases, longer. The information in the sex-offender registry could be accessed via the Internet. The Supreme Court found that the purpose and "principal effect" of the registration and notification provisions were nonpunitive—to protect the public, not to humiliate the registrants. Likening the obtaining of information about a sex offender by visiting a website to browsing through public records in an archive, the Court said: "Our system does not treat dissemination of truthful information in furtherance of a legitimate governmental objective as punishment." Because the threshold requirement for an *ex post facto* violation—punishment— was not met, the Court upheld the constitutionality of the Alaskan statute.

The third and most substantial restriction placed by some states on certain convicted sex offenders is to civilly confine them after they have finished serving their prison sentences. In *Kansas v. Hendricks* (S.Ct.1997), the Supreme Court considered the constitutionality of one of these civil-confinement laws—the Kansas Sexually Violent Predator Act (SVPA). Under this Act, persons found beyond a reasonable doubt to be sexually violent predators can be civilly confined.

To be considered a sexually violent predator, three requirements must be met under the SVPA. First, the person must have been convicted of a sexually violent crime, acquitted of such a crime because of insanity (or related reasons), or found incompetent to stand trial for such a crime. Second, the person must have a "mental abnormality" or personality disorder. The statute defines a "mental abnormality" as a "congenital or acquired condition affecting the emotional or volitional capacity which predisposes the person to commit sexually violent offenses in a degree constituting such person a menace to the health and safety of others." Third, that abnormality or disorder must make it likely that the person will engage in predatory acts of sexual violence in the future. Once confined under the SVPA, a person remains confined until a court determines either that the person is no longer mentally abnormal or no longer dangerous.

Leroy Hendricks was the first person confined under the Kansas Sexually Violent Predator Act. Hendricks was a pedophile who, over a thirty-year period, had been convicted and incarcerated numerous times for sexually molesting children. His most recent conviction, for molesting two thirteen-year-old boys, had resulted in a prison sentence of five to twenty years. (He could have received a maximum sentence of 45 to 180 years in prison.) After serving ten years in prison, Hendricks had been scheduled to be released from prison because of good-time credits he had accumulated. The state then sought to confine him under the Sexually Violent Predator Act.

At a hearing where a jury determined that Hendricks was a sexually violent predator, he admitted that he was a pedophile. He also said that the only way to guarantee that he would not molest more children "is to die." But Hendricks contended that he could not be confined under the SVPA because it was unconstitutional.

Hendricks first argued that the SVPA violated his right to substantive due process. The substantive component of the due-process protection afforded by the Constitution is designed to protect individuals from governmental oppression. Hendricks maintained that due process generally requires that two conditions be met before a person can be civilly confined: first, the person must be "mentally ill," as that term is defined by psychiatrists; and second, the person must pose a danger to himself or others. The Supreme Court responded that a "mental abnormality," as that term had been narrowly defined by the state legislature, combined with dangerousness would suffice for a person's civil confinement to be considered constitutional under the Due Process Clause.

Since the Supreme Court's decision in *Hendricks*, the Court has identified a third requirement that must be met in order for the civil confinement of a sexually violent predator to be constitutional. In addition to proving that a person has a mental abnormality and that the abnormality is likely to cause that individual to commit acts of sexual violence, the government must prove that the person to be confined has a "serious difficulty," though not necessarily a total incapacity, controlling his or her dangerous behavior. *Kansas v. Crane* (S.Ct.2002).

What is still unclear after *Hendricks* and *Kansas v. Crane* is what kinds of "mental abnormalities," other than those that lead to sexual predation, can actuate a civil commitment. For example, could a person who is an alcoholic and has repeatedly been involved in accidents caused by her drunk driving be civilly confined until no longer considered "mentally abnormal" or a threat to the community's safety?

Hendricks had also argued that the SVPA constituted an unconstitutional *ex post facto* law and violated his constitutional right not to be subjected to double jeopardy. As mentioned earlier, the *ex post facto* prohibition forbids a state from increasing the punishment for a crime after it has been committed. The double-jeopardy restriction prohibits a state from punishing a person twice for the same crime.

The Supreme Court held that a prerequisite to a finding of an *ex post facto* or double-jeopardy violation was absent in this case—punishment. The Court concluded that the purpose of the SVPA was not to punish sexually violent predators for their past crimes. In fact, a criminal conviction was not even necessary for confinement under the SVPA. Instead, the primary purpose of the SVPA, according to the Court, was to protect the public by incapacitating a small group of very dangerous individuals. The Court considered it significant that individuals confined under the SVPA, though housed in a prison, were segregated from the rest of the prison population and were supervised by the Department of Health and Social and Rehabilitative Services, not the Department of Corrections.

Four of the Justices disagreed with the Court's conclusion that the SVPA did not constitute an *ex post facto* law. The dissenting Justices' conclusion was grounded in large part on what they considered the state's failure to provide Hendricks with treatment, making his confinement under the SVPA punitive. At the same time, the dissenters emphasized that the SVPA would pose no *ex post facto* problems if it were applied only prospectively—to offenders who committed their crimes after the date of the SVPA's enactment.

A statute authorizing the civil confinement of sexually violent predators that is constitutional on its face cannot, according to the Supreme Court, be challenged on *ex post facto* or double-jeopardy grounds because of the way in which the statute is being implemented in practice. *Seling v. Young* (S.Ct.2001). Thus, in *Seling*, the Court refused to consider whether a petitioner's purported civil confinement was, in actuality, punitive because the conditions that he was forced to endure in the housing unit located on the grounds of a state prison allegedly were worse than those to which the prisoners were subjected. The Court opined that judicial review of such "as applied" challenges to sexually violent predator statutes would be infeasible, since the conditions of confinement under those statutes change continually.

C.   RESTORATION OF RIGHTS AND OTHER STEPS TO LIMIT COLLATERAL SANCTIONS AND CONSEQUENCES

There are a number of different ways that the adverse collateral consequences of a criminal conviction can be reduced. One way is through a pardon. Federal offenders receive pardons from the President, while in the states, the power to grant pardons may be vested in the governor, the parole or pardon board, or the governor working in concert with the parole or pardon board. A pardon does not mean that a person was innocent of the crime of which he or she was convicted; a pardon simply removes at least most of the civil disabilities that attend a criminal conviction. A person pardoned of a crime, for example, can vote or sit on a jury. In some states though, an individual who has received a pardon must still, when requested, reveal the fact of the conviction on an employment application. In addition, the criminal conduct that led to the conviction can in some jurisdictions be considered when determining whether a job applicant meets the character requirements for a particular job.

Political considerations suffuse the pardoning process, which accounts for the reticence to appear ''soft on crime'' by granting many pardons. In part because the pardon power is exercised so sparingly, pardons have proven to be an ineffectual means of restoring convicted offenders' rights and reintegrating them into their communities.

Restoration-of-rights procedures are another common means of mitigating the adverse consequences of a criminal conviction. Under some state statutes, some or all of the rights lost because of a criminal conviction are restored automatically upon the occurrence of a specified event, such as the end of incarceration or the completion of a criminal sentence. In other states, these rights are restored only upon the application of the ex-offender. Whatever the exact mechanism for the restoration of rights, one of their limitations, as with pardons, is that individuals whose rights have been restored may still have to disclose their criminal convictions when asked about them by prospective employers, thereby diminishing the ex-offenders' chances of obtaining employment.

Jurisdictions can take steps, though, to limit the negative effects of a criminal conviction on an individual's employability. For example, some states provide for the expungement or sealing of criminal records in certain circumstances, such as when individuals are sentenced to probation or convicted for the first time of a felony. When expunged, criminal records may be, but sometimes are not, destroyed. When they are sealed, they remain intact, but access to them is limited. Whether the records are expunged or sealed, the end result is that a person with a criminal conviction may, depending on a

state's law, refrain from mentioning the criminal
conviction when applying for a job.

The expungement and sealing of criminal records
also have some drawbacks as reintegration tools.
One of the practical impediments to their efficacy is
that with the evolution of technology, prospective
employers and others frequently can obtain information about an individual's criminal history even
if access to public records about that person's past
criminal convictions has been curtailed.

A few states have taken a different tack to prevent criminal convictions from unduly foreclosing
employment opportunities—generally barring employment discrimination because of prior criminal
convictions. States that have enacted discrimination
bans recognize that some employment limitations
are reasonable and therefore permissible. A person
convicted of child molestation, for example, can and
obviously should be barred from working in a day-
care center.

A statute in effect in Hawaii illustrates one
state's efforts to avert discrimination against convicted offenders without compromising other important interests, including the public's safety. In that
state, employers generally are barred from asking
about or considering a job applicant's criminal record until a conditional job offer has been tendered
to an applicant. Even then, the employer cannot
withdraw the offer because of an applicant's criminal conviction unless it has a "rational relation-

ship" to the duties and responsibilities that attend the job. Haw. Rev. Stat. § 378–2.5(b).

The Constitution also places some limits on the denial of employment to ex-offenders because of their prior convictions. When a person seeks and is denied a government job, there must be a rational connection between the job and the criterion that led to the denial of employment. *Schware v. Board of Bar Examiners* (S.Ct.1957). This due-process requirement may not be met when an individual is denied a government job because of a criminal conviction that really has no bearing on the individual's capability to perform the job.

The American Bar Association has promulgated standards in an effort to encourage jurisdictions to undertake a comprehensive review and overhaul of their laws affecting the imposition of collateral sanctions and discretionary disqualifications on convicted offenders. ABA Standards for Criminal Justice: Collateral Sanctions and Discretionary Disqualification of Convicted Persons (3d ed. 2004). The ABA Standards take a front-end approach to the subject by prescribing strict limits on the imposition of collateral sanctions and discretionary disqualifications. For example, the ABA Standards prohibit the forfeiture of voting rights except while a convicted offender is actually confined. The Standards also call for the establishment of back-end mechanisms through which convicted offenders can obtain, in appropriate circumstances, relief from one or more of the collateral consequences stemming from their convictions.

PART TWO

THE LAW AND POLICY OF CORRECTIONS

CHAPTER 10

PRISONERS' RIGHTS: AN INTRODUCTION

In 1974, the Supreme Court announced in *Wolff v. McDonnell* (S.Ct.1974) that "[t]here is no iron curtain drawn between the Constitution and the prisons of this country." To some people, this statement is heretical. "Prisoners should have no rights," they argue. Yet when pressed, these individuals will generally acknowledge that inmates should be afforded some rights. They should, for example, be fed, be provided with medical care, and be permitted to engage in certain religious practices, such as reading the Bible. So the real question is not whether inmates do or should have constitutional rights, but rather what is the scope of those rights.

A.   HISTORY OF PRISONERS' RIGHTS— A GENERAL OVERVIEW

It is helpful when discussing the subject of the scope of prisoners' rights to explore the evolution of courts' views on this subject. The opinion of the Court of Appeals of Virginia in *Ruffin v. Commonwealth* (Va.1871) typifies the view about prisoners' rights that first prevailed in this country. In that case, the court described prisoners as "slaves of the State." The court observed that prisoners had no rights; any rights that they once had were forfeited, while they were incarcerated, as part of the price they had to pay for their crimes.

The early to mid–1900s marked a subtle shift in courts' views about inmates' rights. Most courts no longer insisted that inmates had no rights. Instead, the courts said that while inmates might have rights, it was not within the courts' province to enforce those rights. Rather, the enforcement of prisoners' rights was the responsibility of the legislative and executive branches of the government.

The courts gave several reasons for embracing what is commonly known as the "hands-off doctrine." First, the courts relied on the constitutionally embedded separation of powers, arguing that judicial enforcement of inmates' rights would interfere with the operation of prisons by the legislative and executive branches of the government. Second, the courts pointed to the principle of federalism subsumed within the Constitution, expressing the concern that federal courts' commands to state officials to respect the constitutional rights of prisoners would unduly encroach on the authority of the states to run their prisons.

Third, the courts observed that judicial involvement in the operation of prisons might jeopardize institutional security and frustrate the goals of incarceration. The judges recognized that they lacked correctional expertise, and they were also concerned that the prospect of liability might sometimes dissuade prison officials from taking the steps needed to protect institutional security, with resultant harm to people and property within the prisons. The courts furthermore recognized the security problems that prisoners' lawsuits would engender, as prisoners who were parties or witnesses in those lawsuits were shuttled to and from court.

A final reason for the courts' adoption of the hands-off doctrine was the concern that opening the litigation spigot would result in the courts being inundated with prisoners' complaints, many of which would, no doubt, be frivolous from a legal perspective. Not only would these lawsuits be a hassle for the courts to deal with, but, it was feared, they would clog up the court system, impeding the adjudication of other legitimate claims.

During the 1960s and '70s, the courts retreated from the view that prisoners' lawsuits are to be shunned and began to acknowledge that courts not only have the power, but the duty, to resolve the constitutional claims of prisoners. Several developments contributed to this shift in the courts' perspective.

First, the '60s were a time of turmoil in this country—a time of war protests, ghetto riots, and assassinations. Prisons were not insulated from this turmoil. As prisoners, particularly black Muslim prisoners, became more militant and assertive, their claims became harder for the courts to ignore.

Second, as a cadre of lawyers committed to civil rights doggedly pursued the goals of improving conditions in the nation's prisons and vindicating inmates' constitutional rights, the horrendous conditions in many prisons were unveiled, making it difficult for the courts to adhere to the view that they could trust the executive and legislative branches of the government to respect the constitutional rights of prisoners. It became even more difficult to rely on this assumption when riots swept through some of the nation's prisons during this time period, particularly the riot in 1971 at the Attica State Prison in New York that resulted in the deaths of forty-three people.

A change in the composition of the Supreme Court was another significant development that catalyzed the abandonment of the hands-off doctrine. Compared to the Court in earlier years, the "Warren Court," named after the Chief Justice who headed the Court during this time, tended to more broadly interpret the scope of civil liberties. The "Warren Court" furthermore was committed to extending the protections of the Constitution to disfavored minorities, including persons accused of crimes and prisoners. It was during this era that the Supreme Court rendered such landmark decisions as *Miranda v. Arizona* (S.Ct.1966) (*Miranda* warnings must precede custodial interrogation) and *Mapp v. Ohio* (S.Ct.1961) (Fourth Amendment exclusionary rule applies to the states).

Some developments in the law also contributed to the formal abandonment of the hands-off doctrine. First, in *Monroe v. Pape* (S.Ct.1961), the Supreme Court removed a legal roadblock that had stood in the way of prisoners wanting to file civil-rights suits under 42 U.S.C. § 1983. In *Monroe*, the Supreme Court clarified the meaning of the requirement in § 1983 that a person must have acted "under color of" a state statute, ordinance, regulation, custom, or usage for a constitutional claim against that person to be cognizable under § 1983.

Monroe v. Pape involved a § 1983 suit brought by several individuals whose home was searched by police officers without a warrant. The state constitution, as well as several state statutes, prohibited the actions undertaken by the police officers. Nonetheless, the Supreme Court held that the under-color-of-state-law requirement of § 1983 could be met even if a state law actually prohibited the actions of the government officials that had allegedly violated the Constitution. The Court noted that § 1983 was enacted to provide a federal remedy for the violation of constitutional rights in large part because the states, in the post-Civil War era, often looked the other way when confronted with violations of state laws. The Court therefore concluded that the under-color-of-state-law requirement is met as long as a constitutional violation stems from the " '[m]isuse of power, possessed by virtue of state law and made possible only because the wrongdoer is clothed with the authority of state law.' "

The second significant legal development that opened the courts to prisoners' civil-rights suits occurred in a series of cases in which the Supreme Court held that certain constitutional provisions that apply to the federal government also apply to the states via the Due Process Clause of the Fourteenth Amendment. A particularly important case for prisoners was *Robinson v. California* (S.Ct. 1962), which held that the Eighth Amendment's prohibition of cruel and unusual punishments extends to the states.

The Supreme Court has now recognized that prisoners have an array of constitutional rights. These rights include the right to freedom of speech, the right to religious freedom, the right to marry, the right to have access to the courts, the right to equal protection of the law, due-process rights, and the right not to be subjected to cruel and unusual punishments. At the same time, vestiges of the hands-off doctrine remain. In a number of cases, the Supreme Court has emphasized the deference due the assessments of correctional officials about what is needed to protect institutional security and effectuate correctional goals. This deference, in turn, has led to decisions narrowly interpreting the scope of prisoners' constitutional rights. The courts

have moved, in short, to what has aptly been described as the "one-hand-on, one-hand-off era" of
prisoners' rights. William C. Collins, *Correctional
Law for the Correctional Officer* 13 (4th ed. 2004).

B. THE PURPOSES OF INCARCERATION

Because the scope of prisoners' constitutional
rights is not only dependent on the demands of
institutional security but also on the purposes of
incarceration, it is important to define what those
purposes are. Traditionally, correctional policymakers and experts have referred to four principal purposes of incarceration—incapacitation, deterrence,
rehabilitation, and retribution. These four goals,
which are briefly defined below, are discussed in
greater depth in Chapter 1.

One purpose of incarceration is incapacitation.
Certain criminal offenders are incarcerated simply
to prevent them, while they are incarcerated, from
being able to commit further crimes against the
public. As was discussed earlier in this book, the
incapacitative goal of incarceration has engendered
much controversy, inciting debate about whether
the comparative costs and benefits of incapacitation
have been assessed accurately.

The second touted purpose of incarceration is
deterrence—dissuading the future commission of
crimes. This deterrent objective has two facets—
specific and general deterrence. The aim of specific
deterrence is to discourage the individual who is
incarcerated from committing additional crimes,

while the focus of general deterrence is on the public. The premise of the theory of general deterrence is that members of the public will refrain from criminal conduct when they see how others are punished for their misdeeds.

Released prisoners' very high recidivism rates undercut the force of arguments underscoring the deterrent effects of incarceration. *See, e.g.*, Bureau of Justice Statistics, U.S. Dep't of Justice, *Prisons and Prisoners Released in 1994*, at 1, 3 (2002) (68% of released prisoners were rearrested for a felony or serious misdemeanor within three years of their release). The deterrent impact of incarceration is limited, in part, because many offenders are under the influence of drugs or alcohol at the time of their crimes and therefore lack the faculties needed for a dispassionate and objective assessment of the costs and benefits of their criminal behavior. The realization of incarceration's deterrent objective is in addition impeded by the fact that most crimes are never solved. Consequently, most people who commit crimes are not deterred by the prospect of imprisonment because they do not expect to be apprehended.

The lack of a discernible correlation, over time, between the crime rate and the rate of incarceration provides further evidence of the limits on incarceration's crime-control benefits, whether derived from its incapacitative or deterrent effects. While the incarceration rate has increased dramatically in this country during the past few decades, the crime rate has fluctuated greatly, sometimes rising sharply and other times falling significantly.

The third reason sometimes cited for incarceration is rehabilitation. The rehabilitative rationale for incarceration is premised on the assumption that by participating in treatment and other programs while in prison, the mores of prisoners will be changed and the underlying problems that contributed to their criminal conduct will be resolved. It is thought that prisoners will then desist from committing further crimes upon their release from prison. Critics, however, argue that the notion that incarceration can be rehabilitative is naive. They point out that the isolation and stigma that attend incarceration, as well as the criminogenic influences to which inmates are exposed while incarcerated, will counteract any beneficial effects of prison programs, assuming that such programs are even available to the inmates in the first place. In addition, the dependency on others that incarceration fosters can, it is felt, be debilitating, compounding the difficulty released prisoners face in reintegrating successfully into their communities upon their release from prison.

The fourth purpose commonly cited for incarceration is retribution. Under this rationale for incarceration, convicted offenders are confined simply because they deserve to be incarcerated as punishment for the crimes they have committed. Many of those who subscribe to the retributive aim of criminal justice also embrace the concept of "just deserts." This limiting principle calls for the imposition of punishment that is no greater than warranted by the severity of the crime of which a person has been convicted.

The chapters that follow discuss the courts' views about the scope of prisoners' constitutional rights. In reading these materials, readers are encouraged to consider what the purposes of incarceration should be and how those identified purposes should affect the scope of prisoners' constitutional rights. Just as important, readers should also contemplate the answer to this policy question: What rights should be afforded prisoners separate and apart from their rights under the United States Constitution? This question is one of import because states have the prerogative to extend rights to prisoners under their own constitutions, statutes, and regulations that go beyond the federal constitutional minima.

CHAPTER 11

FIRST AMENDMENT RIGHTS

A. FREEDOM OF SPEECH

Perhaps no other area of law confirms more clearly the constricted scope of prisoners' rights than the First Amendment area. The First Amendment to the United States Constitution provides in part that "Congress shall make no law ... abridging the freedom of speech." The First Amendment applies directly to federal officials. State and local officials, however, are also subject to the dictates of the First Amendment, since it is applicable to the states via the Due Process Clause found in the Fourteenth Amendment.

The threshold question that had to be resolved when courts were first presented with prisoners' claims alleging abridgments of their free-speech rights was whether the First Amendment provides any protection at all to the communications of prisoners. The Supreme Court had the opportunity to, but ultimately did not, resolve this question in *Procunier v. Martinez* (S.Ct.1974).

In *Procunier*, a group of prisoners challenged the constitutionality of a set of state regulations that governed the censorship of prisoner mail. One of these regulations prohibited letters in which in-

223

mates "unduly complain" or "magnify grievances." Another prohibited writings that expressed "inflammatory political, racial, religious, or other views." And still another proscribed "otherwise inappropriate" letters.

The Supreme Court first noted the confusion that had reigned in the lower courts about the extent to which, if at all, the First Amendment affords protection to the speech of prisoners. Yet the Court declined to immediately alleviate this confusion. Instead, the Court focused upon the fact that the regulations implicated the free-speech interests of nonprisoners, the individuals outside prison with whom the prisoners corresponded. Under these circumstances, the Court noted, the regulations had to meet the requirements of a somewhat stringent two-part test to pass constitutional muster.

First, the regulations had to further an "important" or "substantial" governmental interest not related to the suppression of expression. In other words, the restrictions on speech had to effectuate a goal other than the sheer desire to suppress views with which certain government officials disagreed. The Court cited the government's interests in maintaining institutional security and order and in rehabilitating prisoners as interests that were sufficiently weighty to support restrictions on prisoners' correspondence.

Second, the regulations could not restrict the interest in unimpeded communications more than was "generally necessary" to protect any of the substantial governmental interests outlined above. In discussing this least-drastic-alternative requirement, the Court noted that prison officials needed some leeway in assessing the "probable consequences" of allowing certain speech within the volatile confines of a prison. Therefore, they did not have to show with absolute certainty that a particular letter would, for example, imperil institutional security to justify restrictions placed on the transmission or receipt of that letter. A showing of a general necessity for the restriction would suffice. The Court furthermore noted that when assessing the need for a particular restriction on inmate mail, the policies of other prisons would be relevant, though not controlling.

The Supreme Court then proceeded to apply this two-part test to the censorship regulations before it and concluded, for several reasons, that they were unconstitutional. First, the Court was not persuaded that some of the regulations actually furthered the interests invoked by the prison officials in their defense. For example, although the officials had argued that limitations needed to be placed on inmate complaints in order to prevent riots and promote the rehabilitation of inmates, they had not, according to the Court, explained how complaints contained in letters sent to individuals outside a prison could cause riots or impede inmates' rehabilitation. What is significant about this portion of the Court's opinion is that it showed that there were limits to the deference that the Court would accord the judgments of prison officials about what was needed to protect institutional security or to further other important correctional goals.

The regulations also failed to pass muster under the second prong of the two-part test. The Court observed that there were other ways of achieving the objectives of the censorship regulations that did not impinge so significantly on First Amendment freedoms. For example, the regulation prohibiting writings containing "inflammatory" views was not, as it should be, confined to communications that would provoke violence. Nor was the regulation confined to just incoming mail.

Procunier demonstrates that the censorship of inmate mail may run afoul of other constitutional provisions as well. In *Procunier* itself, the Supreme Court held that the inmates and the individuals with whom they corresponded had not been afforded procedural due process when their mail was censored. To avoid errors and arbitrariness in censorship decisions, the Court said that the following procedural safeguards have to attend the censorship process: (1) notice to an inmate when a letter written to or by the inmate is censored; (2) an opportunity afforded the letter's author to protest the censorship decision; and (3) review of the censorship decision by someone other than the individual who made the initial decision.

In *Pell v. Procunier* (S.Ct.1974), the Supreme Court answered the question left open in *Procunier v. Martinez* and held that prisoners do indeed have some First Amendment rights. Specifically, the

Court held that inmates retain First Amendment rights that do not conflict with their "status" as prisoners or "legitimate penological objectives." The Court expounded upon the list of correctional objectives set forth in *Procunier* that would support curbs on First Amendment freedoms in the prison context, citing not only the interests in maintaining institutional security and rehabilitating prisoners, but also the interests in deterring crime and incapacitating individuals posing a threat to the public's safety.

At issue in *Pell* was the constitutionality of a state regulation that prohibited members of the media from conducting face-to-face interviews with inmates of their choice. In finding this regulation to be constitutional, the Supreme Court emphasized several points. First, the Court noted the conflict between permitting such interviews and maintaining institutional security. For security reasons, the Court observed, prison officials needed to keep the number of prison visitors to a "manageable level." In addition, prison officials had legitimate security reasons for wanting to avert what was known as the "big wheel phenomenon," where inmates who have garnered attention through media interviews wield more influence over other inmates, influence that can then be used towards disruptive ends.

The Court also emphasized in *Pell* that the inmates had other viable means of communicating with the media, both through letters and by sending messages with family members, friends, attorneys, and clergy. *Pell* then was the first of a succession of cases in which the Court, in assessing the constitutionality of prison regulations under the First Amendment, has balanced the governmental interests furthered by a restriction on First Amendment interests against the burden on inmates caused by the restriction.

Pell is also noteworthy because the Supreme Court in that case did not adopt a least-drastic-alternative requirement, as it had in *Procunier v. Martinez* when addressing the First Amendment rights of nonprisoners. In other words, prison regulations that impinge on inmates' First Amendment interests can still be constitutional even if there are less restrictive means through which prison officials can accomplish their correctional objectives. The Court in *Pell* did not, in fact, even bother discussing the less drastic alternatives that were discussed by Justice Powell in his dissenting opinion in the companion case of *Saxbe v. Washington Post Co.* (S.Ct. 1974). One of these suggested alternatives was to limit the number of interviews that could be conducted with any one inmate during a specified time period.

The Supreme Court in *Pell v. Procunier* rebuffed another First Amendment challenge to the regulation restricting media interviews of inmates. Certain media members had contended that the regulation abridged the freedom of the press protected by the First Amendment. The Court simply responded that members of the press have no greater right to have access to prisons than do members of the general public. Dissenting from this portion of the

Court's opinion, Justice Powell, joined by Justices Brennan, Marshall, and Douglas, observed that because the public is dependent on the media for information about prisons, the right of the press to have access to prisons is not coextensive with that of the public's.

In cases decided since *Pell*, the Supreme Court has continued to focus on security concerns and the availability of alternative means of expression when evaluating the free-speech claims of prisoners. In *Jones v. North Carolina Prisoners' Labor Union* (S.Ct.1977), for example, the Court upheld three state regulations that curbed inmate involvement in a prisoner labor union. The first regulation barred inmates from soliciting other inmates to join the union; the second prohibited union meetings in the state's prisons; and the third prohibited bulk mailings of union materials for redistribution to inmates. Prison officials argued that these restrictions were needed to protect institutional security. They contended, for example, that a prisoner union might encourage work slowdowns or stoppages that might in turn culminate in riots.

In responding to the prisoners' argument that these predictions about the disruptive effects of prisoner unions were not supported by any evidence of actual disruptions in the past, the Supreme Court showed great deference towards correctional officials' opinions about what was needed to protect institutional security. The Court simply noted that the prison officials' concerns were "reasonable" and that they had not been "conclusively shown to be wrong." Prison officials, according to the Court, did not have to wait until a prison was on the verge of a riot before they could take steps to thwart a prison disruption.

The Court in *Jones* also noted the alternative outlets available for the expression impaired by the prison regulations. For example, inmates had other ways to communicate their complaints to prison officials, including prison grievance procedures. In addition, although union materials could not be mailed in bulk to prisoners because of the ease with which contraband can be hidden in bulk mailings, the mailing of union materials to individual inmates was permitted.

In *Bell v. Wolfish* (S.Ct.1979), the Supreme Court again found a correctional regulation constitutional in the face of a First Amendment challenge. The regulation at issue prohibited inmates and pretrial detainees from receiving hardbound books mailed from a source other than a bookstore, a book publisher, or a book club. Noting the difficulty of detecting contraband hidden in the bindings of hardbound books, the Court concluded that the restriction was a "rational response" to "an obvious security problem." The Court also underscored that the burden caused by the restriction was dissipated by several factors. First, the inmates and detainees were still permitted to receive magazines and softbound books from any source. Second, they had access to a well-stocked library. And third, the pretrial detainees were affected by the regulation for a relatively short period of time, because the vast majority of them were released within sixty days.

In a dissenting opinion, Justice Marshall objected to applying the same watered-down First Amendment test that was applied to convicted criminals to pretrial detainees not yet convicted of a crime and presumed innocent of any criminal wrongdoing. In defending its decision not to differentiate between the First Amendment claims of inmates and those of pretrial detainees, the majority responded that pretrial detainees often pose the same, and sometimes greater, threats to institutional security as individuals incarcerated for crimes of which they have been convicted. For example, pretrial detainees awaiting trial for very serious crimes may be more dangerous and present a heightened risk of escape compared to inmates convicted of less serious crimes and sentenced to a short period of incarceration.

Pell, Jones, and *Bell* were the prelude to *Turner v. Safley* (S.Ct.1987), a pivotal Supreme Court case that fleshed out the contours of the test to be applied to prisoners' First Amendment claims. One of the regulations whose constitutionality was at issue in *Turner* generally prohibited inmates from writing to each other unless they were close relatives or were corresponding about legal matters. In enunciating the test to be applied in determining whether this regulation was constitutional, the Supreme Court stated that "when a prison regulation impinges on inmates' constitutional rights, the regulation is valid if it is reasonably related to legitimate penological interests."

The Court then discussed four factors to be considered under this reasonable-relationship test. First, there must be a "valid, rational connection" between the regulation and the interest it is designed to further. In other words, the connection between the regulation and its purpose must not be so attenuated as to produce arbitrary or irrational results. In addition, the interest that a regulation purportedly furthers must be both "legitimate" and "neutral." The Court in *Turner* seemed to suggest that to meet the neutrality requirement, a regulation's application cannot hinge on the content of the expression being regulated.

Second, a court must examine the extent to which inmates have other ways of exercising the right in question. This factor, as mentioned earlier, bears on the burden on inmates caused by a particular restriction.

The third factor to be considered is the effect that recognizing the claimed right will have on other inmates, correctional officers, and prison resources, and the fourth and final factor looks at the extent to which there are less drastic means of achieving the legitimate objectives of the regulation—means that do not so greatly impinge upon the asserted rights of prisoners. But while the existence of less drastic alternatives is a relevant factor to be weighed under the *Turner* test, there is no least-drastic-alternative requirement that must be met under the *Turner* test, in contrast to the test applied by the Court in *Procunier v. Martinez* when assessing the scope of nonprisoners' rights under the First Amendment.

The factors outlined in *Turner* as relevant to the reasonableness inquiry simply represented a more detailed exposition of a balancing process that had begun years earlier in *Pell v. Procunier*. What was noteworthy about *Turner* was the way in which the Court construed some of these factors so as to almost foreordain a finding in favor of the constitutionality of most prison regulations and practices. For example, when applying the second factor to the facts of the case before it, the Court broadly construed what constitutes an available alternative to a claimed right. Noting that the inmates had not been deprived of "all means of expression," the Court seemed unconcerned that the ban on inmate-to-inmate correspondence totally prevented inmates from communicating with certain individuals with whom they wanted to correspond.

The Court similarly construed the fourth factor in a way that makes it exceedingly difficult for inmates to prevail on their First Amendment claims. The Court said that if an alternative means of achieving the government's objectives entails more than "*de minimis* costs" to legitimate penological objectives, it is not to be considered a viable option and consequently is not an indicator of a regulation's unconstitutionality. It is unlikely then that this factor will often weigh in favor of inmates' constitutional claims, because extending almost any right to prisoners will have security implications. As the United States District Court for the District of New Jersey observed in *Valentine v. Englehardt* (D.N.J.1979), "A naked man in chains poses no risk. From that point on, every increase in freedom brings at least some decrease in security."

Not surprisingly, the Supreme Court found in *Turner* that the regulation prohibiting inmate-to-inmate correspondence did not unconstitutionally abridge inmates' free-speech rights under the First Amendment. The Court first observed that there was the requisite rational connection between this regulation and legitimate security interests, because inmates at different prisons could use the mail to coordinate gang activity and plan assaults, murders, and other activities inimical to the safety and security of individuals within the state's prisons. The second factor, according to the Court, weighed in favor of the regulation's constitutionality because, as mentioned earlier, the inmates had other means of expression available to them, even though they were forbidden from communicating with some of the individuals with whom they perhaps most wanted to communicate. Third, permitting inmates to correspond with each other would have harmful effects on the inmates and staff whose safety would be jeopardized by such correspondence. Finally, the Court noted that there were no "obvious, easy alternatives" to the ban on inmate-to-inmate correspondence. Screening inmates' mail would consume valuable staff resources, and risks to institutional security would remain because of encoded messages that might be missed during the screening process.

Although it is now an uphill battle for an inmate to prevail on a constitutional claim to which the *Turner* test is applied, *Turner* itself demonstrates that it is not impossible for an inmate to do so. While the Supreme Court in *Turner* upheld the ban on inmate-to-inmate correspondence, the Court also struck down another regulation that prohibited inmates from getting married without the warden's consent. Under this regulation, the warden was not supposed to approve inmate marriages unless there was a "compelling" reason for the marriage, such as pregnancy or the birth of a child.

The Supreme Court found that there was no reasonable relationship between the marriage prohibition and the interests invoked in its defense— security and rehabilitation. In finding that the threshold requirement of a logical connection between the prohibition and security interests was absent, the Court noted that the "love triangles" that prison officials argued might lead to violence could develop whether or not inmates were married. The Court also felt that there were less drastic means of achieving the security objectives of the marriage prohibition. Prison officials could, for example, just prohibit marriages that posed a distinct threat to institutional security rather than institute an across-the-board ban on inmate marriages.

The Court also noted that the prohibition on inmate marriages was broader than necessary to achieve the rehabilitative goals asserted by the prison officials. The prison officials had argued that female inmates, many of whom have been victims of abuse in the past, needed to learn to become self-reliant while in prison, a task that would be more difficult if they were married. In highlighting the regulation's overbreadth, the Court noted that the regulation encompassed marriages about which the prison officials had expressed little concern—marriages involving male inmates and inmate marriages to civilians who were not ex-felons.

The progression of Supreme Court cases in which inmates' free-speech rights were narrowly construed culminated in *Thornburgh v. Abbott* (S.Ct. 1989). In *Thornburgh*, the Supreme Court considered the constitutionality of some prison regulations that governed the censorship of publications that were sent to prisoners. Like the censorship regulations that were at issue in *Procunier v. Martinez*, these regulations had an impact on the free-speech interests of nonprisoners as well as prisoners. The Court, however, refused to apply the two-part *Procunier* test to the regulations, narrowly construing *Procunier* in the process.

Despite the breadth of the language in *Procunier* discussing when the two-part test enunciated in that case would apply in the prison context and despite the fact that the regulations at issue in *Procunier* had applied to both incoming and outgoing correspondence, the Supreme Court in *Thornburgh* claimed that *Procunier* had primarily concerned just outgoing personal correspondence. Such outgoing correspondence, the Court said, was to be distinguished from incoming publications, which tend to circulate widely within a prison and whose contents therefore pose a much greater potential threat to institutional security. Accordingly, the Court held that the *Turner* test should apply to incoming publications and overruled *Procunier* to the extent that it suggested otherwise. Although the only issue actually before the Court in *Thornburgh* was the standard to be applied to incoming publications and not the standard to be applied to incoming personal correspondence, the Court sweepingly announced that application of the *Procunier* test was to be confined to outgoing correspondence.

While the Court in *Thornburgh* insisted that the *Turner* test is not a "toothless" one, *Thornburgh* itself confirmed the ease with which prison regulations can survive that test. The Court, for example, took pains to note that there was no need to demonstrate that a particular publication was "likely" to cause violence to justify banning it from a prison; all that was necessary was that the publication pose "an intolerable risk of disorder."

The Court also qualified what it had said earlier in *Procunier v. Martinez* regarding the relevance of other prisons' policies to the constitutionality of prison regulations. The Court noted that just because a publication was admitted into some prisons, and not others, did not mean that prison officials were necessarily acting irrationally or arbitrarily. The Court observed that prisons can differ greatly from one another and even the same prison can vary significantly over time as far as the steps needed to preserve its security.

The Court also expounded upon what it had meant in *Turner* when it had referred to a "neutral" interest to which a restriction on prisoners' rights must be rationally connected. The Court in *Turner* had indicated that this neutrality requirement meant that application of a regulation could not be contingent on a communication's content. That definition obviously posed a problem in *Thornburgh*, where incoming publications might or might not be admitted into a prison, depending on their content. However, because the regulations in *Thornburgh* only allowed censorship to further a governmental interest—institutional security—"unrelated to the suppression of expression" (they specifically disallowed censorship for other reasons), the Court said that the regulations were "neutral" in the technical sense required by *Turner*.

Perhaps the most revealing portion of the Court's opinion in *Thornburgh* was its discussion of whether there were viable, less drastic alternatives to the way in which publications were censored under the regulations. Under the regulations, if a passage or article in a publication was censorable, the entire publication could be withheld from prisoners. Justice Stevens, in dissent, described this "all-or-nothing rule" as "a meat-ax abridgement" of the First Amendment rights of both free citizens and prisoners. The Court responded that the regulations were still constitutional because the belief of prison officials that inmates would get upset if they received publications with parts missing was "reasonably founded." The Court in addition noted that it would be "inconvenient" for prison officials to have to take the time to remove censorable materials out of incoming publications.

B. FREEDOM OF ASSOCIATION

Another right protected by the First Amendment and applicable to the states through the Due Process Clause of the Fourteenth Amendment is known as the freedom of association. A threshold question concerning this First Amendment right is whether it even extends to prisoners. In *Jones v. North Carolina Prisoners' Labor Union* (S.Ct.1977), the Supreme Court seemed to assume that inmates retain some associational rights, although the Court in that case ultimately concluded that certain restrictions on the activities of a prisoner labor union did not unconstitutionally abridge inmates' freedom of association.

Assuming that prisoners retain some degree of freedom of association despite their incarceration, the next question concerns the scope of their associational rights. At least some answers to this question were provided by the Supreme Court in *Block v. Rutherford* (S.Ct.1984), a case involving the rights, not of prisoners, but of pretrial detainees. In *Block*, a group of pretrial detainees challenged the constitutionality of a jail policy that prohibited contact visits between pretrial detainees and their visitors, including family members. A contact visit is one in which there is no physical barrier, such as a plexiglas window, between inmates or detainees and their visitors.

The Supreme Court analyzed the constitutionality of this ban on contact visits under the Due Process Clause of the Fourteenth Amendment. The pivotal question, according to the Court, was whether this ban was tantamount to punishment, since the Due Process Clause prohibits the punishment of individuals who have not been convicted of any crime. Such proscribed punishment will be found when a policy or practice is designed to punish pretrial detainees. Even in the absence of proof of an intent to punish, punishment will be found to exist when a policy or practice that has a negative effect on pretrial detainees is not "reasonably related to a legitimate governmental objective."

The latter way in which *Block* said punishment can be established seems to mirror the reasonable-relationship test that the Court later said in *Turner v. Safley* should be applied to the First Amendment claims of prisoners. Yet the way in which the Court applied the reasonable-relationship test in *Block* stands in marked contrast to the way in which it was subsequently applied in *Turner*.

In *Block*, the Court noted that contact visits can cause a lot of security problems in correctional facilities. Visitors can smuggle drugs, weapons, and other contraband that poses a direct threat to institutional security to the detainees with whom they are visiting. There is also always the risk that detainees might harm visitors, using them, for example, as hostages in an escape attempt.

The district court had readily conceded the legitimacy of the security concerns spawned by contact visits, but the court believed that the ban on contact visits was an excessive response to those concerns. The district court therefore crafted an order that it felt addressed the security risks posed by contact visits without so drastically impinging upon the interest of pretrial detainees in maintaining, through contact visits, ties with their family members and friends. Because the impact of the contact-visitation ban fell most heavily on detainees incarcerated for lengthy periods of time, the district court generally lifted the ban for detainees incarcerated for a month or more. Mindful of the security risks posed by contact visits, however, the district court authorized continuing the ban for long-term detainees who had drug-use or escape propensities. In addition, the court placed a cap on the total number of contact visits that the jail officials had to allow each month.

The Supreme Court criticized the lower court for its balancing of the security interests that prompted the contact-visitation ban against the burden on detainees caused by that ban. The Court brusquely said that once the district court found that contact visits actually threaten institutional security, its analysis should have ended. By instead balancing these interests against the interests of the detainees, the district court had, according to the Supreme Court, impermissibly supplanted the judgment of jail administrators about what was needed to maintain jail security with its own view.

This rejection of a balancing of interests is at odds with the long line of cases discussed earlier in this chapter in which the Supreme Court has done exactly what it said the lower court should not have done. And in most of those cases, such as *Pell v. Procunier* (S.Ct.1974) and *Turner v. Safley* (S.Ct. 1987), the Court was analyzing the rights of prisoners, not detainees who are presumed innocent of any criminal wrongdoing.

Even if the Court in *Block*, however, had applied a balancing test, the end result of the case might very well have been the same, particularly if the Court had applied a test whose factors are as tilted in favor of correctional officials as are those considered under the *Turner* test. The Court in *Block*, for example, had noted that the detainees, although not allowed contact visits, were still permitted unmonitored noncontact visits during most of the day. This fact would weigh in favor of the contact-visitation ban's constitutionality under the second factor of the *Turner* test—the alternative means available to inmates to exercise the right in question.

In addition, because the Supreme Court had expressed concerns in *Block* about the risks of allowing even detainees classified as low-security risks to have contact visits, the other *Turner* factors appear to support the constitutionality of the contact-visitation ban. The Court had observed that even detainees who are classified as low-security risks might be induced or coerced by other detainees to smuggle contraband into the jail. In addition, the Court had stated that allowing contact visits for some detainees and not others might fuel tensions between them. Finally, the Court had noted the fallibility of the classification systems through which detainees are assigned a risk level.

In *Overton v. Bazzetta* (S.Ct.2003), the Supreme Court rejected a First Amendment challenge to an array of restrictions imposed on prisoners' visiting privileges. One of the restrictions provided for the total forfeiture of visiting privileges for two years when a prisoner had violated departmental substance-abuse rules two or more times. Skirting, once again, the question whether the First Amendment right to freedom of association extends to prisoners, the Supreme Court found that the restriction comported with the First Amendment in any event because it was reasonably related to institutional security. Specifically, the Court noted that the withdrawal of visiting privileges is a commonly employed way of inducing prisoners to comply with prison rules.

The Supreme Court conceded in *Overton* that the impact of this across-the-board visitation ban was "severe" but added that inmates subject to the ban had alternative ways to communicate with friends and family members—through letters and phone calls. The prisoners argued that these alternatives were not viable means of communicating with small children and that writing letters was not a feasible alternative for illiterate inmates. But the Court responded that under the *Turner* test, the alternatives avenues for exercising a right "need not be ideal; . . . they need only be available."

Even when correctional officials can constitutionally restrict family members' access to prisoners, the officials must decide whether particular restrictions are sound from a policy perspective. Institutional-security considerations will, of course, be factored into this policy assessment. In addition, the results of research finding that maintaining and nurturing ties between inmates and their families decrease recidivism rates clearly have a bearing on the question of the types of restrictions that should be placed on inmates' visiting privileges. *See, e.g.*, N.E. Schafer, *Exploring the Link Between Visits and Parole Success: A Survey of Prison Visitors*, 38 Int'l J. Offender Therapy & Comp. Criminology 17 (1994).

C. FREEDOM OF RELIGION

Another First Amendment right upon which much prisoners' rights litigation has focused is the right to religious freedom. The Supreme Court confirmed that inmates have the right to freedom of religion in *Cruz v. Beto* (S.Ct.1972). In that case, a Buddhist inmate claimed that prison officials violated his right to religious freedom by making accommodations for inmates of other faiths that they did not make for him. He charged, for example, that other inmates were permitted to use the prison chapel, while he was not, and that the state only paid for Catholic, Jewish, and Protestant clergy and Jewish and Christian Bibles.

In holding that the district court had erred in dismissing the plaintiff's complaint, the Supreme Court noted that inmates must be afforded "reasonable opportunities" to practice their religious faith and that these opportunities must be comparable to those afforded prisoners of other religions. At the same time, the Court emphasized that prison officials need not provide different religious sects with identical facilities and personnel to facilitate the exercise of inmates' religious freedom; the number of inmate adherents to a particular religion can rather be taken into account when making personnel decisions and decisions regarding the use of facilities.

In *O'Lone v. Shabazz* (S.Ct.1987), the Supreme Court embellished upon the scope of inmates' right to religious freedom. In that case, a group of Muslim inmates challenged the constitutionality of several prison regulations, one of which required inmates assigned to work details outside the prison to remain with those details throughout the day. The effect of these regulations was to prevent the Muslim inmates from being able to attend Jumu'ah, a group worship service that, according to the Koran, must be held at a certain time on Friday afternoons.

The Supreme Court applied the *Turner* test in assessing the constitutionality of these regulations. The Court first found a logical connection between the prohibition on returns to the prison during the day and legitimate penological interests. Inmates returning to the prison posed security risks at the main gate through which they returned because of the heavy amount of traffic that also traveled through the gate during the day. Letting inmates leave work early, according to the Court, also interfered with the rehabilitative purpose of the work details.

Turning to the second *Turner* factor, the Court acknowledged that the Muslim inmates had no alternative way of attending Jumu'ah. Nonetheless, this fact, in the opinion of the Court, did not weigh against the regulations' constitutionality, because the Muslim inmates were not deprived of "all forms of religious exercise." They could meet together at other times to worship; they were provided special pork-free meals; and they were permitted to eat at different times than other inmates during the holy month of Ramadan. The state also paid for an imam, a Muslim prayer leader, to provide religious services to the Muslim inmates.

This portion of the Court's opinion drew a sharp rebuke from Justice Brennan, who objected to treating religious practices as though they are interchangeable. Justice Brennan, who was joined in his dissenting opinion by three other Justices, insisted that the deprivation in this case was total and that this fact therefore weighed heavily against the regulations' constitutionality.

Justice Brennan also disagreed with the way in which the majority spurned the less drastic alternatives proffered by the Muslim inmates as ways to eliminate the security concerns caused by inmates leaving their work details while preserving the Muslim inmates' ability to attend Jumu'ah. One of the plaintiffs' suggestions was to have the Muslim inmates not work on Fridays so that they could remain in the prison to attend Jumu'ah and then work on weekends to compensate for the work missed on Fridays. The majority of the Court, however, did not consider weekend work details to be a viable option. The Court cited three concerns the prison officials had raised about this alternative— that it would be difficult to supervise work details on weekends, when staffing is already sparse; that work details comprised only of Muslim inmates would be "affinity groups" that would be more likely to challenge the authority of prison officials; and that other inmates would resent what they perceive as the special treatment of Muslim inmates.

One of Justice Brennan's objections to these reasons for opposing weekend work details comprised of Muslim inmates was that they seemed, in his opinion, to reflect an anti-Muslim bias. He noted that the prison officials did not seem at all concerned about the staff needed on weekends to accommodate the religious needs of Christian and Jewish inmates who wanted to attend group worship services. Nor did they seem concerned about affinity groups when the inmates working together were Christians. Finally, the prison officials seemed to give no thought to the resentment ensuing when

Muslim inmates, denied the opportunity of participating in Jumu'ah, saw prison officials making accommodations to enable Christian and Jewish inmates to attend their own group worship services.

The Supreme Court has never acknowledged the apparent tension between the admonition in *Cruz v. Beto* that inmates must be afforded "reasonable opportunities" to practice their religion and the Court's niggardly construction of the scope of inmates' religious rights in *O'Lone v. Shabazz*. But with the lower courts generally following the Supreme Court's lead in *O'Lone*, prisoners often have not prevailed on their freedom-of-religion claims grounded on the First Amendment. However, some prisoners have had a measure of success in some lower-court cases in which they asserted a constitutional right to a special diet and a right to utilize a religious name in addition to the name under which they were committed to prison. *See, e.g., DeHart v. Horn* (3d Cir.2000) (special diet); *Hakim v. Hicks* (11th Cir.2000) (name change).

Two of the more frequently asserted freedom-of-religion claims are brought by inmates who, for religious reasons, want to wear their hair long or grow a beard. The majority of the courts have upheld prison regulations restricting the length of prisoners' hair and prohibiting beards. *See, e.g., Green v. Polunsky* (5th Cir.2000) (beards); *Diaz v. Collins* (5th Cir.1997) (long hair). One of the reasons why courts consider these restrictions reasonably related to institutional security is that they can impede the efforts of inmates to alter their appearance and avoid being identified after they have committed a crime or disciplinary infraction or escaped from prison.

Even if *O'Lone v. Shabazz* were not on the books, many prisoners' First Amendment freedom-of-religion claims would still fail (including the claim asserted by the prisoners in *O'Lone*) due to a rule propounded in another Supreme Court case. The plaintiffs in that case, *Employment Div. v. Smith* (S.Ct.1990), were Native Americans who had been fired from their jobs at a drug-rehabilitation center after ingesting peyote during a Native–American religious ceremony. Because they were fired for work-related misconduct, the plaintiffs' applications for unemployment-compensation benefits were later denied. The plaintiffs contended that this denial abridged their First Amendment right to freely exercise their religion, but the Supreme Court disagreed. The Court held that when the burden on a religious practice is "merely the incidental effect of a generally applicable and otherwise valid provision" rather than the result of a governmental regulation whose purpose is to restrict religious practices, the First Amendment is simply not violated.

Because of the restrictions on religious freedom that would be upheld under the Supreme Court's decision in *Employment Div. v. Smith,* Congress attempted to reverse the effects of that decision by enacting the Religious Freedom Restoration Act of 1993 (RFRA). That Act, which includes prisoners within the scope of its protection, provides that actions taken by government officials that place a "substantial burden" on a person's exercise of religion are illegal unless they further a "compelling" governmental interest and are the "least restrictive means" of furthering that interest. 42 U.S.C. § 2000bb–1(a), (b). In *City of Boerne v. Flores* (S.Ct.1997), however, the Supreme Court held that the RFRA was unconstitutional, as applied to the states, because Congress had exceeded its enforcement powers under § 5 of the Fourteenth Amendment when enacting the RFRA. The RFRA is therefore no longer binding on state and local correctional officials, although courts have held that it still applies to federal restrictions on religious freedom, including restrictions imposed on federal prisoners. *See, e.g., O'Bryan v. Bureau of Prisons* (7th Cir.2003).

After the Supreme Court's decision in *City of Boerne v. Flores*, Congress enacted the Religious Land Use and Institutionalized Persons Act (RLUIPA) as part of its ongoing effort to protect religious practices. 42 U.S.C. § 2000cc to 2000cc–5. The RLUIPA prohibits state and local governments from placing a "substantial burden" on inmates', including pretrial detainees', exercise of their religion unless the restriction furthers a compelling governmental interest and is the least restrictive means of achieving the government's objective. *Id.* § 2000cc–1. Unlike the RFRA, application of the Religious Land Use and Institutionalized Persons Act is confined to programs that receive federal funding and to those in which the burden on religious freedom or the removal of that burden affects interstate or international commerce or commerce with Native–American tribes. But since all states receive federal funding for their prisons, prisons officials need to comply with the requirements of the RLUIPA.

In *Cutter v. Wilkinson* (S.Ct.2005), the Supreme Court held that the RLUIPA does not, on its face, promote religion, in contravention of the First Amendment's Establishment Clause, by affording heightened protection to inmates' religious activities. The Court viewed the Act as a permissible way of accommodating the religious needs and interests of inmates who, because of obstacles stemming from their incarceration by the government, are handicapped in meeting those needs themselves. Inmates who, for religious reasons, believe that they must or should follow certain dietary restrictions, for example, would have difficulty adhering to those restrictions without some accommodations being made by prison officials.

CHAPTER 12

RIGHT OF ACCESS TO
THE COURTS

While the protection that the Constitution affords inmates is not as broad as the protection afforded the citizenry at large, prisoners still, as mentioned earlier, have a number of constitutional rights. These rights mean nothing, as a practical matter though, if inmates have no means of enforcing them.

The primary vehicle for enforcing inmates' constitutional rights has been civil-rights suits filed in federal or state courts, primarily under 42 U.S.C. § 1983. Prisoners have, however, sought and continue to seek access to courts for reasons other than to challenge the conditions of their confinement or their treatment while confined. They also contest the legality of their convictions through habeas corpus petitions and other postconviction complaints, and, like other individuals, they turn to the courts to resolve such civil matters as divorces and parental-rights disputes.

Since inmates, who are insulated from public view, are so dependent on the courts to enforce their rights, the question of the extent to which inmates have a right of access to the courts is an important one. It is clear from the decisions of the Supreme Court that a right of access to the courts is embedded within the Constitution. The Due Process Clauses of the Fifth and Fourteenth Amendments are one source of this right. *Procunier v. Martinez* (S.Ct.1974). In addition, the Supreme Court has said that the First Amendment right to petition the government for a redress of grievances includes the right to have access to the courts. *California Motor Transport Co. v. Trucking Unlimited* (S.Ct.1972).

It is also clear from Supreme Court decisions that the litmus test for determining whether the right of access to the courts has been violated is whether inmates have been provided with "meaningful access" to the courts. *Bounds v. Smith* (S.Ct.1977). But what exactly does that mean?

The Supreme Court has provided some definitive answers to this question, although many questions still remain. It is clear, for example, that prison officials cannot refuse to mail a prisoner's legal papers to a court because the officials believe that the papers are not in proper form. It is rather for the courts, and the courts alone, to decide whether the documents that an inmate wants to file meet procedural and substantive requirements. *Ex parte Hull* (S.Ct.1941). Preventing inmates from filing legal documents can also violate their right to the equal protection of the law, since individuals outside of prison who wish to file similar documents enjoy relatively unencumbered access to the courts. *See Cochran v. Kansas* (S.Ct.1942) (equal protection violated when prison officials prevented prisoner from filing papers needed to appeal his conviction).

The Supreme Court has also held that the constitutional rights of inmates are not violated when mail sent to them by an attorney is opened and inspected for contraband, at least when the inspection occurs in the inmate's presence. In *Wolff v. McDonnell* (S.Ct.1974), the Court noted that there was no risk of censorship under the inspection scheme in question, because inmates' mail was not read. Nor was there any risk that communications between inmates and attorneys would be chilled by the fear that prison officials might read their correspondence, because that risk was obviated by the inmate's presence.

While the Court in *Wolff* added that the prison officials might even have gone beyond the requirements of the Constitution by allowing inmates to be present when attorney-inmate mail was inspected, most of the lower courts have held that inmates must be present or be afforded the opportunity to be present during the inspection of this confidential mail. *See, e.g., Cody v. Weber* (8th Cir.2001). Furthermore, most courts have held that correctional officials cannot, at least usually, read attorney-inmate mail. *Id.* (reading attorney-inmate mail abridges right of access to the courts unless "reasonably related to a legitimate penological interest"). However, some courts have held that prison officials can "scan" legal mail to confirm that an attorney sent the mail or is its intended recipient. *See, e.g., Bell–Bey v. Williams* (6th Cir.1996). The line between unconstitutional reading of attorney-inmate mail and what, to some courts, is permissible "scanning" of that mail is not, at this point, altogether clear.

If correctional officials do read correspondence between inmates and their attorneys, they may violate not only inmates' right of access to the courts in most instances but also, in the case of inmates awaiting trial or sentencing, their Sixth Amendment right to counsel. The Supreme Court's decision in *Maine v. Moulton* (S.Ct.1985) arguably suggests that asserted security reasons for reading the attorney-inmate mail would not obviate the Sixth Amendment problem, at least usually. *Moulton* involved a defendant who had been indicted, thereby triggering his Sixth Amendment right to counsel. When the defendant met with his codefendant to plan their trial strategy, the police electronically monitored their conversation through a wire worn by the codefendant. They did so for two reasons: one, in order to protect the codefendant's safety in the event that the defendant discovered that he was working with the police; and two, to determine whether the defendant was planning to kill a witness as he had previously threatened. Despite the conceded legitimacy of the safety interests served by the monitoring of the defendant's conversation, the Supreme Court held that the government had abridged the defendant's Sixth Amendment right to have counsel serve as an intermediary between the defendant and the government once the government had committed itself to prosecute the defendant.

In *Procunier v. Martinez* (S.Ct.1974), the Supreme Court fleshed out the analysis to be undertaken when resolving inmates' right-of-access claims, although the Supreme Court subsequently modified this analytical framework in *Lewis v. Casey* (S.Ct.1996). In *Procunier*, the issue before the Court concerned the constitutionality of an across-the-board ban on interviews of inmates by law students and paralegals who were working for attorneys. The Court first cited the "substantial burden" that this ban placed on inmates' right of access to the courts. The Court observed that travelling to a prison to interview a prisoner is time-consuming and expensive for an attorney, particularly because so many prisons are located far away from urban areas. To preclude attorneys from defraying the expenses of assisting an inmate by using law students or paralegals to conduct inmate interviews would therefore discourage many attorneys from providing any legal assistance to inmates.

The Court noted though that just because inmates' right of access to the courts was substantially burdened by the regulation restricting who could interview inmates did not necessarily mean that that regulation violated the right of access to the courts. To complete the analysis, the burden that the regulation imposed on inmates had to be weighed against any "legitimate interest in penal administration" that it furthered. In other words, the burden caused by the regulation had to be weighed against the need for it. If the need for the regulation outweighed the burden that it caused, the regulation would be constitutional despite the "substantial burden" on inmates' access to the courts.

In *Procunier*, the Supreme Court concluded that the legitimate penological interest in maintaining institutional security that was invoked in the regulation's defense did not warrant the across-the-board ban on interviews of inmates by law students and paralegals working for attorneys. Noting that the ban was not limited to law students and paralegals who posed a "colorable threat" to security or to interviews of "especially dangerous" inmates, the Court concluded that the prison officials had not demonstrated that a more narrow restriction would "unduly burden" or impede their task of screening and monitoring visitors to maintain institutional security.

It is interesting to note the difference between the Court's discussion in *Procunier v. Martinez* of the significance of the existence of less drastic alternatives to right-of-access claims and its discussion of less drastic alternatives in the First Amendment context. In *Procunier*, the Court seemed to be placing the burden on prison officials of proving that there were no viable, less restrictive means of achieving the objectives of a regulation that impinged on inmates' access to the courts. By contrast, the Court in *Turner v. Safley* suggested that it was incumbent on inmates asserting First

Amendment claims to demonstrate the viability of less restrictive alternatives when it said:

> [P]rison officials do not have to set up and then shoot down every conceivable alternative method of accommodating the claimant's constitutional complaint. But if an inmate claimant can point to an alternative that fully accommodates the prisoner's rights at *de minimis* cost to valid penological interests, a court may consider that as evidence that the regulation does not satisfy the reasonable relationship standard.

The Supreme Court's decision in *Johnson v. Avery* (S.Ct.1969) is further confirmation of the fact that the Court, at least until its decision in *Lewis v. Casey* (S.Ct.1996), treated prisoners' right-of-access claims differently than their First Amendment claims. *Johnson* involved the constitutionality of a regulation that prohibited inmates from providing legal assistance to other inmates. The Supreme Court recognized that there were sound reasons for this regulation. Jailhouse lawyers, as they are popularly known, can endanger institutional security. They sometimes extract an extortionate price for their services, even demanding sexual favors from the inmates they are assisting. In addition, because of jailhouse lawyers' legal knowledge and their willingness to challenge the authority of prison officials in court, they can become power figures within a prison, exerting a disproportionate, and often negative, influence on other prisoners. The Court also noted the burden on courts caused by the complaints and other legal documents that are ineptly drafted by some jailhouse lawyers.

Nonetheless, the Supreme Court struck down the ban on jailhouse lawyers because of the burden that it placed on inmates' right of access to the courts. The Court noted that the effect of the ban was to prevent illiterate and poorly educated inmates from seeking and obtaining habeas corpus relief when they were unconstitutionally confined. The rigor with which the Court in *Johnson* applied the balancing test it had enunciated is to be contrasted with the more perfunctory balancing that has occurred in cases where the Court has applied the *Turner* test, under which the existence of more than *de minimis* costs of accommodating an inmate's constitutional rights weighs heavily against the inmate's constitutional claim.

The Supreme Court in *Johnson v. Avery* did say that prison officials can place "reasonable restrictions" on the activities of jailhouse lawyers. Prison officials can, for example, limit the times and places that jailhouse lawyers can render assistance to other inmates, and they can bar jailhouse lawyers from receiving any form of compensation for their labors.

In addition, the Court observed that prison officials can avoid the security and other types of problems caused by jailhouse lawyers and can ban them altogether if the officials provide some form of "reasonable alternative" assistance to inmates. The Court provided some clues as to what might constitute "reasonable alternative" assistance in its discussion of some legal-assistance programs that already existed in some of the states. Some of these programs used public defenders to provide legal assistance to inmates; one used senior law students for this purpose; and still another utilized lawyer volunteers to consult with the prisoners. Whatever the alternative devised, the Court made it clear that it must enable inmates to prepare their habeas corpus petitions with "reasonable adequacy."

In *Wolff v. McDonnell* (S.Ct.1974), the Supreme Court held that the right to receive assistance from a jailhouse lawyer or some "reasonable alternative" is not confined to inmates in need of assistance when preparing habeas corpus petitions. The right also extends to inmates who wish to bring civil-rights suits challenging the conditions of their confinement or their treatment while incarcerated.

One of the questions not resolved in *Johnson v. Avery* or *Wolff v. McDonnell* was whether permitting jailhouse lawyers to operate within a prison is enough to ensure that inmates' access to the courts is indeed "meaningful." Even if prison officials permit jailhouse lawyers to provide legal assistance to other inmates, there is a concern that some inmates, so many of whom are illiterate or poorly educated and some of whom cannot even speak English, will still be unable to prepare their legal documents with "reasonable adequacy." Some jailhouse lawyers may, for example, be incompetent, and even those who are competent may refuse to help some inmates who need assistance.

The right to assistance discussed in *Johnson v. Avery* and *Wolff v. McDonnell* clearly does not mean that inmates generally have a constitutional right to the assistance of an attorney when litigating a civil-rights claim or even when seeking habeas corpus relief. In *Pennsylvania v. Finley* (S.Ct.1987), the Supreme Court specifically rejected the claim that an indigent inmate challenging the validity of a conviction in a state postconviction proceeding has the right to the assistance of an appointed attorney. And in *Murray v. Giarratano* (S.Ct.1989), the Court went even further, rejecting the claim that an inmate facing the death penalty has the right to such assistance.

In *Murray*, however, Justice Kennedy, who wrote the concurring opinion that provided the fifth vote needed to reject the prisoner's claim, emphasized the special circumstances of the case before the Court. Justice Kennedy noted, for example, that there was no evidence that any inmate on death row in the state in question had actually been unable to find a lawyer willing to assist the inmate in a postconviction proceeding. In addition, while the state did not hire attorneys to represent inmates in the postconviction proceedings, attorneys were assigned to the prisons to assist inmates on death row in drafting their postconviction petitions. The possibility remains then that the Court might find, in a case with different facts, that an indigent inmate on whom the death penalty has been imposed has a constitutional right to the assistance of an attorney when challenging the validity of his or her conviction in a postconviction proceeding.

While inmates do not, at least generally, have the constitutional right to the assistance of counsel when litigating civil-rights claims or claims raised in postconviction proceedings, they may, by statute, be accorded such a right. For example, as is discussed more fully in Chapter 18, federal courts have the discretion under 28 U.S.C. § 1915(e)(1) to appoint counsel to represent indigent inmates who have filed a civil-rights suit.

If jurisdictions do choose to appoint attorneys to assist inmates in litigating civil-rights and habeas corpus actions, they clearly will have satisfied, and even exceeded, the constitutional requirements stemming from the right of access to the courts that were described by the Supreme Court in *Bounds v. Smith* (S.Ct.1977) and *Lewis v. Casey* (S.Ct.1996). In *Bounds*, the Court held that inmates either must be afforded access to "adequate" law libraries or be provided with "adequate" assistance from persons "trained in the law." The Court stated that without such access or assistance, the opportunity of inmates to litigate their constitutional claims would not be, as the Constitution requires, "reasonably adequate." Inmates often would not know such basics, for example, as where their lawsuits should be filed, against whom their lawsuits can and should be brought, and the information that should be included in their complaints to state an actionable claim.

The Court in *Bounds* did not define what constitutes an "adequate" law library, but it is clear that the failure of a library to stock the books needed for inmates to meaningfully pursue their constitutional claims in court may lead to a violation of the constitutional right to have "meaningful" access to the courts. *See, e.g., Gilmore v. Lynch* (N.D.Cal. 1970) (absence of U.S. Supreme Court Reports, other federal reporters, the United States Code, annotated copies of the state's code, many local federal district rules, and *U.S. Law Week* from prison law library violates right of access to the courts). Placing undue limits on the time that inmates can spend in the law library to do their legal research may also result in a violation of their constitutional right of access to the courts. *See, e.g., Ramos v. Lamm* (10th Cir.1980) (striking down regulation that resulted in inmates having access to the law library only three hours every thirteen weeks).

To prevail on a right-of-access claim, however, a prisoner must show something more than that a prison law library is not stocked with the right books or that access to the law library has been substantially impeded by prison officials. In *Lewis v. Casey*, the Supreme Court held that a prisoner also must prove that he or she suffered some "actual injury" because of deficiencies in a prison law library or the legal assistance with which the inmate was provided. A prisoner might, for example, show that he or she was unable to even file a complaint because a law library was so inadequate.

Or, according to the Court, a prisoner might show that a complaint was dismissed for failure to meet a "technical requirement" of which the prisoner was unaware because of deficiencies in the system through which prisoners are afforded legal assistance.

While inadequacies in a prison's law library will not necessarily give rise to a constitutional violation, providing inmates with sufficient access to even a well-stocked law library will not necessarily satisfy constitutional requirements. In *Lewis v. Casey*, the Supreme Court backtracked from its statement in *Bounds* that seemed to suggest that correctional officials could satisfy their constitutional obligations by providing inmates with physical access to an "adequate" law library. In *Lewis*, the Court observed that prisoners have the right to a "reasonably adequate opportunity to file nonfrivolous legal claims challenging their convictions or conditions of confinement." The Court underscored that simply allowing illiterate or non-English-speaking inmates to turn pages in a law library does not mean that they have been afforded this opportunity.

While the Supreme Court made it clear in *Lewis* that providing access to a law library will not protect all inmates' right of access to the courts, the Court did not prescribe any particular program or procedures that correctional officials should adopt to ensure that the right is protected. Instead, the Court emphasized that it had in *Bounds* encouraged "local experimentation" as correctional officials devise ways to protect prisoners' constitutional right of access to the courts. In a potentially telling comment, however, the Court noted that one possible experiment "might replace libraries with some minimal access to legal advice and a system of court-provided forms ... forms that asked the inmates to provide only the facts and not to attempt any legal analysis."

In one sense, the Supreme Court in *Lewis* more expansively interpreted the scope of the right of access to the courts than it had been interpreted previously. Correctional officials cannot, as many had thought, satisfy their constitutional obligations by simply installing a law library in a prison. Instead, they must do something more or different to ensure that those inmates who cannot utilize a law library effectively have a "reasonably adequate opportunity" to present certain nonfrivolous claims to a court.

In other ways though, the Supreme Court more narrowly construed the scope of the right of access to the courts compared to the way in which many correctional officials (and courts) had previously understood the scope of that right. The Court identified two significant limitations on the scope of the right of access. First, the Court noted that the constitutional right is confined to what is needed to give a prisoner the capability to present a grievance to a court. The Court said that correctional officials need not do anything, at least as far as the Constitution is concerned, to help inmates "discover grievances" or "litigate effectively" once they are in court.

Second, the Supreme Court observed that the Constitution does not require correctional officials to take steps to facilitate the bringing of all types of legal claims by prisoners. The Court stated: "*Bounds* does not guarantee inmates the wherewithal to transform themselves into litigating engines capable of filing everything from shareholder derivative actions to slip-and-fall claims." Instead, according to the Court, the affirmative assistance that must be provided to prisoners as part of the right of access to the courts is confined to what is needed for them to challenge their convictions or sentences, whether directly on appeal or collaterally, and to challenge the conditions of their confinement.

Lewis v. Casey is also significant because the Supreme Court in that case announced that the *Turner* test should be applied to prisoners' claims alleging infringements of their constitutional right of access to the courts. In upholding restrictions on segregated inmates' access to law libraries that resulted in lengthy delays in their receipt of legal materials and assistance, the Court held that the restrictions need only be "reasonably related to legitimate penological interests" to pass constitutional muster. If this test is met, restrictions that impede access to the courts are constitutional, even if they result in an "actual injury" to prisoners who want to file lawsuits.

In *Shaw v. Murphy* (S.Ct.2001), the Supreme Court once again confronted questions regarding the applicability of the *Turner* test. The plaintiff in that case was a prisoner who was disciplined by prison officials after he sent a letter to a fellow inmate counseling him not to plead guilty to a charge of assaulting a correctional officer. The plaintiff contended that the imposition of these disciplinary sanctions impinged on his First Amendment right to correspond with other inmates about legal matters. The plaintiff furthermore argued that in addressing the merits of this claim, a test more rigorous than the *Turner* test should be applied.

The Supreme Court refused, however, to vary the protection afforded prisoners' correspondence based on its content. The Court noted that legal correspondence, like other correspondence, can be used by prisoners to distribute contraband and instructions for making drugs and weapons to other prisoners. The Court also evinced a concern that legal correspondence could be used as a subterfuge to disseminate "clearly inappropriate comments" throughout a prison. The Court therefore concluded that courts should apply the *Turner* test when determining the constitutionality of restrictions on legal correspondence between prisoners.

When inmates exercise their right of access to the courts and file lawsuits against correctional officials, some correctional officials respond by retaliating against the inmates. This retaliation can come in a variety of forms, including transferring the inmates to other prisons or parts of the same prison with worse conditions of confinement, firing the inmates from their prison jobs, and taking other steps to generally make the inmates' lives more miserable. Such retaliation for pursuing litigation is itself an abridgment of the right of access to the courts for which the inmate can seek redress in a civil-rights suit. *See, e.g., Gomez v. Vernon* (9th Cir.2001). Retaliation against an inmate for filing an administrative grievance against a correctional official also violates this constitutional right, because a federal statute, 42 U.S.C. § 1977e(a), requires prisoners to exhaust their administrative remedies before filing a federal claim contesting the legality of the conditions of their confinement. *De-Walt v. Carter* (7th Cir.2000).

To prevail on a retaliation claim, a prisoner must prove that he or she engaged in activities protected by the Constitution or a statute; that the defendant took an adverse action against the plaintiff that would dissuade a person of "ordinary firmness" from engaging in the protected activity; and that the adverse action was motivated, at least in part, by the protected conduct. *Smith v. Campbell* (6th Cir.2001). Some courts have held that once the prisoner proves that protected conduct precipitated the retaliatory response, the burden shifts to the defendant to prove that the action that had an adverse impact on the prisoner would have been taken even if the prisoner had not engaged in the protected activity. *See Rauser v. Horn* (3d Cir.2001). Other courts have placed the burden on the prisoner of proving that the adverse action would not have occurred in the absence of the retaliatory animus. *See, e.g., Peterson v. Shanks* (10th Cir.1998).

CHAPTER 13

PRISON DISCIPLINARY PROCEEDINGS

A. PROCEDURAL DUE PROCESS

Both prison officials and inmates have a critical stake in the proper functioning of the disciplinary process in a prison. For prison officials, what is at stake is their ability to maintain order in a prison by disciplining inmates who violate prison rules. For inmates, what is at stake in a disciplinary proceeding will depend on the nature of an inmate's alleged misconduct and the penalties authorized for such misconduct. Often, inmates face the prospect of losing good-time credits if they are found guilty of violating prison rules, which means that the length of time that they will be incarcerated will be prolonged. Alternatively or in addition, inmates may be placed in segregation for their disciplinary infractions, where they will have to remain in their cells almost all of the time and will lose many of the privileges afforded inmates in the general-population unit of the prison. For less serious violations of prison rules, prisoners may remain in the general-population unit but lose one or more privileges, such as television or commissary privileges, for a defined period of time.

Because of the sanctions that may ensue from a finding of guilt of disciplinary misconduct, inmates obviously have an interest in ensuring that they are only punished for a disciplinary violation of which they are actually guilty. The Supreme Court has held that in some disciplinary proceedings, though not all, this interest triggers constitutional protections. In *Wolff v. McDonnell* (S.Ct.1974), the Court held that when an inmate may lose good-time credits if found guilty of violating prison rules, due process requires that certain procedural safeguards attend the disciplinary process in order to protect the inmate from being arbitrarily deprived of those credits. On the other hand, in *Sandin v. Conner* (S.Ct.1995), the Court held that confinement in a prison's disciplinary segregation unit for thirty days did not deprive a prisoner of the liberty that gives rise to the protections of due process. *Sandin* and the approach taken by the Supreme Court in identifying liberty interests protected by the Due Process Clause are discussed in the next chapter.

In *Wolff*, the Court outlined five procedural safeguards to which inmates are constitutionally entitled during disciplinary proceedings that may result in a loss of good-time credits. First, the inmates must receive written notice at least twenty-four hours before their disciplinary hearings of the infractions with which they have been charged. The purpose of this notice is to both make sure that the inmates are aware of the actual charges confronting them and to enable them to collect evidence and otherwise prepare their defense.

Second, inmates have the right to call witnesses to testify at their disciplinary hearings and the right to present documentary evidence at the hearings, except when the exercise of those rights would be "unduly hazardous to institutional safety or correctional goals." The Court gave some examples of when it would be permissible to restrict inmates' general right to call witnesses at disciplinary hearings—when the witness's testimony would be irrelevant, when the witness's testimony would be unnecessary, and when calling the witness would create a risk of retaliation against the witness or "undermine authority." The Court did not fully flesh out the contours of some of these exceptions, failing to explain, for example, when calling a witness might "undermine authority" or be unnecessary. But Justice Marshall, in his opinion partially concurring in, and partially dissenting from, the majority's opinion, provided an example of when a witness's testimony would be unnecessary, noting that a disciplinary decisionmaker is not required to hear the duplicative testimony of numerous witnesses.

While the Supreme Court in *Wolff* held that inmates have a general right to call witnesses at disciplinary hearings, the Court at the same time said that a disciplinary decisionmaker need not explain at a disciplinary hearing why a request to call a witness was denied. In the subsequent case of *Ponte v. Real* (S.Ct.1985), however, the Court held that if such a contemporaneous explanation is not provided and an inmate later brings suit challenging the denial of a request to call a witness, due process requires that the reason or reasons for the denial be tendered in a "limited manner" to the court. The Court added that when disclosure of the reasons in open court might cause security problems, the reasons can be presented to the court *in camera*.

The third right to which inmates are entitled during disciplinary hearings is the right to assistance in preparing and presenting a defense to a disciplinary charge. This right to assistance is a limited one. In *Wolff*, the Supreme Court said that illiterate inmates are entitled to assistance as are inmates facing disciplinary charges raising issues whose complexity makes it unlikely that the inmates can adequately mount a defense. The Court did not purport to enunciate an all-inclusive list of the instances when an inmate might have a constitutional right to assistance at a disciplinary hearing. Inmates with certain kinds of debilitating mental illnesses and inmates who do not speak English would, for example, seem to be in similar need of such assistance.

While some inmates have the right to assistance during disciplinary proceedings, that right does not include the right to the assistance of an attorney. The Court in *Wolff* observed that injecting attorneys into the disciplinary process would make the process adversarial in nature, contrary to its rehabilitative objectives. The Court also underscored the delay that would ensue if attorneys were involved in disciplinary proceedings as well as the cost of providing counsel to inmates charged with disciplinary infractions. The Court therefore held that the right to assistance means only that an inmate be permitted to obtain the assistance of another inmate or, alternatively, be provided with "adequate substitute aid" from a staff member or a "sufficiently competent" inmate selected by the correctional officials.

The fourth procedural right identified in *Wolff* is the right of inmates found guilty of a disciplinary violation to receive a written statement recounting the evidence relied on by the disciplinary decisionmaker and the reasons for the disciplinary action taken. This procedural safeguard is designed to serve multiple purposes—to protect an inmate from adverse "collateral consequences," such as the denial of parole or transfer to a prison with a higher security level, that might follow from a misunderstanding of the import of the guilty finding; to enable an inmate to challenge, in court or elsewhere, what occurred in a disciplinary proceeding when there are grounds for such a challenge; and to induce disciplinary decisionmakers to render their decisions with care by reminding them that their actions may be reviewed by others. The Supreme Court recognized that sometimes, for security reasons, the disciplinary decisionmaker might appropriately omit reference to a particular piece of evidence upon which the disciplinary decision was founded, such as the identity of a confidential informant. The Court stated that the fact of this omission must then be denoted in the written statement.

The final right outlined in *Wolff*, though somewhat sketchily, is the right to have a "sufficiently impartial" decisionmaker adjudicate a disciplinary charge. While the Court did not say much about this right, it is clear that the fellow employees of a correctional official who has brought a disciplinary charge against an inmate can adjudicate that charge without necessarily impinging upon the inmate's due-process rights. In *Wolff* itself, the disciplinary committee whose composition survived the Court's constitutional scrutiny was comprised of an associate warden, the director of the reception center through which incoming prisoners are processed, and the director of the prison industries program. While one might expect that correctional officials might feel some pressure to give credence to the allegations of coworkers over the conflicting statements of an inmate, the Court observed that the record before it did not reveal that this disciplinary committee posed a sufficient risk of "arbitrary decisionmaking" to give rise to due-process concerns. Even Justice Marshall, who dissented from other portions of the Court's opinion, saw no inherent constitutional problem in having correctional officials employed at the facility where a disciplinary charge was filed adjudicate the charge. He noted, however, that a violation of due process would occur if any of these officials had investigated or prosecuted the charge or had some other "personal involvement" in the case.

One of the rights that due process does not accord inmates during disciplinary proceedings, according to the Supreme Court, is the right to confront and cross-examine adverse witnesses. The primary impetus for this conclusion was the Court's concern that the tension that ensues when an inmate confronts and cross-examines an adverse witness might culminate in violence in the volatile confines of a prison. Over the long run, this threat of violence would impede the functioning of the disciplinary process by dissuading witnesses from bringing disciplinary charges or testifying about the misconduct of inmates against whom disciplinary charges have been filed. The Court also noted that extending the right of confrontation and cross-examination to inmates during disciplinary proceedings would prolong those proceedings in a way that the Court believed might interfere with the rehabilitative effects of swiftly disciplining inmates for their misconduct.

Justice Marshall sharply disagreed with this conclusion of the Court, noting that greater procedural fairness during a disciplinary proceeding would enhance, rather than detract from, the proceeding's rehabilitative aims. Justice Marshall emphasized the value of cross-examination in uncovering a witness's bias or malice, mistakes about identity, and memory and perception problems, all of which diminish the weight to be given a witness's testimony. While Justice Marshall acknowledged that sometimes, for security reasons, the right of confrontation and cross-examination would have to be curtailed, he accused the majority of letting "the tail ... wag the constitutional dog" by condoning across-the-board restrictions on what he believed to be a constitutional right. Even when it would be constitutionally permissible to prohibit an inmate from personally confronting and cross-examining an adverse witness, Justice Marshall asserted that due process requires the disciplinary decisionmaker to question the witness *in camera* to assess the credibility of the witness.

The Court in *Wolff* took pains to emphasize that its decision was not "graven in stone." The Court seemed to be suggesting that it might be willing at some point in the future to revisit such questions as the extent to which, if at all, inmates have a right to confront and cross-examine adverse witnesses.

There was also no suggestion in the Court's opinion that the list of procedural rights that it was enunciating was all-inclusive. In fact, in the later case of *Superintendent, Massachusetts Correctional Institution at Walpole v. Hill* (S.Ct.1985), the Court identified another right that inmates have during disciplinary proceedings, although it is one that affords inmates just a modicum of protection. In that case, the Court held that the decision to revoke an inmate's good-time credits must be supported by "some evidence" in the record that the prisoner violated prison rules, a standard of proof that is considerably lower than a preponderance of the evidence.

Sometimes confidential information that points to an inmate's culpability of a disciplinary infraction may be relayed to a correctional official and, in turn, the disciplinary decisionmaker. Most courts have held that to comply with the requirements of due process, the disciplinary decisionmaker must take steps to verify that the confidential informant's tip is reliable—in other words, truthful—in order for the tip to support a guilty finding. *Broussard v. Johnson* (5th Cir.2001). The disciplinary committee or hearing officer cannot simply rely on a correctional officer's or investigator's assertion that the information relayed by the confidential informant is reliable.

The question that remains after *Wolff* and *Hill* is the extent to which inmates have other procedural rights during prison disciplinary proceedings. Several lower courts have held that inmates have the right to be apprised of the rules for whose violation they may be disciplined. *See, e.g., Reeves v. Pettcox* (5th Cir.1994). Examples of some other procedural safeguards to which inmates may or may not be entitled as a matter of due process include: the right to be apprised of the procedural safeguards, such as the limited right to assistance, to which the inmate is entitled during the disciplinary process (*cf. Vitek v. Jones* (S.Ct.1980) (inmates facing possible transfer to a mental hospital must be apprised of the rights they have during the transfer proceedings)); the right to have disciplinary reports submitted under oath; the right to a reasonably prompt disciplinary hearing; and the right to have exculpatory evidence considered by the disciplinary decisionmaker. *Whitford v. Boglino* (7th Cir.1995). Even if certain procedural safeguards are not encompassed by due process, statutes and correctional regulations may accord inmates rights that go beyond the constitutional minima. *See, e.g.*, Mich. Comp. Laws § 791.251(6) (hearing officer must be an attorney); 28 C.F.R. § 541.15(i) (all inmates have the right to receive assistance from a staff member during disciplinary hearings).

B.   *MIRANDA* AND THE PRIVILEGE AGAINST SELF–INCRIMINATION IN THE CORRECTIONAL CONTEXT

In *Miranda v. Arizona* (S.Ct.1966), the Supreme Court held that for statements obtained from a person subjected to custodial interrogation to be admissible in a criminal prosecution, the custodial interrogation must have been preceded by the giving of what are known as the *Miranda* warnings and the obtaining of a valid waiver of the rights to which the warnings refer, such as the right to remain silent. Two general questions arise concerning the applicability of *Miranda* in the prison context. First, must inmates questioned by correctional or other governmental officials first be given *Miranda* warnings in order for any statements that they make to be admissible in a disciplinary hearing? And second, must inmates, since they are always, in a literal sense, in custody, be given *Miranda* warnings in order for any statements that they make in response to questioning to be admissible in a criminal prosecution?

The Supreme Court has provided a clear answer to the first question, holding that *Miranda* does not apply to prison disciplinary proceedings. *Baxter v. Palmigiano* (S.Ct.1976). In other words, statements obtained without first apprising inmates of their rights under *Miranda* are admissible in a prison disciplinary proceeding.

The answer to the second question is not, at this point, altogether clear. In *Mathis v. United States* (S.Ct.1968), the Supreme Court held that an inmate incarcerated for a state crime should have been given *Miranda* warnings before being questioned by an IRS agent about a suspected federal tax crime. Because he was not, the Court held that his incriminating statements should not have been admitted at his trial.

On the other hand, in *Illinois v. Perkins* (S.Ct. 1990), the Supreme Court held that a defendant's *Miranda* rights were not violated when he was questioned about a murder by an undercover police officer with whom he was incarcerated in the same jail cell while awaiting trial for another crime. The Court observed that since the defendant was unaware that his cellmate was an undercover officer, he was not subjected to the kind of overbearing pressures, with which *Miranda* was concerned, that threaten a person's Fifth Amendment privilege against self-incrimination.

Perkins is significant because it tells us that there will be times when *Miranda* does not apply even though, in a technical sense, a person is both in custody and subjected to interrogation. The intriguing question that remains after *Perkins* is whether correctional officials who wish to question an inmate about suspected misconduct that constitutes both a disciplinary infraction and a crime must first give the inmate *Miranda* warnings in order for any statements of the inmate to be admissible in a subsequent criminal prosecution. Some lower courts have held that *Miranda* does not apply in this context unless the inmate is subject to constraints on his or her freedom above and beyond those that normally attend day-to-day confinement. *See, e.g., Garcia v. Singletary* (11th Cir.1994). The Supreme Court in *Perkins* added fuel to the speculation that statements made without the giving of *Miranda* warnings during some or all of the steps of the prison disciplinary process might still be admissible in a criminal prosecution when the Court volunteered that "[t]he bare fact of custody may not in every instance require a warning even when the suspect is aware that he is speaking to an official."

While inmates have no right to be given *Miranda* warnings at a disciplinary hearing in order for their incriminating statements to be considered as evidence of guilt by the disciplinary decisionmaker and while they may or may not have such a right in order for their statements to be admissible in a subsequent criminal prosecution, they can still invoke their privilege against self-incrimination during a disciplinary hearing. In *Baxter v. Palmigiano* (S.Ct.1976), however, the Supreme Court held that a disciplinary decisionmaker can draw an adverse inference against an inmate who invokes that privilege. In other words, the inmate's silence can constitutionally be treated as evidence of his or her guilt of the disciplinary infraction. At the same time, the Court emphasized that under the state disciplinary procedures whose constitutionality the Court was upholding, a guilty finding could not be based solely on an inmate's silence.

The effect of *Baxter* is that it may put some inmates in a damned-if-you-do, damned-if-you-don't situation. If the inmates do not speak during their disciplinary hearings to refute the charges against them, their silence may provide the final quantum of evidence needed to support a finding of guilt. On the other hand, if they testify during the hearings, they may make incriminating statements that will lead the disciplinary decisionmaker to find them guilty of misconduct and that, in addition, may later be used against them in a criminal prosecution.

CHAPTER 14

TRANSFERS, CLASSIFICATION, AND DISPARITY IN PROGRAMMING OPPORTUNITIES

A. PROCEDURAL DUE PROCESS

In addition to the steps taken to discipline inmates found guilty of violating prison rules or regulations, prison officials make decisions on a daily basis that have adverse, and sometimes substantially adverse, effects on prisoners. Prison officials often, for example, transfer prisoners to prisons where they have fewer privileges and the conditions of confinement are much worse. Other transfers occur within the confines of the prison itself—from, for example, a general-population unit to an administrative-segregation unit where privileges are sparse and inmates' freedom of movement is curtailed substantially. Prisoners also often lose prison jobs and other privileges for a variety of reasons, including the concern that an inmate will in the future abuse the privilege in question.

The question that arises is whether prison officials must take any steps to ensure that the actions they take against an individual inmate are well-founded—that they are not based on misinformation or personal animosity towards the inmate. The question, in short, is whether due process requires the emplacement of certain procedural safeguards in the decisionmaking processes to avoid unfounded decisions that can have such negative effects on prisoners.

1. Liberty Interests

In order for a prisoner, like any other individual, to be entitled to the protections of due process, the prisoner must be deprived of an interest falling within the scope of the Due Process Clause—life, liberty, or property. Much litigation has focused on the question of what constitutes "liberty," the deprivation of which triggers due-process protections. According to the Supreme Court, there are two kinds of liberty interests—those that stem from the Constitution itself and those that are created by state law. In a series of cases, the Court has attempted to flesh out when either type of liberty interest exists in the prison context.

In *Meachum v. Fano* (S.Ct.1976), the Supreme Court held that the transfer of a prisoner from one prison to another does not implicate a constitutionally-derived liberty interest. The Court explained that when convicted of a crime through a process that is replete with due-process protections, people lose their liberty to the extent that they can be confined or transferred to any prison that correctional officials deem most suitable. The Court noted that confinement in any prison is "within the normal limits or range of custody which the conviction has authorized the State to impose." It does not matter that a prisoner is being transferred to a prison with substantially more onerous conditions of confinement or is being transferred because the prisoner violated prison rules. *Montanye v. Haymes* (S.Ct.1976). Even the transfer of a prisoner out of state, to a prison thousands of miles from his or her family, does not deprive the prisoner of a constitutionally-derived liberty interest. *Olim v. Wakinekona* (S.Ct.1983) (prisoner transferred from Hawaii to a prison in California 2500 miles away).

The same rationale underlying the Supreme Court's conclusion in *Meachum* that interprison transfers do not deprive prisoners of any constitutionally-derived liberty interest led the Court to conclude in *Hewitt v. Helms* (S.Ct.1983) that inmates are not deprived of any liberty that stems from the Constitution itself when they are transferred from the general-population unit of a prison to the administrative-segregation unit. The Court observed that the transfer of an inmate from one part of a prison to another with less palatable conditions is "well within the terms of confinement ordinarily contemplated by a prison sentence" and that prisoners should "reasonably anticipate" undergoing such a transfer sometime during the period of their incarceration.

Meachum v. Fano and *Hewitt v. Helms* are to be contrasted with the Supreme Court's decision in *Vitek v. Jones* (S.Ct.1980). In *Vitek*, the Court considered whether an inmate transferred from a prison to a mental hospital had been deprived of liberty without due process of law. In addressing the threshold question whether such a transfer deprives a prisoner of liberty within the meaning of the Due Process Clause, the Court once again applied the "within-the-sentence test." This time, however, the Court concluded that confinement in a mental hospital is not within the range of conditions implicitly authorized by a conviction. The Court cited two reasons for this conclusion—one, the stigma that attends confinement in a mental hospital, and two, the behavioral-modification programs that an inmate may be forced to participate in while confined in a mental hospital.

The within-the-sentence test applied by the Supreme Court when determining whether a prisoner has been deprived of a constitutionally-derived liberty interest has been criticized by some members of the Court as knowing "few rivals for vagueness and pliability." *See, e.g., Kentucky Dep't of Corrections v. Thompson* (S.Ct.1989) (Marshall, J., dissenting). The way in which the Court has said states can create liberty interests has also engendered controversy and debate, both within and outside the Court.

Over the years, the Supreme Court has substantially modified the test to be applied when determining whether a state has created a liberty interest protected by due process. Several cases illustrate the way in which the Court used to approach this subject in the prison context.

In *Meachum v. Fano*, the Court held that prisoners who were transferred from one prison to another were not deprived of any state-created liberty interest, since a state statute left the decision whether to transfer a prisoner within the unconfined discretion of correctional officials. By contrast, the transfer of the prisoner from the general-population unit to the administrative-segregation unit that was at issue in *Hewitt v. Helms* did deprive the prisoner of a state-created liberty interest, according to the Supreme Court, because of the limits placed by state law on the discretion of prison officials when ordering such transfers. A state statute authorized such transfers only in certain delineated situations, such as when an inmate's continued presence in the general-population unit posed a serious threat of harm to the inmate or others. Similarly, the prisoner who brought suit in *Vitek v. Jones* was deprived of a state-created liberty interest when he was transferred from a prison to a mental hospital, because a state statute made such a transfer contingent on a finding that the prisoner was suffering from a mental disease or defect that could not adequately be treated in the prison.

In *Kentucky Dep't of Corrections v. Thompson* (S.Ct.1989), the Supreme Court clarified that it requires more than what it called "substantive predicates" governing the exercise of official discretion for state statutes or regulations to create a liberty interest. The Court noted that at least the most common means of creating a liberty interest required not only substantive criteria that limit officials' discretion when making a decision that has negative repercussions on an inmate, but also a mandated result, such as a transfer, when those criteria are met.

The Court in *Thompson* held that the plaintiffs, inmates who had lost the privilege of visiting with certain friends and family members whom prison officials thought had abused their visiting privileges, had not been deprived of any state-created liberty interest. One of the points emphasized by the Court was that while the pertinent prison regulations spelled out reasons why visiting privileges might be curtailed, the list did not purport to be all-inclusive. Visitors might be excluded, according to the regulations, for reasons not set forth on the list. The Court concluded that prisoners could not, therefore, "reasonably form an objective expectation" that they would be allowed a visit unless one of the restrictions specified in the regulations applied. The kind of mandated outcome that the Court said was needed to create a liberty interest through state law was consequently absent.

Some of the Justices on the Supreme Court belittled the Court's majority for making the existence of a liberty interest, which triggers the important protections of due process, hinge on the presence or absence of a few words in a state statute or regulation. Justice Stevens, for example, pointed out that predicating the applicability of due-process safeguards on the language that happens to be inserted in a state statute or regulation gives individuals only ephemeral constitutional protection, because the liberty that the government grants today can summarily be taken away tomorrow by changing the language of a statute or regulation. *Hewitt v. Helms* (S.Ct.1983) (Stevens, J., dissenting). Finding that states have created liberty interests when they constrain official discretion through "substantive predicates" and mandated outcomes might also discourage states from making laudable attempts to control the exercise of governmental officials' discretion. The end result might be more arbitrary decisionmaking, a result that seems palpably at odds with one of the very core purposes of the Due Process Clause. See *Wolff v. McDonnell* (S.Ct.1974) ("The touchstone of due process is protection of the individual against arbitrary action of government.").

These and other concerns led the Supreme Court in *Sandin v. Conner* (S.Ct.1995) to reexamine its approach to state-created liberty interests. The plaintiff in *Sandin* was a prisoner serving a sentence of thirty years to life for a number of crimes, including murder. In his § 1983 lawsuit, the plaintiff contended that he was deprived of his right to due process during a disciplinary proceeding that resulted in his confinement in a disciplinary-segregation unit for thirty days. Specifically, he claimed that the disciplinary committee unconstitutionally refused to hear the testimony of witnesses who would have exonerated him.

In resolving the threshold question whether the plaintiff had been deprived of a state-created liberty interest, the Court announced that it was abandoning the "mechanical" test applied in earlier cases in which the existence of a liberty interest was contingent on a finding of the requisite "substantive predicates" and mandatory language in a state law or regulations. Instead, the litmus test for a state-created liberty interest was whether a restriction "imposes atypical and significant hardship on the inmate in relation to the ordinary incidents of prison life."

The Court then applied this test to the facts of the case before it and concluded that it was not met by the plaintiff's thirty-day confinement in disciplinary segregation. The Court first emphasized that the conditions in the disciplinary-segregation unit were very similar to those in the prison's administrative-segregation and protective-custody units, parts of the prison where prison officials had the discretion to place any prisoner. The Court also underscored that the plaintiff had succeeded, after his release from segregation, in getting the guilty finding expunged from his prison record. Finally, the Court noted that the prisoner's release from prison would not "inevitably" be delayed because of what had transpired during the disciplinary process.

The Court was closely divided in *Sandin*, with four Justices dissenting. Justice Ginsburg, joined by Justice Stevens in dissent, felt that disciplinary confinement in segregation has such a substantial impact on the conditions of a prisoner's confinement that it gives rise to a liberty interest that stems, not from state law, but from the Due Process Clause itself. Justice Ginsburg also criticized the majority for creating a nebulous category of liberty interests emanating from deprivations significant enough to create a liberty interest via state law, but not significant enough to create a liberty interest directly under the Constitution.

In a separate dissenting opinion, Justice Breyer, joined by Justice Souter, also concluded that the plaintiff's disciplinary confinement effected a deprivation of a constitutionally-derived liberty interest. Justice Breyer emphasized that prisoners confined in the disciplinary-segregation unit where the plaintiff had been confined are released from their cells only fifty minutes a day while prisoners in the general population are out of their cells eight hours a day.

Justice Breyer also concluded that the plaintiff had been deprived of a state-created liberty interest. Justice Breyer urged the Court not to completely abandon the "discretion-cabining" test for state-created liberty interests. While Justice Breyer agreed that this test need not be applied to relatively trivial deprivations, such as restrictions on television privileges, he believed that looking to see whether, and how, officials' discretionary power has been limited by a state can assist courts in determining whether a deprivation is "atypical" and significant enough to give rise to due-process protection.

The Supreme Court's decision in *Sandin* does not necessarily mean that a prisoner's confinement in a disciplinary-segregation unit will never implicate due process. The possibility remains open after *Sandin* that disciplinary confinement for much longer periods of time than thirty days or in conditions much different than those experienced by other prisoners in a prison triggers the protections of due process. *See, e.g., Colon v. Howard* (2d Cir.2000) (confinement for 305 days in disciplinary segregation deprived prisoner of a liberty interest). In addition, the significance of the expungement of the guilty finding from the plaintiff's institutional records to the Court's finding in *Sandin* that he had not been deprived of a state-created liberty interest is still not entirely clear.

The conditions to which the prisoners who filed suit in *Wilkinson v. Austin* (S.Ct.2005) were subject exemplify the kind of "atypical and significant hardship" compared to the "ordinary incidents of prison life" that will give rise to a state-created liberty interest. The prisoners contended that their placements in a supermaximum-security prison in Ohio were not effectuated in accordance with due process. Prisoners incarcerated at the supermax prison were confined in their cells twenty-three hours a day. They could leave their cells one hour each day to exercise, but the recreation cells were small and indoors. The light in each inmate's cell was always on, and inmates who tried to cover up the light so they could sleep were disciplined. The isolation of the inmates from other human beings was, in the words of the Supreme Court, "extreme." Unlike the conditions in any other prison in the state, including the segregation units, the cells in the supermax prison had solid metal doors, which prevented inmates from conversing or communicating with other inmates. In addition, prisoners were fed in their cells.

The Supreme Court's conclusion that the assignment of inmates to the supermax prison inflicted an "atypical and significant hardship" on them, depriving them of a state-created liberty interest, did not rest alone on the fact that the prisoners incarcerated there had virtually no human contact or exposure to any other "environmental or sensory stimuli." The Court noted two other potentially distinguishing features of the supermax confinement. First, confinement in the supermax facility was indefinite, although prison officials periodically assessed whether that confinement should continue. Prisoners assigned to the supermaximum-security prison therefore might remain there for years and perhaps for the rest of their lives. Second, while confined in the supermax prison, inmates were ineligible for parole.

Most courts have held that pretrial detainees, unlike at least most prisoners, are entitled to the protections of due process before being transferred to disciplinary segregation. *See Benjamin v. Fraser* (2d Cir.2001) (listing cases). The courts have reasoned that since pretrial detainees have not been sentenced for a crime, their confinement in disciplinary segregation cannot be an implicit term of a sentence that has never been, and may never be, imposed.

2. Procedural Safeguards

Once it has been determined that an action contemplated by prison officials, if taken, would deprive a prisoner of a liberty interest falling within the scope of the protection of due process, the next question to be addressed concerns the procedural safeguards that must be incorporated into the process attending the deprivation. In *Hewitt v. Helms* (S.Ct.1983), the Supreme Court's answer to the question of what "process" is "due" an inmate deprived of a liberty interest through a transfer from general population to administrative segregation was, "Not much." Assuming that, after *Sandin v. Conner,* a transfer to administrative segregation can, in some circumstances, still effect a deprivation of liberty within the meaning of the Due Process Clause, the inmate subject to transfer first must be afforded "some notice" of the reason for the transfer. The Court in *Hewitt* did not say, however, that this notice must be in writing.

Second, the inmate must be given the chance to communicate his or her views about the transfer to the person who will decide whether the inmate's confinement in administrative segregation is warranted. But in most instances, an inmate has no right to appear in person to explain why the confinement in administrative segregation is unjustified or not needed. The Court said that "ordinarily," permitting the inmate to submit a written statement will suffice.

Third, the inmate has the right to have the transfer decision and the evidence upon which it was founded reviewed by a prison official within a "reasonable time" after the transfer. This informal review does not have to occur during a hearing because, as mentioned earlier, an inmate generally has no right to be present when the transfer decision is being reviewed.

Finally, if the inmate remains confined in the administrative-segregation unit, prison officials periodically must assess the need for continued confinement. According to the Supreme Court, an inmate does not "necessarily" have the right to submit any evidence or even a written statement to be considered during this periodic-review process. The Court explained that, in its opinion, any facts about the prisoner needed to make the decision whether to keep the prisoner in the administrative-segregation unit will already have been obtained during the initial review process. In addition, the retention decision will often be based on predictions about the future behavior of the prisoner and other inmates that would not be aided by the formal introduction of evidence.

In a dissenting opinion, Justice Stevens disagreed with the majority's assessment of the value of the contribution that a prisoner might make to the decision whether to continue the prisoner's confinement in the administrative-segregation unit. Justice Stevens argued that a prisoner has a right to appear in person to state his or her views as to why continued confinement in administrative segregation is unwarranted.

In addition, Justice Stevens insisted that if the decision is made to continue to keep a prisoner in segregation, the decisionmaker has to provide the prisoner with at least a brief written statement recounting the reasons for this decision. According to Justice Stevens, this statement will provide guidance to the prisoner as to the steps that he or she can take to procure release from segregation. The statement will also enable the inmate to bring any errors upon which the segregation decision has been founded to the attention of prison authorities and will prompt those conducting the review to make their decision with greater care. Finally, such a written statement will facilitate the administrative and judicial review of segregation decisions.

The dearth of procedural safeguards that, according to the Supreme Court, must attend transfers to administrative segregation when state law creates a liberty interest in remaining in the general-population unit is to be contrasted with the many procedural safeguards that must surround transfers of an inmate from a prison to a mental hospital. In *Vitek v. Jones* (S.Ct.1980), the Supreme Court agreed with the district court that the following procedures are constitutionally mandated when transferring prisoners to mental hospitals: (1) written notice of the contemplated transfer far enough in advance of the hearing to permit the prisoner to adequately prepare for it; (2) a hearing that the inmate has a right to attend; (3) the right to make an oral statement at the hearing; (4) the right to be apprised of the information upon which the transfer recommendation is predicated; (5) the right to present documentary evidence in opposition to the transfer; (6) the right to call witnesses to testify on the prisoner's behalf unless there is "good cause" for not permitting the prisoner to call a particular witness to testify; (7) the right to confront and cross-examine adverse witnesses unless there is "good cause" for prohibiting the exercise of these rights; (8) the right to have an "independent decisionmaker" make the transfer decision (although this decisionmaker need not come from outside the prison or mental hospital to be considered sufficiently "independent"); (9) the right to receive a written statement outlining the evidence relied on and the reasons for the transfer; and (10) "effective" and "timely" notice of all of the above rights.

The district court in *Vitek* had also held that an inmate facing a possible transfer to a mental hospital is entitled to be represented by an attorney at the transfer hearing, a conclusion with which four Justices on the Supreme Court agreed. Justice Powell, however, wrote a separate concurring opinion in which he set forth his view that due process is satisfied as long as the prisoner contesting the recommended transfer to a mental hospital receives assistance from someone who is both "qualified" and "independent." He explained that a prisoner can be adequately and perhaps even better assisted by a licensed psychiatrist or other mental-health professional during a transfer proceeding, since the focus of the hearing is on a medical issue. An inmate confronted with a possible transfer to a mental hospital must therefore receive assistance from someone who is "qualified" and "independent," but not necessarily an attorney, as the eleventh procedural safeguard mandated by due process.

The vast difference between the paltry amount of procedural safeguards that must attend those transfers to administrative segregation that implicate due process and the breadth of procedural protection that surrounds transfers of prisoners to mental hospitals is due to the balancing test discussed earlier in this book that courts customarily apply when determining what "process" is "due" when a person faces a deprivation of life, liberty, or property. *See* page 50 in Chapter 3. Under this test, which was first enunciated in *Mathews v. Eldridge* (S.Ct. 1976), courts balance the following three factors: (1) the private interest that is at stake; (2) the effect on governmental interests of incorporating a particular procedural safeguard into the decisionmaking process; and (3) the safeguard's value and the risk of an erroneous deprivation of the private interest at stake if the safeguard were not put in place.

When the Supreme Court applied the *Mathews* balancing test in *Hewitt v. Helms* and *Vitek v. Jones*, one of the chief differences in the Court's analysis in the two cases was in its discussion of the private interest at stake. In *Hewitt*, the Court asserted that an inmate's interest in remaining in the general-population unit and not being transferred to administrative segregation is "not of great consequence." The Court noted that no great stigma attaches to such a transfer, because a prisoner can be transferred to administrative segregation for an array of reasons, some of which have nothing to do with a suspicion of wrongdoing. In addition, there was no evidence in the record that confinement in administrative segregation might reduce a prisoner's chances of being released on parole. By contrast, the Court in *Vitek v. Jones* emphasized the opprobrium that accompanies the label "mentally ill," as well as the intrusiveness of the unwanted medical treatment to which individuals in mental hospitals are subjected.

When balancing the remaining two factors under the *Mathews* balancing test in *Hewitt v. Helms*, the Supreme Court seemed to deviate from the way in which it normally analyzes those factors. The second factor, as mentioned earlier, generally focuses on the extent to which inserting a particular procedural safeguard into a process will advance or detrimentally affect a governmental interest or interests. To the extent that an important governmental interest will be adversely affected by inclusion of the procedural safeguard in the process, it is less likely that the safeguard is constitutionally mandated. On the other hand, to the extent that the safeguard will promote a significant governmental interest, it is more likely that the procedural safeguard will be considered part of due process.

In *Hewitt v. Helms*, the Supreme Court narrowed its traditional focus when it examined the second factor under the *Mathews* balancing test. The Court simply identified "the governmental interests involved" in the prisoner's transfer to administrative segregation and then assessed how important those interests were. According to the Court, two interests were implicated in the case before it when the prisoner was transferred to administrative segregation after a prison riot in which he was suspected of participating. One was the interest in isolating a prisoner who posed a risk of harm to other prisoners or correctional staff. The other was the interest in confining the prisoner away from other prisoners while his involvement in the riot was investigated, to prevent him from hurting or coercing witnesses who might attest to his involvement.

The Court underscored the centrality of each of these interests, and that was essentially the end of its analysis. Had the Court gone on to analyze the extent to which each of these interests would have been affected by a particular procedural safeguard, such as letting the inmate be present when the need for segregating the inmate was reviewed, the Court might have concluded that the governmental interests implicated by the transfer would not have been adversely affected by affording the inmate this safeguard.

The Supreme Court skewed its application of the *Mathews* balancing test in another way that may have contributed to the dearth of procedural protections that the Court concluded must be afforded an inmate deprived of liberty through a transfer to administrative segregation. When examining the third factor under the *Mathews* balancing test—the value of the claimed safeguard and the risk of an erroneous deprivation of the private interest at stake if the safeguard is not provided, the Court discussed the value that a "detailed adversary proceeding" would have on the reliability of the decision to transfer an inmate to administrative segregation. The Court ultimately concluded that such an adversary process would not be overly helpful because of the complexity and subjectivity of the assessments made by prison officials when deciding whether an inmate needs to be confined in administrative segregation. Such a decision may not even be grounded on specific facts about what an inmate has done, since even untrue rumors about an inmate might justify the isolation of the inmate to protect the inmate from retaliation from those who believe the rumors to be true. In addition, transfers are often based on predictions about what an inmate or others might do in the future.

The problem with the Court's analysis is that by lumping all procedural safeguards into one amorphous category—"detailed adversary proceeding"—the Court failed to examine the potential value of individual safeguards subsumed within that general category. For example, while it might be true that there would not be any great benefit in turning a transfer review into a "detailed adversary proceeding," that does not necessarily mean that the reliability of the process would not be enhanced by, for example, permitting an inmate, as Justice Stevens proposed, to appear in person before those individuals charged with periodically reviewing the need for the inmate's continued confinement in administrative segregation. In sum, the way in which the Supreme Court truncated the *Mathews* balancing test in *Hewitt v. Helms* catalyzed its finding that when transfers to administrative segregation implicate due process, they need to be accompanied by few procedural safeguards.

In *Wilkinson v. Austin* (S.Ct.2005), the Supreme Court considered some questions regarding the procedural safeguards that must attend a prisoner's assignment to a supermaximum-security prison. In answering these questions, the Court applied the *Mathews* balancing test. Although, as mentioned earlier in this chapter, prisoners confined in the supermaximum-security prison in question had almost no contact with any other human being, the Supreme Court characterized the private interest in avoiding an unfounded transfer to a supermax prison as "minimal," because prisoners already and inevitably suffer a curtailment of their freedoms due to their incarceration.

Turning to the risk of an erroneous placement in the supermax prison and the value of additional procedural safeguards in averting such an erroneous placement, the Court opined that the correctional policy that governed these placements afforded inmates the core protections of due process: they received notice of the recommended assignment and a "fair opportunity" to rebut the reasons asserted for the assignment. For example, they could attend the hearing before the classification committee charged with deciding whether to recommend that an inmate be confined in the supermax prison. At that hearing, the inmate could explain why the placement was unwarranted and tender a written statement as well. Any recommendation to assign the prisoner to the supermax prison had to undergo several levels of review, and before the final review, the prisoner had the right, under the policy, to once again proffer objections to that assignment and the reasons asserted for it.

The risk of an erroneous placement was further reduced, according to the Court, by periodic reviews of the soundness of the inmate's placement in the supermax facility. The first review occurred thirty days after the initial placement, and further reviews were conducted every year thereafter.

In completing its analysis under the *Mathews* balancing test, the Supreme Court observed that the state's interest in protecting the safety of other prisoners, correctional personnel, and the public was a "dominant consideration" in its assessment of the procedural safeguards that must attend a placement in a supermaximum-security prison. The Court pointed to the peril prison gangs pose to the safety of others. Prison gang members commonly are directed by gang leaders to kill other inmates and prison staff, and the prospect of being punished through the criminal-justice system for their crimes might have little deterrent effect on gang members already serving life sentences. The Court felt that according inmates the kinds of procedural safeguards that typically attend an "adversary hearing" would compromise the important state interest in safeguarding institutional security and the safety of others furthered by prisoners' assignments to the supermax prison.

The right to call witnesses was one of the procedural safeguards that the Supreme Court specifically said was a "formal, adversary-type" procedure ill-suited to a proceeding at which the appropriateness of assigning a prisoner to the supermax facility was being decided. The Court was unconvinced that crafting an exception to this right when a witness's participation in the hearing would be dangerous would alleviate the state's safety concerns. The Court noted, for example, the difficulty of determining when a witness's testimony might lead to a reprisal against the witness or others.

The Supreme Court also alluded to the state's interest in conserving resources as counseling against affording inmates more procedural protections than they were afforded already under the state's supermaximum-placement policy. Citing the high costs of incarcerating a prisoner in a super-maximum-security facility compared to a maximum-security prison, the Court said that courts should be reticent to require prison officials to spend even more money for "elaborate procedural safeguards" when a decision has been made that, for safety and security reasons, a prisoner needs to be housed in a supermax prison.

In capsulizing its holding in *Wilkinson*, the Supreme Court said that when a deprivation of liberty stems, like in the case before it, from the exercise of prison officials' expertise, and when it has repercussions on the safety of inmates and prison staff, due process only requires "informal, nonadversary procedures" like those outlined in *Hewitt v. Helms* (S.Ct.1983) and *Greenholtz v. Inmates of Nebraska Penal and Correctional Complex* (S.Ct.1979). (*Greenholtz*, which is discussed on page 189, dealt with the procedural safeguards that must attend some parole-release decisions.) The Court considered a prisoner's confinement in a supermaximum-security prison to be unlike the revocation of good-time credits for a disciplinary infraction, which the Court has held requires "more formal, adversary-type procedures." *See Wolff v. McDonnell* (S.Ct. 1974), which is discussed on page 271.

In *Washington v. Harper* (S.Ct.1990), the Supreme Court addressed some questions concerning the requirements of procedural due process when psychotropic drugs are administered involuntarily to a mentally ill inmate. The Court first concluded that such involuntary administration of antipsychotic medication deprives an inmate of a constitutionally-derived liberty interest. Applying the "discretion-cabining" test later discarded in *Sandin v. Conner*, the Court noted that the inmate who had brought suit in *Harper* had been deprived of a state-created liberty interest as well.

Turning to the question of what "process" is "due" an inmate to whom government officials wish to compulsorily administer antipsychotic medication, the Court first rejected the inmate's claim that the decision whether such involuntary medication is warranted has to be made by a judge. The Court recognized the substantiality of the private interest at stake; antipsychotic drugs can cause severe side effects—even death. The Court nonetheless believed that inmates' interest in avoiding unwanted medical treatment can be protected, and perhaps even better protected, by having independent mental-health professionals make the medication decision. At the same time, the Court emphasized that in the state of Washington, an inmate could obtain judicial review of the determination that the involuntary administration of psychotropic drugs was justified.

The Court in *Harper* also gave short shrift to the inmate's claim that he was entitled to be represented by an attorney at the hearing where it would be determined whether to administer antipsychotic drugs to him over his objection. The requirements of due process would be satisfied, the Court observed, as long as the inmate was represented by a person who was "independent" and understood the psychiatric issues in the case.

The Court furthermore rejected the inmate's claim that the need to administer antipsychotic drugs over his objection had to be proven by "clear, cogent, and convincing evidence" before such forced drugging could occur. The Court gave no reason for this conclusion other than opining that this standard of proof was "neither required nor helpful" when this type of medical determination is being made.

There are a number of questions that remain after *Harper* about the procedural safeguards that must surround the involuntary administration of psychotropic drugs to inmates. The state of Washington, by policy, afforded inmates who were involuntarily medicated a broad measure of procedural protection, including review of the advisability of continuing the involuntary medication seven days after the treatment had begun and every fourteen days thereafter. The Supreme Court therefore had no opportunity to consider in *Harper* whether the safeguards already afforded by the state were constitutionally mandated. In determining what procedural safeguards are required by due process in this context, courts will apply the *Mathews* balancing test. In addition, they will turn to other relevant Supreme Court cases, such as *Vitek v. Jones*, for guidance.

B.   THE FIFTH AMENDMENT PRIVILEGE AGAINST SELF–INCRIMINATION

In *McKune v. Lile* (S.Ct.2002), the Supreme Court considered whether a prisoner's participation in a treatment program for sex offenders could constitutionally be conditioned on his disclosure of his sexual history, including sex crimes with which he had not been charged previously. To participate in the treatment program, prisoners also had to admit their culpability of the crime for which they were serving time even if they had testified at their trial, as had the prisoner in this case, that they were innocent. Under the rules governing the treatment program in question, prisoners who refused to disclose the required information or to admit their guilt of the crime for which they were incarcerated were transferred from the medium-security unit to a maximum-security unit. In addition, their privileges, including visitation rights, work opportunities, earnings, and access to television, were curtailed substantially. However, the refusal to disclose inculpatory information did not adversely affect their parole prospects or otherwise lengthen the period of their incarceration.

The plaintiff in *McKune*, a convicted sex offender, contended that the threatened loss of privileges and transfer to a maximum-security unit constituted the compulsion to incriminate himself proscribed by the Fifth Amendment. The Court responded that whether the defendant was subjected to compulsion within the meaning of the Fifth Amendment depended on the severity of the consequences that would ensue from his refusal to comply with the treatment program's disclosure requirements. And a plurality of the Court concluded that the consequences would not be severe enough to implicate the Fifth Amendment unless they met the *Sandin* test. In other words, a prisoner had to be threatened with "atypical and significant hardships in relation to the ordinary incidents of prison life" in order for those threats to be tantamount to compulsion.

Although providing the critical fifth vote for upholding the constitutionality of the disclosure and admission-of-guilt conditions, Justice O'Connor agreed with the four dissenters that the Court should not import the *Sandin* test into its Fifth Amendment analysis. At the same time, she agreed with the plurality that the effects of the diminution in the plaintiff's privileges and his transfer to a maximum-security unit were not onerous enough to effectively compel him to incriminate himself. Emphasizing that the plaintiff had not proven the degree to which a maximum-security unit is more dangerous than a medium-security unit, Justice O'Connor seemed to intimate that the outcome of the case might have been different had the plaintiff adduced such proof. *McKune* also left unresolved whether the conditioning of parole release on compliance with a treatment program's protocols mandating disclosure of, and admission of responsibility for, past crimes violates the Fifth Amendment privilege against self-incrimination.

C. EQUAL PROTECTION OF THE LAW

In prisons, racial tensions abound. The discord between races that often simmers in the free world can explode when combined with the anger, frustration, loneliness, and resentment that permeate the lives of prisoners.

Some prison officials have attempted to respond to the reality of racial hatred in prisons and the threat of violence that it creates by separating prisoners of different races. In *Washington v. Lee* (M.D.Ala.1966), the United States District Court for the Middle District of Alabama struck down such a segregation scheme as violative of the Equal Protection Clause found in the Fourteenth Amendment. At the same time, the court recognized that in some "isolated instances," segregation by race might be constitutionally permissible for a "limited period" of time.

In its summary affirmance of the district court's judgment, the Supreme Court seemed to agree that the interest in maintaining institutional security can sometimes override the interest in averting the racial discrimination that inheres in attempts to keep prisoners of different races apart. *Lee v. Washington* (S.Ct.1968). In a concurring opinion, Justice Black clarified what he felt was implicit in the majority's opinion: that prison officials must have acted in good faith and in response to "particularized circumstances" to trigger the limited exception to the general rule that the Constitution will not countenance racial discrimination—even in a prison.

In *Johnson v. California* (S.Ct.2005), the Supreme Court was asked to clarify when racial segregation in prisons violates the Constitution. The policy whose constitutionality was at issue in that case provided for the double celling of only inmates of the same race during their first sixty days at a correctional reception center. The policy applied both to inmates newly admitted into the state's prison system and to those being transferred from one prison to another. The professed justification for this racial segregation was to avert race-related violence while inmates were assessed individually at the reception center for the risk of violence they posed to other inmates.

The specific question before the Court in *Johnson* was whether the *Turner* test should be applied when determining whether racial segregation in a prison violates the equal protection of the law guaranteed by the Constitution. In earlier Supreme Court cases, the Court had said that the *Turner* test is to be applied in "all circumstances" when prisoners' constitutional claims implicate the administration of prisons. *See, e.g., Washington v. Harper* (S.Ct.1990). But in *Johnson v. California*, the Supreme Court held that a strict-scrutiny test should be applied when assessing the constitutionality of racial classifications in prisons. Specifically, the Court held that a race-based classification, like the one before it, was unconstitutional unless the government proved both that it furthered a "compelling" governmental interest and was "narrowly tailored" to achieve that goal. The Court then ordered that the case be remanded back to the district court to provide the defendants with an opportunity to attempt to meet this stringent constitutional standard.

One of the particularly noteworthy features of the Court's opinion in *Johnson* is its discussion of the dividing line between cases in which the *Turner* test is to be applied to prisoners' constitutional claims and those in which some other test applies. The Court insisted that in the past it had applied the *Turner* test "*only* to rights that are 'inconsistent with proper incarceration.' " (emphasis in the original) And in explaining why the *Turner* test was inapposite in the case before it, the Court said that the right not to be subjected to racial discrimination was not a right that "necessarily" had to be limited in order to accommodate the needs of "proper prison administration."

These comments drew a caustic rebuke from Justice Thomas, who was joined by Justice Scalia in his dissenting opinion. Justice Thomas charged that the "inconsistency-with-proper-prison-administration test" propounded by the majority would nullify the purport and intent of the *Turner* test: As courts strove to determine whether recognition of an asserted constitutional right would "necessarily" conflict with "proper prison administration," courts would have to make decisions about how prisons can and should be operated, decisions that Justice Thomas considered at odds with the deference the *Turner* test accorded prison officials' judgments on these matters.

After *Johnson*, even when the concerns of prison officials about racial conflict are well-founded, they cannot segregate inmates by race if there are viable alternative ways to preserve institutional security. Some of the potentially feasible alternatives mentioned by the lower courts have included increasing the supervision of inmates, disciplining and isolating assaultive inmates, and decreasing the prison population to enhance officials' ability to supervise and control the prisoners. *See, e.g., Blevins v. Brew* (W.D.Wis.1984).

One theme that has permeated the court cases striking down the segregation of inmates by race is that segregation can, over the long term, actually aggravate racial tensions. *See, e.g., Stewart v. Rhodes* (S.D.Ohio 1979) (holding unconstitutional a policy of double celling only inmates of the same race during the eight-week processing period following their entry into the prison system). *White v. Morris* (S.D.Ohio 1993) represents one of the exceptional cases where a court upheld race-based segregation, though for a limited period of time. In that case, the district court agreed to permit prison officials to house only prisoners of the same race together in double cells. But the court emphasized that the prison officials were faced with an emergency situation. In part because of racial tensions exacerbated by interracial cell assignments, prisoners had recently rioted. Nine inmates and one correctional officer were killed during the riot, and the records needed to assess the security risks posed by individual inmates were destroyed. The court therefore authorized the prison officials to make race-based cell assignments for four months, while the records were reconstructed. But the court emphasized that it would not approve any long-term segregation by race.

Thus far, some, though not all, courts have refused to apply the *Turner* test to inmate claims alleging gender-based discrimination. Many of these claims have centered on the diminished work and educational opportunities afforded female inmates compared to their male counterparts. In reviewing these claims, some lower courts have required that female inmates receive "parity of treatment." *See, e.g., McCoy v. Nevada Dep't of Prisons* (D.Nev. 1991). Parity of treatment does not mean identical treatment. A class offered, for example, at a men's prison does not have to be included automatically in course offerings at a women's prison. The facilities, programs, and privileges of female inmates must, however, be "substantially equivalent ... in substance if not form" to those of male inmates. *Glover v. Johnson* (E.D.Mich.1979). Male inmates cannot, for example, be trained for high-paying jobs, while female inmates are consigned to training programs that will enable them to perform only low-paying, menial work.

Before a court will find that the differential treatment of female inmates violates their right to the equal protection of the law, the court first must find that the female inmates are "similarly situated" to the male inmates who are allegedly receiving more favorable treatment. Unless the female and male inmates are similarly situated, no equal-protection violation can exist because the dissimilar treatment of dissimilar persons is constitutional.

In recent years, the factors that some courts have said should be considered when determining whether female inmates are similarly situated to their male counterparts have made it increasingly difficult for female inmates to prevail on their equal-protection claims. For example, in *Klinger v. Department of Corrections* (8th Cir.1994), the Eighth Circuit Court of Appeals held that female prisoners at one prison were not similarly situated to male prisoners at another prison for a number of reasons, including differences in the size of the prisons' populations, the prisons' different security levels, and the longer sentences of the male inmates.

According to courts applying heightened scrutiny to claims of gender discrimination in the prison context, if female inmates are considered "similarly situated" to male inmates and the facilities, programs, and privileges offered female inmates are not substantially equivalent to those offered male inmates, the government has the burden of proving that the differences are "substantially related to the achievement of important government objectives." *Pitts v. Thornburgh* (D.C.Cir.1989). When this burden is not met, a finding that the female inmates' equal-protection rights have been violated will follow. In addition, disparities in the educational opportunities afforded female inmates may violate Title IX of the Education Amendments of 1972. 20 U.S.C. §§ 1681–1688. This federal statute prohibits gender-based discrimination in educational programs or activities that receive federal financial assistance. *See Jeldness v. Pearce* (9th Cir.1994).

Even though there are some equal-protection claims asserted in the correctional context, such as claims alleging racial or gender discrimination, that have triggered more stringent review by the courts, courts have analyzed the brunt of prisoners' equal-protection claims under a rational-basis test. For example, in *Jones v. North Carolina Prisoners' Labor Union* (S.Ct.1977), a case discussed earlier in this book in Chapter 11, some prisoners contended that regulations that prohibited the bulk mailing of prisoner union materials and the convening of prisoner union meetings violated their right to the equal protection of the law. The basis for their equal-protection claim was the fact that inmates in two other organizations, the Jaycees and Alcoholics Anonymous, were permitted to send such group mailings and hold group meetings.

The Supreme Court rejected the prisoners' claim, noting that there was a "rational basis" for the differential treatment of inmates in the Jaycees and Alcoholics Anonymous. Those two organizations, the Court noted, had rehabilitative objectives, while the principal goal of the prisoners' union was to require prison officials to engage in collective bargaining with the union, a practice that was illegal under state law.

CHAPTER 15

SEARCHES, SEIZURES, AND PRIVACY RIGHTS

In prisons, privacy is a rare commodity. Often, prisoners' letters to and from family members and friends are opened and read by prison officials. Prisoners' movements throughout the prison are observed, monitored, and regulated, and there is no place where they can go for a private respite. Most inmates share a cell with one or more other inmates or live in dormitories filled with many other prisoners. Even for those fortunate few inmates who have their own cells, privacy is nonexistent. They can be observed in their cells or rooms through cellbars or windows at any moment, even when defecating or urinating in a toilet within the cell. And every inch of their cells and every piece of property that they own can and often will be inspected as correctional officials attempt to fulfill their responsibility of ferreting contraband out of the institution.

Because of the demands of maintaining institutional security, inmates' privacy must necessarily be curtailed. The question that remains is whether inmates have any residual privacy rights that are protected by the Constitution.

A.   THE FOURTH AMENDMENT

One of the primary purposes of the Fourth Amendment is to prevent unreasonable incursions on individuals' privacy by the government. The Fourth Amendment protects our "persons, houses, papers, and effects" from "unreasonable searches and seizures" and also sets forth the requirements that must be met in order for a warrant to be valid. But does the Fourth Amendment extend any protection to prisoners?

In *Hudson v. Palmer* (S.Ct.1984), the Supreme Court provided a partial answer to this question. In that case, a prisoner had brought a lawsuit in which he contended that his Fourth Amendment rights were violated when his cell was searched and personal property destroyed for no other reason than to harass him. The Supreme Court disagreed, holding that the predicate for a finding of a violation of the Fourth Amendment did not exist in this case; according to the Court, no search or seizure had occurred that would even trigger further analysis under the Fourth Amendment.

The Supreme Court first held that the inspection of the prisoner's cell was not a "search" within the meaning of the Fourth Amendment. In arriving at this conclusion, the Court, as it has in other contexts, departed from the literal meaning of the word "search." Instead, the Court said that for a search in the Fourth Amendment sense to occur, there must be an intrusion by the government into an area where a person has a "legitimate" or "reasonable'' expectation of privacy. In order for an expectation of privacy to be considered legitimate or reasonable, the Court explained, it must be one that ''society is prepared to recognize as 'reasonable.' '' The Court then stated that any expectation that inmates have that they will have some measure of privacy in their cells is not reasonable because of the obvious need for correctional officials to have uninhibited access to cells in order to find weapons, drugs, and other contraband, discover evidence of impending escapes, and ensure that the cells are sanitary.

In addition to rejecting the plaintiff's claim that the search of his cell violated his Fourth Amendment rights, the Supreme Court in *Hudson* gave short shrift to his claim that the destruction of his property constituted an ''unreasonable seizure'' proscribed by the Fourth Amendment. In a footnote, the Court cursorily addressed this claim, simply noting that prisoners cannot contest seizures of their property under the Fourth Amendment for the same reasons that they cannot contest searches of their cells. In analogizing searches of cells and seizures of property, the Court did not respond to, or even acknowledge, the argument of Justice Stevens in dissent that seizures of property are different from searches of property because they implicate not just privacy, but also possessory, interests. Instead, the Court summarily announced that prison officials need the freedom to confiscate items that, in their opinion, threaten ''legitimate institutional interests.''

At the same time, the Court assured prisoners that they are not remediless when their property is unjustifiably destroyed by correctional officials. They can, for example, seek redress under state law. In addition, the destruction of property, such as the eyeglasses of an almost blind inmate, sometimes violates the Eighth Amendment's prohibition of cruel and unusual punishments. The destruction of an inmate's property may abridge other constitutional provisions as well, including the First Amendment (if correctional officers burned a Bible, for example) or the right of access to the courts (if the officers, for example, shredded the inmate's legal papers). The irony of this portion of the Court's opinion is that the Court was saying that the Fourth Amendment provides no protection to inmates whose property has been destroyed, because prison officials must be free to seize items which, under other portions of the Constitution, they are forbidden from seizing.

In other cases, the Supreme Court has held that inmates and pretrial detainees do not even have a right to observe searches of their cells to avert the theft or the unnecessary confiscation or destruction of their property. *See Block v. Rutherford* (S.Ct. 1984); *Bell v. Wolfish* (S.Ct.1979). The Court's rationale is that the presence of inmates while their cells are being searched might spark confrontations between the inmates and the correctional officers searching through their personal belongings. In addition, inmates might frustrate the purposes of cell searches by passing contraband from one cell to another as the searches are being conducted.

While the claims before the Supreme Court in *Hudson v. Palmer* concerned only the search of a cell and the destruction of personal property, the Court, in rejecting those claims, used broad language that arguably suggested that prisoners might have no rights at all under the Fourth Amendment. At one point in its opinion, the Court said, "We are satisfied that society would insist that the prisoner's expectation of privacy *always* yield to what must be considered the paramount interest in institutional security." (emphasis added).

The question that remains after *Hudson* then is to what extent, if at all, inmates retain any rights under the Fourth Amendment. In particular, does the Fourth Amendment place any constraints on the observation or touching of inmates' bodies?

Most, though not all, of the lower courts that have addressed this question have held that the Fourth Amendment does place some limits on searches of inmates' bodies. *See Wilson v. City of Kalamazoo* (W.D.Mich.2000) (listing cases). It is clear, however, from the Supreme Court's decision in *Bell v. Wolfish* (S.Ct.1979) that if the Fourth Amendment extends to inmates when their bodies are being searched, the protection afforded by that amendment is quite limited.

Bell involved a challenge by convicted inmates, as well as pretrial detainees, to visual body-cavity inspections to which they were subjected after contact visits. As mentioned earlier in this book, contact visits are those that occur without a physical barrier between inmates and their visitors. During the inspection at issue in *Bell*, male inmates had to bend over and lift their genitals to permit correctional officials to visually inspect their rectums, and female inmates had to let correctional officers visually inspect their vaginal and anal cavities.

The Supreme Court began its analysis of the constitutionality of these inspections by assuming, without deciding, that inmates and pretrial detainees retain some Fourth Amendment rights. The Court then proceeded to conclude that visual body-cavity inspections can be conducted after contact visits even when correctional officials do not have any particular reason to believe an inmate is attempting to smuggle contraband into the institution.

In reaching this conclusion, the Court applied the balancing test that it typically applies when assessing the constitutionality of what it deems to be "special needs" searches—searches whose principal, immediate purpose is something other than the apprehension of a criminal or the detection of evidence of a crime to be introduced in a criminal prosecution. Under this balancing test, the Court weighs the intrusiveness of a search against the need for that kind of search.

In *Bell*, the Court acknowledged that visual body-cavity inspections are extremely invasive. Yet the Court upheld such inspections, even in the absence of any suspicion of wrongdoing on the part of an inmate, because of the need to not only detect, but deter, the inflow of contraband, such as weapons and drugs, into an institution.

In assessing the need for visual body-cavity searches after contact visits, the Supreme Court rejected the argument that the existence of less intrusive means of achieving the objectives of the searches would necessarily mean that the searches are unreasonable and hence unconstitutional. In subsequent cases, the Court has explained that the question under the Fourth Amendment is not simply whether an alternative was available, but whether an official was unreasonable in failing to recognize or implement the alternative. *See United States v. Sharpe* (S.Ct.1985). Consequently, in *Bell v. Wolfish*, the Court rebuffed the suggestion that the correctional officials had acted unreasonably in conducting visual body-cavity inspections because they could, alternatively, have used metal detectors to thwart the smuggling of contraband into the facility or could have more closely observed inmates and their visitors during contact visits. The Court noted the drawbacks of these alternatives. Metal detectors cannot detect nonmetallic contraband, such as drugs, while the closer monitoring of contact visits would interfere with their purpose of fostering and maintaining family and other ties by enabling inmates to converse with loved ones in a somewhat private setting.

Bell was a close case, with the Court splitting 5–4 on the issue of the constitutionality of the visual body-cavity inspections. Three of the dissenting Justices—Justices Marshall, Stevens, and Brennan—would have required probable cause to believe an inmate was attempting to smuggle contraband into a facility before permitting such a search. Justice Powell, on the other hand, insisted that such searches be predicated on at least "reasonable suspicion," a more lax standard than probable cause.

While the majority of the Court concluded that there is no individualized-suspicion requirement applicable to visual body-cavity inspections conducted after contact visits, the Court hastened to add that such inspections must be conducted in a "reasonable manner." This caveat raises the possibility of successful Fourth Amendment challenges to visual body-cavity inspections because of where they were conducted, who conducted them, or who else observed them. In addition, *Bell* leaves unanswered questions about the circumstances under which manual body-cavity inspections, those involving the physical touching of body cavities, are constitutional. In answering these questions, the need for manual inspections in certain circumstances would, under the Fourth Amendment balancing test, have to be weighed against their intrusiveness.

The Fourth Amendment test under which a court assesses the need for a search and weighs that need against the search's "nature" also dictates when a visual body-cavity inspection can be conducted during the intake process at a jail. Thus far, most courts have held that strip searches and body-cavity inspections conducted during the processing into a jail of a person arrested for a "minor crime" must be grounded on reasonable suspicion that the detainee is carrying a weapon or contraband. *See Roberts v. Rhode Island* (1st Cir.2001) (listing cases).

B.   RIGHT OF PRIVACY

In addition to the protection afforded privacy interests by the Fourth Amendment, there is, according to the Supreme Court, a more general right of privacy subsumed within the Constitution. The Court has vacillated as to the source of this right. In some cases, the Court has said that the right springs from the "penumbras" of several constitutional provisions—the First Amendment right to freedom of association; the Third Amendment, which prohibits the government from forcing individuals to shelter soldiers in their homes during times of peace; the Fourth Amendment; the Fifth Amendment privilege against self-incrimination; and the Ninth Amendment, which states that individual rights are not limited to those listed in the Constitution. *See, e.g., Griswold v. Connecticut* (S.Ct.1965). In other cases, the Court has simply said that the right of privacy is encompassed within the "liberty" protected by the Due Process Clauses of the Fifth and Fourteenth Amendments. *See, e.g., Zablocki v. Redhail* (S.Ct.1978).

The Supreme Court has never explicitly held that the right of privacy extends to inmates, but the Court seemed to implicitly acknowledge as much in

Turner v. Safley (S.Ct.1987). In that case, which was discussed earlier in Chapter 11, the Court struck down a regulation, which restricted inmate marriages, because it unconstitutionally impinged upon the right to marry. In other cases, the Supreme Court has noted that this right to marry is a component of the more general constitutional right of privacy. *See, e.g., Zablocki v. Redhail* (S.Ct.1978).

Most of the lower courts have assumed or held that inmates retain a limited right to privacy under the Constitution. *See Oliver v. Scott* (5th Cir.2002) (listing cases). The courts are divided, however, regarding the source of this right. Some courts have held that the origin of inmates' residual right to privacy is the Fourth Amendment, while other courts have applied the Eighth Amendment when analyzing inmates' right-to-privacy claims. Still other courts have found that the right to privacy is rooted in substantive due process. *Compare Moore v. Carwell* (5th Cir.1999) (cross-gender strip and body-cavity searches should be analyzed under the Fourth, not the Eighth, Amendment); *Peckham v. Wisconsin Dep't of Corrections* (7th Cir.1998) (constitutionality of strip searches "more properly" analyzed under the Eighth Amendment, rather than the Fourth); and *Oliver v. Scott* (5th Cir.2002) (substantive due process, not the Eighth Amendment, governs challenges to cross-gender surveillance of inmates showering and going to the bathroom).

The courts have expended much energy in recent years in attempting to define the scope of inmates' right to privacy. Inmates generally have had little luck with right-to-privacy claims in which they objected to persons of the same sex viewing their nude bodies or observing them going to the bathroom. For example, in *Michenfelder v. Sumner* (9th Cir. 1988), the Ninth Circuit Court of Appeals found that strip searches conducted in the hallway in full view of other inmates were reasonably related to institutional security and therefore constitutional. The court noted that adopting measures to protect inmates' privacy during the searches posed security risks: searching inmates in their cells or moving them to a more private place to be searched might prove dangerous to the correctional officers conducting the searches.

Much of the litigation in the right-to-privacy area has centered on questions concerning the extent to which correctional officers of a different gender can search inmates or observe them while they are bathing, dressing, or using the toilet. The courts have really struggled with these questions because of the clash between several competing interests that are at stake—inmates' interest in their privacy; the interest of correctional officers, both male and female, in having equal employment opportunities; and the institutional interest in maintaining security.

Another interest is also arguably implicated by cross-gender searches of inmates and observation of them while they are nude or going to the bathroom—that of rehabilitation. Some courts have argued that the presence, for example, of female correctional officers in a men's prison is rehabilitative.

See, e.g., Bagley v. Watson (D.Or.1983). These courts contend that with women working in prisons, the prisons will be more like "the real world," facilitating inmates' ability to adjust, and their ability to relate positively to women, upon their release from prison. Detractors of this rehabilitation argument maintain that the presence of female correctional officers in men's prisons is dehumanizing and therefore actually anti-rehabilitative. They point out that in the "real world," persons of one sex do not normally watch strangers of the other sex undress, bathe, urinate, and defecate. *See, e.g., Bowling v. Enomoto* (N.D.Cal.1981).

The state of the law in this area is in flux, but some areas of general consensus have emerged. First, the courts generally concur that the right of privacy is not violated by the inadvertent or infrequent observation of a nude inmate by a correctional officer of a different gender. *See, e.g., Michenfelder v. Sumner* (9th Cir.1988). Second, the courts agree that inmates' right of privacy is not abridged when a person of the opposite sex is in the inmates' living area for a short, but designated, period of time, because the inmates can take steps during those predetermined times to avoid being seen in the nude or using the toilet. *See, e.g., Avery v. Perrin* (D.N.H.1979). Finally, the courts agree that whatever limitations the Constitution places on the observation or touching of inmates by correctional officers of the opposite sex, those limitations can be overridden in an emergency situation. *See, e.g., Lee v. Downs* (4th Cir.1981) (no abridgment of the right to privacy when two male correctional officers restrained the arms and legs of a female inmate, a very big and strong woman, while a female nurse searched her vagina for matches after the inmate had set fire to her paper dress).

Rather than holding that inmates' interest in their privacy must always give way to the interest in providing equal employment opportunities to men and women or, conversely, that inmates' privacy interests always supersede the interest of others in equal employment opportunities, the courts have usually sought to accommodate both interests without undermining institutional security. Where the courts have differed is on how far correctional officials must go to accommodate inmates' interest in their privacy.

The different responses of the trial court and the Eighth Circuit Court of Appeals to the inmates' right-to-privacy claims asserted in *Timm v. Gunter* (8th Cir.1990) exemplify the variation in views about the degree to which accommodations must be made. In that case, male inmates at a maximum-security prison contended that pat-down searches conducted by female correctional officers and visual surveillance by these officers of inmates when they were dressing, showering, using the toilet, and sleeping violated their constitutional right of privacy. The district court agreed and ordered the prison officials to take a number of steps to avoid impinging on the inmates' privacy interests. One of those steps was to permit an inmate to request that a male correctional officer search him when both a male and a female correctional officer were working at the same post. Another was to limit the extent to which female correctional officers could observe inmates who were undressed or using the toilet, by altering work schedules, admonishing female correctional officers to avoid looking at unclothed inmates or those who were using the toilet, and making modifications to the facility, such as the addition of toilet doors in one unit.

The Eighth Circuit Court of Appeals reversed the lower court's order, holding that none of these accommodations were constitutionally required. In explaining its conclusion, the court of appeals emphasized the adverse effects on security of some of the accommodations, as well as their costs, both financial and administrative. The prescribed modifications to the facility's physical plant, for example, would be quite expensive and would impede the observation of inmates needed to preserve institutional security. Modifying female correctional officers' work schedules, on the other hand, would create scheduling problems. And permitting inmates to request that they be searched by a male, instead of a female, correctional officer would diminish the perceived authority of female correctional officers, to the detriment of the institution's overall security.

The court of appeals in *Timm v. Gunter* also expressed concern about the impact of some of the accommodations on employment opportunities for women. The court noted the resentment felt by male correctional officers when they saw female correctional officers assigned to different, and generally less dangerous, posts because of their gender. The court also observed that limiting the job opportunities and responsibilities of female correctional officers would make them less knowledgeable, and therefore less effective, if they were later promoted to supervisory positions.

Finally, the court of appeals stated that the incursions on inmates' privacy were, in its opinion, really quite minimal. The court noted that there were already some physical obstructions that limited the viewing of inmates in the nude or going to the bathroom, such as the three-sided wall surrounding the urinal in the prison yard. In addition, the prisoners could take steps to further protect their privacy, such as covering themselves with a towel when using the toilet.

There is certainly no uniformity in the decisions of the lower courts as to the scope of inmates' right to privacy. Some courts have concluded that inmates have the right to be protected from the unrestricted viewing of their genitals or their use of the toilet by members of the opposite sex. *See Baker v. Welch* (S.D.N.Y.2003) (listing cases). Others have disagreed or expressed doubts that such a right exists. *See, e.g., Somers v. Thurman* (9th Cir.1997). But more courts seem to be moving in the direction taken by the court of appeals in *Timm v. Gunter*— towards countenancing incursions on inmates' privacy by correctional officers of the opposite sex. This trend is most apparent in cases contesting pat-down searches and visual surveillance of living and bathing areas by such officers. One of the themes repeated in many of these cases is that as long as the correctional officers act professionally when performing pat-down searches or monitoring living and bathing areas, the intrusion on inmates' privacy will be limited, just as it is limited when a doctor examines a patient of a different gender.

While the courts are increasingly permitting correctional officers of the opposite sex to perform tasks that intrude upon inmates' privacy, some courts are drawing the line at strip searches, holding that these searches generally cannot be performed or observed by correctional officers of a different gender. *See, e.g., Canedy v. Boardman* (7th Cir.1994) (listing cases). Other courts have held that cross-gender strip searches undertaken for legitimate penological reasons are constitutional provided that the searches are not conducted in a way deliberately designed to humiliate and harass an inmate. *See, e.g., Calhoun v. DeTella* (7th Cir.2003).

Many courts have required or permitted greater restrictions on searches and surveillance of female inmates by male correctional officers than those imposed on searches and surveillance of male inmates by female correctional officers. In rejecting the argument that this differential treatment violates the equal-protection rights of male inmates, the courts have asserted an assortment of justifications for the disparate treatment. Some, such as the court of appeals in *Timm v. Gunter*, have cited the greater risks to security posed by male inmates because of their more serious criminal backgrounds and their greater propensity to use violence while they are incarcerated. Others have pointed to the large number of female inmates who have been sexually or otherwise physically abused by men and who would suffer severe emotional trauma if male officers patted down their bodies, including their breasts and genital areas, in a search for contraband. *See, e.g., Jordan v. Gardner* (9th Cir.1993). Finally, at least one court has concluded that maximizing the number of tasks that female correctional officers can perform in men's prisons, while not permitting male correctional officers to perform similar functions in women's prisons, is a defensible means of ensuring that women have adequate employment opportunities in prisons, which still predominantly house male inmates. *Madyun v. Franzen* (7th Cir.1983).

Restrictions sometimes may be placed on the work to be performed by correctional officers of one gender in prisons housing inmates of another gender for reasons other than to accommodate what is believed to be inmates' right to privacy. Safety and security interests may also, at least in some circumstances, justify such restrictions. In *Dothard v. Rawlinson* (S.Ct.1977), the Supreme Court upheld an Alabama regulation that prohibited women from working in positions in maximum-security prisons for men where they would frequently be physically near the inmates. The Court rejected the argument that this regulation violated Title VII of the Civil Rights Act of 1964, 42 U.S.C. § 2000e, which prohibits gender-based employment discrimination. In-

stead, the Court found that the ban on the employment of women was permissible under the statutory
exemption that permits sex-based discrimination
when gender is "a bona fide occupational qualification reasonably necessary to the normal operation
of that particular business or enterprise." *Id*.
§ 2000e–2(e).

The Court acknowledged that the "bfoq exception" is "an extremely narrow" one. Nonetheless,
the Court held that the ban on the employment of
women in contact positions in Alabama's maximum-
security prisons fell within this exception because
there was a substantial risk that prisoners confined
in those prisons would sexually assault female correctional officers.

Justice Marshall was incensed by what he described as the Court's paternalistic attitude towards
women. He noted that "[o]nce again, '[t]he pedestal
upon which women have been placed has . . . , upon
closer inspection, been revealed as a cage.'" Let
women decide for themselves, he argued, whether
they were willing to undergo the risk of being
sexually assaulted. The majority responded that
more than the safety of prospective female employees was at stake, since an increase in assaults in a
prison would undercut the officials' control of prisoners and thereby undermine the safety and security of other correctional officers and the inmates.

By underscoring in *Dothard* that Alabama's maximum-security prisons for men, with their "jungle
atmosphere," were "not typical," the Supreme

Court seemed to be intimating that the case before it was an exceptional one and that normally women cannot be barred from working in contact positions in prisons for security reasons. Many of the conditions in the Alabama prisons that the Court cited as distinguishing characteristics, however, exist in other correctional facilities as well—rampant violence, understaffing, dormitory living arrangements, and the commingling of sex offenders within the general prison population.

The Sixth Circuit's decision in *Everson v. Michigan Dep't of Corrections* (6th Cir.2004) is an example of another of the few cases holding that Title VII permits prison officials, for safety reasons, to bar individuals of one gender—in this case, male—to work in units housing inmates of the opposite gender. The court of appeals cited the "endemic problem of sexual abuse" in women's prisons in Michigan in concluding that being female was a bona fide occupational qualification for employment as a correctional or residential unit officer in those prisons.

It seems clear from the Supreme Court's resolution of another Title VII claim in *Dothard v. Rawlinson* that while women may sometimes be barred from working in contact positions in some men's prisons because of their "very womanhood," they cannot be excluded because prison officials assume they are less strong than men. In *Dothard*, the Court struck down certain height and weight requirements that an individual had to meet in order to be hired as a correctional officer in Alabama. These requirements had led to a disproportionate number of women being disqualified from employment as correctional officers. The defendants had argued that the height and weight standards were needed to ensure that persons hired as correctional officers were strong enough to perform their duties. The Supreme Court responded that if a certain amount of strength is needed to perform the duties of a correctional officer, then an applicant's strength should be measured directly, instead of employing surrogate indicators of strength whose application has a discriminatory impact on female job applicants.

CHAPTER 16

DUE-PROCESS CLAIMS FOR PERSONAL INJURIES AND PROPERTY DEPRIVATIONS; RESTRICTIONS ON INMATE LABOR

A. DUE PROCESS

As was discussed in the previous chapter, the Supreme Court in *Hudson v. Palmer* (S.Ct.1984) observed that while the destruction of a prisoner's property cannot be challenged under the Fourth Amendment, it might give rise to claims cognizable under other provisions of the Constitution. One question is whether prison officials' destruction or loss of an inmate's property violates the inmate's right to due process of law, a right, as mentioned earlier, accorded federal inmates by the Fifth Amendment and state and local inmates by the Fourteenth Amendment. In order for a due-process violation to have occurred, the inmate must have been "deprived" of that property within the meaning of the Due Process Clause, and the deprivation must have occurred "without due process of law."

In *Daniels v. Williams* (S.Ct.1986), the Supreme Court addressed the question of what constitutes a "deprivation" within the meaning of the Fourteenth Amendment's Due Process Clause. In that case, a jail inmate brought a § 1983 suit against a deputy sheriff after slipping on a pillow negligently left on the stairs in the jail and injuring himself. The issue before the Supreme Court was whether negligence can effect a "deprivation" that triggers due-process requirements.

In resolving that issue, the Court noted that the purpose of the Due Process Clause is to avert and redress the " 'affirmative abuse of power' " by governmental officials. The Court then concluded that the negligence of governmental officials—their simple failure to act with reasonable care—does not involve the abuse of power with which the Due Process Clause is concerned. Thus, while the plaintiff in *Daniels* may have been deprived, in a literal sense, of his liberty interest in not being injured, according to the Court he suffered no deprivation in the constitutional sense. The Court emphasized that its conclusion did not mean that claims grounded on the negligence of governmental officials are unimportant; it simply meant that these claims are more suitable for consideration in a different forum—in a tort action filed in a state court.

While the Supreme Court in *Daniels* held that the negligence of governmental officials would not support a due-process claim, the Court noted that the intentional actions of the officials would. The Court said that it was leaving unresolved the question whether officials acting with a state of mind falling somewhere in between negligence and intent can effect a deprivation in the constitutional sense. Specifically, the question that *Daniels* purported to leave open is whether gross negligence or recklessness, which generally requires some subjective appreciation of the substantial risk that harm will ensue, will suffice to support a due-process claim.

In *Davidson v. Cannon* (S.Ct.1986), a case decided on the same day as *Daniels v. Williams*, the Supreme Court reaffirmed that the negligence of prison officials will not give rise to a due-process claim. *Davidson* involved a lawsuit brought by an inmate who, after being threatened by another inmate, apprised certain prison officials of the threats. The officials took no steps to protect the plaintiff, and he was eventually seriously injured when he was assaulted by the inmate who had previously threatened him.

The Supreme Court rejected the plaintiff's argument that the defendants' failure to protect him violated his right to due process of law, invoking the rationale and holding of *Daniels v. Williams* that negligence alone will not suffice to violate due process. In a dissenting opinion, Justice Blackmun distinguished the facts of the case in *Davidson* from those in *Daniels*. Justice Blackmun conceded that ordinarily negligence alone will not effect a due-process deprivation, but he noted that in this case, the plaintiff had been deprived by the state of all means of protecting himself. He could not possess or use weapons, he could not fight back without exposing himself to disciplinary sanctions, and he could not escape. Being deprived of all means of self-protection, the plaintiff was totally dependent on the prison officials to protect him. Justice Blackmun concluded that under these circumstances, the prison officials' negligence in ignoring the probable risk of harm to the plaintiff did constitute the requisite abuse of governmental authority needed to trigger the protections of due process.

When an inmate has suffered a deprivation of liberty or property within the meaning of the Due Process Clause, the next question is whether the inmate was afforded due process. The Supreme Court discussed the requirements of procedural due process in *Parratt v. Taylor* (S.Ct.1981). In that case, the plaintiff, a prisoner, filed a § 1983 suit after his hobby kit worth $23.50 was lost due to the negligence of some prison officials. The Court first held that the negligence of the defendants had effected a constitutional deprivation, a holding later overruled in *Daniels v. Williams*. The Court then turned to the question whether the deprivation of the plaintiff's property had occurred without due process.

The Supreme Court began by acknowledging that normally due process requires a predeprivation hearing, in other words, a hearing where a person can raise objections to a contemplated deprivation before it occurs. The Court recognized that sometimes a predeprivation hearing will not be feasible, such as when property must be immediately seized because of an emergency. The Court then found that a predeprivation hearing is not feasible and therefore not constitutionally required when a prisoner is deprived of property through the random and unauthorized act of a governmental official. The Court observed that in such a situation, the government realistically cannot be expected to provide the prisoner with a predeprivation hearing, because the government does not know when the deprivation will occur. Under these circumstances, the Court noted, due process is satisfied as long as the prisoner is afforded a "meaningful" postdeprivation hearing.

In *Hudson v. Palmer* (S.Ct.1984), the Supreme Court held that postdeprivation hearings can satisfy due process even when a prisoner has been intentionally deprived of property through the random and unauthorized act of a governmental employee. Although the offending employee in such a situation may know when a deprivation is about to occur, the state cannot know when an employee will deliberately disregard its rules. Consequently, the state cannot realistically provide a prisoner with a predeprivation hearing.

Despite some of the statements of the Court in *Parratt v. Taylor* and *Hudson v. Palmer*, it is now evident that just because the actions of a governmental employee that cause a deprivation of liberty or property are unauthorized does not mean that the existence of a tort remedy will always, or even usually, satisfy the requirements of procedural due process. In *Zinermon v. Burch* (S.Ct.1990), the Supreme Court narrowly construed *Parratt* and *Hudson* and held that a due-process violation still ensues if safeguards could have been put in place that would have prevented a "foreseeable" deprivation from occurring in the first place. Thus, if procedures could have been adopted that would have averted, for example, the erroneous and foreseeable deprivation of an inmate's property resulting from the intentional actions of a prison official, the failure to implement these procedures would, it appears, constitute a violation of due process.

In addition, a postdeprivation hearing will not satisfy due process when the deprivation of a prisoner's property or liberty occurs, not through the random and unauthorized actions of a prison official, but through some "established state procedure." *Logan v. Zimmerman Brush Co.* (S.Ct.1982). When a deprivation occurs through such an "established state procedure," affording a prisoner a predeprivation hearing is feasible.

In those circumstances when due process does not require a predeprivation hearing, the question arises as to what constitutes a "meaningful" postdeprivation hearing. In *Parratt*, the Supreme Court addressed this question. The plaintiff in that case had the option of filing a tort suit in the state court to obtain redress for the loss of his property. The plaintiff contended that this tort remedy did not satisfy the dictates of due process because it did not provide him with some of the benefits that attend the filing of a civil-rights suit under 42 U.S.C. § 1983. In the state action, the plaintiff could not recover punitive damages and could only sue the state and not employees of the state. The plaintiff also had no right to a jury trial. The Supreme Court nonetheless concluded that the tort remedy clearly provided the plaintiff with the due process to which he was constitutionally entitled since he could be compensated fully for the loss of his property.

B.   RESTRICTIONS ON INMATE LABOR

Apart from questions that arise in the correctional context regarding whether inmates are constitutionally entitled to compensation because of a loss suffered due to the actions or inaction of correctional officials are questions concerning inmates' right to be compensated for work they perform while incarcerated. Inmates who are confined following a conviction generally have no constitutional right to receive compensation for their work. The Thirteenth Amendment to the Constitution, which prohibits involuntary servitude, specifically exempts from that prohibition prisoners who are forced to work as part of the punishment for their crimes.

Courts have also held that requiring pretrial detainees to perform tasks that are reasonably related to the correctional facility's operation, such as cleaning a housing unit or working in food services, does not abridge the Thirteenth Amendment or contravene the prohibition, grounded in due process, on punishing persons who have not been convicted of a crime. *See, e.g., Tourscher v. McCullough* (3d Cir.1999). According to the courts, such compulsory work assignments do not reflect the punitive intent needed to establish a violation of the Thirteenth Amendment or due process.

Even though prisoners may have no constitutional right to be compensated for their labor, they often do have a right to compensation under statutes or prison regulations. Typically, the statutes and regulations provide for a very low rate of compensation compared to compensation rates in the outside world. Wages of less than, and often much less than, fifty cents per hour for prisoners are quite common.

Prisoners have filed a number of lawsuits claiming that they are entitled to be paid for their work the minimum wage required by the Fair Labor Standards Act (FLSA). 29 U.S.C. § 206. Thus far, the vast majority of the courts have rejected these claims. These courts often have cited the FLSA's purpose of ensuring that workers are compensated enough to meet basic needs, such as for food, shelter, clothing, and medical care. Prison officials, these courts point out, already meet these basic needs for prisoners.

While prisoners' FLSA claims generally have failed, most courts have refused to hold that prisoners are categorically excluded from the FLSA. *See, e.g., Danneskjold v. Hausrath* (2d Cir.1996). In concluding that the FLSA can, in certain circumstances, apply to prisoners, courts have focused on another purpose of the FLSA—the prevention of the unfair competition that ensues when employers pay employees subminimum wages. These courts have expressed concerns about the unfair competition that can occur when inmate-produced goods or services compete with goods or services produced in the outside world. *See, e.g.*, *Watson v. Graves* (5th Cir.1990) (construction company owned by sheriff's daughter and son-in-law used inmate-laborers, paying them twenty dollars a day).

The risks of this kind of unfair competition already are somewhat limited by a ban on the interstate transportation of inmate-produced goods. 18 U.S.C. § 1761(a). But this ban has been criticized for impeding the adoption and expansion of prison industries programs. These programs can be useful in curtailing the inmate idleness that can cause problems in the management and control of inmates. Through these programs, inmates also can learn work skills that may facilitate their successful reintegration into society upon their release from prison. Consequently, Congress has exempted some pilot projects from this ban, subject to the caveat that the inmates participating in the pilot programs must be paid no less than the prevailing wages for comparable work in the community. *Id.* § 1761(c). In addition, the interstate-transportation ban does not apply to goods produced for federal, state, and local governments or for nonprofit organizations. *Id.* § 1761(b).

Despite these limits on the interstate-transportation ban, it has continued to serve as a substantial impediment to the establishment and operation of prison industries programs. To nurture the development, and safeguard the viability, of the federal prison industries program, Congress consequently adopted a number of years ago what has become known as the "mandatory-source rule." Under this rule, most federal agencies had to purchase goods produced in the federal prison industries program if they met the agencies' requirements and did not exceed market prices. This rule ignited forceful protests from domestic manufacturers, such as furniture makers. Congress responded by enacting an appropriations bill in 2004 prohibiting federal agencies from purchasing goods or services from the federal prison industries program unless they offered the purchasing agency the "best value" for its financial outlay. Whether this legislation leads to the enactment of more permanent restrictions on the purchase of goods and services from the federal prison industries program remains to be seen.

CHAPTER 17

CRUEL AND UNUSUAL PUNISHMENT

The Eighth Amendment to the United States Constitution prohibits the imposition of "cruel and unusual punishments." This amendment is applicable to the states via the Due Process Clause of the Fourteenth Amendment.

An Eighth Amendment claim can be raised in a number of different contexts. We have already discussed constraints the Eighth Amendment places on the imposition of the death penalty and, in unusual cases, on noncapital sentences. See Chapters 6 and 7. The way in which an inmate is treated while in prison or jail can also violate the Eighth Amendment. Eighth Amendment claims in this context generally concern alleged deficiencies in medical care, the use of force by correctional officers, the failure to afford protection from attacks by other inmates, and the conditions of the inmates' confinement.

The Eighth Amendment applies to individuals convicted of, and sentenced for, a crime. When pretrial detainees assert similar claims, their claims are analyzed under other constitutional provisions, usually the Due Process Clause. The lower courts are divided on whether a person convicted of, but not yet sentenced for, a crime is to be considered a pretrial detainee or a prisoner when analyzing a constitutional claim contesting the person's conditions of confinement or treatment while incarcerated.

A.   MEDICAL AND PSYCHIATRIC CARE

1.   The Right to Receive Medical Treatment

Inmates are dependent on correctional officials to get the medical care they need. The failure to provide inmates with that care can, in some circumstances, violate the Eighth Amendment. It is clear that not every inadequacy in the medical care afforded inmates gives rise to an Eighth Amendment claim. Negligence alone will not suffice. A governmental official must have acted with "deliberate indifference" to an inmate's "serious medical needs" for that official's actions or inaction to be considered cruel and unusual punishment. *Estelle v. Gamble* (S.Ct.1976). If the official's actions constituted mere negligence—the failure to act reasonably—an inmate cannot prevail on an asserted Eighth Amendment claim; usually, the inmate's only litigation option is to pursue a tort remedy in the state courts.

In *Estelle v. Gamble*, the Supreme Court helped to illuminate the boundary between negligence and deliberate indifference in its analysis of the inmate's claim before the Court. After hurting his back, the inmate who brought the suit in *Estelle* saw three different doctors and a medical assistant seventeen times over a three-month period. The medical personnel responded to his complaints of pain in a number of different ways—by prescribing bed rest, muscle relaxants, and pain relievers. Nonetheless, the inmate claimed that his back pain persisted and that the failure to adequately diagnose the source of his pain and treat it constituted cruel and unusual punishment. Specifically, the inmate claimed that the doctors were remiss in failing to order an X-ray of his back. The Supreme Court, however, held that this failure was, at most, medical malpractice for which the Eighth Amendment provides no redress.

In *Farmer v. Brennan* (S.Ct.1994), the Supreme Court identified three requirements that must be met before it can be said that a correctional or medical official acted with deliberate indifference. First, the official must have known the facts revealing that an inmate faced a substantial risk of serious harm. Second, the official must have actually deduced from these facts that the inmate was at significant risk of being seriously harmed. Third, the official must have failed to take reasonable steps to prevent the harm from occurring. In other words, even if an official was actually aware of a significant risk of serious harm to an inmate, the official did not act with deliberate indifference if the official acted reasonably, though unsuccessfully, to protect the inmate from harm.

While the Supreme Court in *Farmer v. Brennan* held that deliberate indifference requires that an official be subjectively aware of the significant threat of serious harm posed to an inmate, the Court noted that the official's awareness of the risk of harm can often be deduced from the obviousness of the risk. The Court underscored, however, that if an official was actually unaware of the risk of harm, despite its obviousness and despite the fact that a reasonable person would have recognized the risk, then the deliberate-indifference requirement is not met.

Deliberate indifference to the serious medical needs of an inmate can be manifested in a number of different ways. Correctional officers, for example, may act with the requisite deliberate indifference when they prevent an inmate from getting needed medical treatment or delay the obtaining of such treatment. Doctors, on the other hand, may act with deliberate indifference when they take no steps or only perfunctory steps in response to an inmate's medical complaints.

The existence of deliberate indifference can also sometimes be inferred from facts that go beyond the rendition of medical care to a particular inmate. For example, a recurring failure to adequately attend to a particular type of medical problem may reveal the presence of deliberate indifference when a review of just one of the incidents involving such a failure might suggest that only negligence has occurred. In addition, the risks posed by systemic problems in a correctional facility's medical-care system might be so substantial, and the need to rectify those problems so apparent, that the failure to do so supports

an inference of deliberate indifference. Such systemic problems often arise in the areas of medical
staffing, procedures, facilities, equipment, and
recordkeeping. *See, e.g., Bass v. Wallenstein* (7th
Cir.1985) (sick-call procedures failed to ensure
prompt access to medical care); *Wellman v. Faulkner* (7th Cir.1983) (two of three prison doctors could
barely speak English; failure to stock necessary
medical supplies, such as colostomy bags); *Madrid
v. Gomez* (N.D.Cal.1995) (gross understaffing
caused lengthy delays in medical treatment and, in
turn, deaths and serious injuries).

When pretrial detainees complain that the medical care they have received does not meet constitutional requirements, their claims are not analyzed
under the Eighth Amendment. The claims of pretrial detainees are instead analyzed under the Due
Process Clauses of either the Fifth or the Fourteenth Amendment. According to the Supreme
Court, the Constitution affords pretrial detainees at
least as much protection, in terms of the medical
care with which they must be provided, as inmates
serving criminal sentences. *City of Revere v. Massachusetts Gen. Hosp.* (S.Ct.1983). Consequently, the
deliberate indifference of correctional officials to the
serious medical needs of a pretrial detainee clearly
constitutes a violation of due process.

Even if correctional officials act with deliberate
indifference to an inmate's medical needs, no violation of the Eighth Amendment ensues unless the
inmate's medical need is "serious." The Supreme
Court has not defined what it meant in *Estelle v.*

Gamble by a "serious" medical need, but the lower courts have attempted to flesh out the meaning of this requirement. Most have agreed that a medical need should be considered serious if either a doctor has determined that medical treatment is required or the need for treatment is so obvious that even a layperson would recognize the need for treatment. *See, e.g., Zentmyer v. Kendall County* (7th Cir.2000). Whether the need for medical treatment would be considered obvious to a layperson depends on a number of different factors, including the type of medical problem; the likelihood that pain or injury would result if the medical problem is not attended to; the severity of that pain or injury; and the extent to which pain or injury has already occurred.

The courts have recognized that mental problems can cause suffering that is as unbearable as that caused by physical ailments. Accordingly, a mental affliction may constitute a serious medical need that, in conjunction with the deliberate indifference of governmental officials, will trigger liability under the Eighth Amendment. In order for a mental or emotional problem to be considered "serious" within the meaning of *Estelle v. Gamble*, an inmate must allege more than that he or she has felt depressed, because almost every person confined in prison feels depressed at times.

Some lower courts have applied a three-part test that must be met in order for a psychiatric or psychological problem to rise to the level of a "serious" medical need. Under that test, a doctor or other health-care provider must have concluded that: (1) the prisoner's symptoms stem from a serious disease or injury; (2) the prisoner can be cured or his or her symptoms substantially alleviated; and (3) the risk of harm to the prisoner is great if treatment is delayed or denied. *See, e.g., Bowring v. Godwin* (4th Cir.1977).

In addition to the care and treatment to which sick and disabled inmates are entitled under the Constitution, statutes may serve as a separate source of protection. Perhaps the most significant example of the breadth of protection that may be afforded by a statute is the Americans with Disabilities Act, codified at 42 U.S.C. §§ 12101–12213. That Act prohibits state and local governments and other public entities from discriminating against any "qualified individual with a disability" and from excluding individuals from programs, services, or activities because of their disability. *Id.* § 12132. A "qualified individual with a disability" is defined as "an individual with a disability who, with or without reasonable modifications to rules, policies, or practices, the removal of architectural, communication, or transportation barriers, or the provision of auxiliary aids and services, meets the essential eligibility requirements for the receipt of services or the participation in programs or activities provided by a public entity." *Id.* § 12131(2). Because of this Act, state and local officials have had to take a number of steps, including some physical-plant modifications, to ensure that disabled inmates can participate in programs and receive services available to nondisabled inmates. Another federal statute, the

Rehabilitation Act of 1973, also prohibits federal agencies, as well as state and local agencies that receive federal financial assistance, from discriminating against individuals because of their disabilities. *See* 29 U.S.C. § 794.

2.   The Right to Refuse Medical Treatment

Some prisoners assert claims, not to receive medical treatment, but to avoid being subjected to certain forms of treatment. Generally these claims asserting a constitutional right to refuse medical treatment arise when mentally ill inmates resist the administration of medication to temper the effects of their illnesses.

In *Washington v. Harper* (S.Ct.1990), the Supreme Court addressed several constitutional questions concerning the involuntary administration of antipsychotic medication to a mentally ill inmate. The questions regarding the procedural safeguards that must attend the involuntary administration of such medication were discussed in Chapter 14. Another question before the Court involved the parameters of substantive due process: When can antipsychotic medication be administered to an inmate over the inmate's objection?

The prison policy whose constitutionality the Supreme Court was analyzing permitted antipsychotic drugs to be involuntarily administered when an inmate "suffers from a mental disorder and as a result of that disorder constitutes a likelihood of serious harm to himself or others and/or is gravely disabled." The plaintiff in *Harper* contended that this policy abridged his substantive-due-process rights. He underscored the invasiveness of such unwanted medical treatment—not only the physical intrusion that results from such treatment, but also the degradation of having someone else decide what to do with his body. In addition, he noted the serious, and sometimes lethal, side effects that can be caused by antipsychotic drugs, including catatonia, swelling of the brain, drowsiness, restlessness, high blood pressure, nausea, vomiting, headaches, constipation, blurred vision, impotency, eczema, tremors, muscle spasms, and involuntary movements so disabling that a person cannot perform such basic tasks as driving a car. Antipsychotic drugs can also cause neuroleptic malignant syndrome, which is fatal in 30% of the cases in which people suffer from this affliction.

Because of the indignity of being forced to take drugs that he did not want to take, as well as the negative effects of those drugs, the plaintiff in *Harper* contended that medication could not be forced on him unless he was incompetent to make decisions concerning his medical welfare. He further argued that even if he was incompetent, the medication could still not be administered to him, over his objection, unless a finding was made that he would have consented to such treatment if he were competent.

The Supreme Court refused to put so many roadblocks in the path of officials trying to prevent mentally ill inmates from harming themselves or others. Applying the *Turner* test discussed earlier in

Chapter 11, the Court instead observed that a prison policy governing the involuntary administration of antipsychotic drugs is constitutional if it is "reasonably related to legitimate penological interests."

The Supreme Court ultimately concluded that this test was met in this case. The Court noted the obligation of prison officials to not only protect others from prisoners, but also to protect prisoners from themselves. In addition, the Court emphasized the absence of any viable alternatives that could accommodate inmates' desire not to be forcibly drugged, at only *de minimis* cost to legitimate penological objectives. The Court had doubts, for example, about the soundness, from a medical perspective, of either secluding or physically restraining mentally ill inmates who posed a risk of harm to themselves or others. The Court also noted the harm that inmates could inflict on themselves, even when physically restrained, and the injuries they could inflict on others attempting to place restraints on them. (Interestingly, the Court did not address the implications of the fact that inmates to whom antipsychotic medication is about to be involuntarily administered could also inflict such injuries on others.)

The Supreme Court concluded by holding in *Washington v. Harper* that if inmates have a "serious mental illness," antipsychotic drugs can be administered involuntarily to them as long as two requirements are met: one, the inmates pose a danger to themselves or others; and two, the treatment is in their "medical interest." The dissenters

in *Harper* pointed out what they considered one of
the ironies of the majority's opinion: that the prison
policy upheld by the Court in that case did not, on
its face, actually meet the substantive-due-process
requirements described by the Court. Nowhere in
that policy was there a requirement that the medication decision be made with the medical interests
of the inmate in mind. The Court, however, apparently assumed that doctors would prescribe medication only to meet the medical needs of their
patients. In fact, the Court referred in its opinion to
the ethical duty of doctors to refrain from prescribing medication for any other reason. The dissenters,
on the other hand, emphasized what they considered to be the very real risk that antipsychotic
drugs would be prescribed, not to advance inmates'
medical interests, but to make it easier for officials
to control unruly inmates.

B. CONDITIONS OF CONFINEMENT

The conditions of inmates' confinement can, unquestionably, in some circumstances inflict cruel
and unusual punishment on them. Inmates have
asserted a variety of claims contesting the constitutionality of the conditions of their confinement.
They have, for example, complained about inadequate food, poor ventilation, rodent and insect in-
festation, fire hazards, inoperable toilets, and rampant violence. One of the most common complaints
has concerned the crowded conditions to which inmates are subjected in so many of the nation's
prisons and jails.

As was mentioned in Chapter 1, the United States has the highest incarceration rate of any country in the world. To house the ever increasing number of inmates, federal, state, and local governments have, in recent years, built hundreds of new prisons and jails, at a cost of billions of dollars to American taxpayers. Even with the enormous diversion of resources from other governmental programs for the construction and operation of these new correctional facilities, construction has not been able to keep pace with the demand for prison and jail space. With too many inmates and not enough space for them, correctional officials have been forced sometimes to set up beds for inmates in gymnasiums, dayrooms, hallways, and many other places throughout their correctional facilities. Correctional officials have also responded to the need for bed space by housing two, and sometimes more, inmates in cells, many of which were designed for only one inmate.

It is clear that the double celling of prisoners is not *per se* unconstitutional. In *Bell v. Wolfish* (S.Ct. 1979), the Supreme Court considered the constitutionality, under the Due Process Clause of the Fifth Amendment, of housing federal pretrial detainees two to a cell in cells that were designed to hold only one person. Each cell had seventy-five square feet of cell space.

In rejecting the plaintiffs' argument that double celling them in effect punished them in violation of their right to due process of law, the Supreme Court emphatically declared that there is no "one man,

one cell" principle subsumed within the Constitution. At the same time, the Court emphasized two
factors that supported its conclusion that the double
celling in that case did not abridge any constitutional rights. First, most of the detainees were not
confined in the detention center for very long. Almost all of them were released within sixty days.
Second, even while they were confined in the correctional center, the detainees had a great deal of
freedom of movement. They had to stay in their
cells only seven to eight hours a day, during which
time they slept, thereby mitigating any hardships
ensuing from the double celling.

In *Rhodes v. Chapman* (S.Ct.1981), the Supreme
Court confirmed that just because inmates are double-celled does not mean that their constitutional
rights have been violated. The inmates who brought
suit in *Rhodes* were double-celled because the prison, built with 1620 cells, housed 2300 inmates.
Each cell was sixty-three square feet in size, but
much of this space was consumed by a bunk bed,
sink, toilet, and cabinets. Because the prison in
question was a maximum-security facility, most of
the inmates within it were more serious offenders
serving long prison sentences, who could expect to
be subjected to the conditions about which they
complained for many years.

The Supreme Court nonetheless balked at the
suggestion that the double celling of the inmates
constituted cruel and unusual punishment. The
Court underscored that the trial judge had toured
the prison and had found it to be "unquestionably a

top-flight, first-class facility." The food was adequate, the ventilation system worked reasonably well, the noise level was not too high in the cellblocks, and the temperature within the prison was neither too hot nor too cold. Although it was true that violence had increased within the prison in recent years, the Court considered it significant that there was no evidence that this increase was attributable to the double bunking of inmates.

A fact that the Court considered particularly significant was that most inmates did not have to remain within their cells during the day. They could go to a dayroom next to their cellblock from 6:30 in the morning until 9:30 at night. Each dayroom had a television, card tables, and chairs and was, according to the Court, the equivalent of a living room or den.

The Supreme Court concluded that these conditions did not violate the Eighth Amendment. They did not conflict with the "evolving standards of decency that mark the progress of a maturing society," constitute the "unnecessary or wanton infliction of pain," or lead to punishment that was "grossly disproportionate" to the severity of the crimes warranting imprisonment. The Court conceded that the amount of living space accorded each inmate was much less than the amount prescribed by the standards of numerous professional organizations at that time, such as the American Correctional Association (60–80 square feet per inmate) and the National Sheriffs' Association (70–80 square feet). The Supreme Court observed that while the opinions of experts are relevant to the question whether conditions of confinement constitute cruel and unusual punishment, they are not conclusive. Far more important, in the Court's opinion, are the views of the general public as to the acceptability of a particular punishment, and the Court could find no evidence of public opposition to the double celling of inmates. To the extent that the conditions of the inmates' confinement were unpleasant and even harsh, that, according to the Court, was simply part of the price that they had to pay for the crimes they had committed. The Constitution, in the Court's words, "does not mandate comfortable prisons."

The Supreme Court in *Rhodes v. Chapman* also acknowledged that work and educational opportunities for inmates had diminished at the prison because of double celling and the resultant overcrowding. But the Court considered this fact irrelevant to the constitutional question before it. The Court observed: "[L]imited work hours and delay before receiving education do not inflict pain, much less unnecessary and wanton pain; deprivations of this kind simply are not punishments."

The conditions of confinement whose constitutionality the Court upheld in *Rhodes v. Chapman* and *Bell v. Wolfish* are to be contrasted with the conditions in Arkansas prisons that the district court found, and the Supreme Court agreed, were unconstitutional in *Hutto v. Finney* (S.Ct.1978). The question before the Court in *Hutto* was the propriety of a district-court order limiting inmates' confinement in punitive-isolation cells to no more than thirty days as a means of alleviating the unconstitutional conditions in those cells. The cells were only eighty square feet in size, but held four, and sometimes up to ten or eleven, inmates. The cells contained no windows or furniture, and the toilet within each cell could only be flushed from outside the cell, creating obvious odor and sanitation problems if correctional officers refused to flush the toilets. Each night, the inmates slept on mattresses brought into the cells, but because the mattresses were intermingled each day, inmates slept on mattresses previously used by inmates with hepatitis and other infectious diseases. The inmates in punitive isolation were also poorly fed, receiving less than one thousand calories a day, less than half the amount required by basic nutritional standards.

The Supreme Court considered the district court's order limiting the duration of an inmate's confinement in a punitive-isolation cell a reasonable response to the sordid and unconstitutional conditions in those cells. Noting that the length of time that an inmate is subjected to certain conditions is relevant to the question whether those conditions constitute cruel and unusual punishment, the Court observed, "A filthy, overcrowded cell and a diet of 'grue' might be tolerable for a few days and intolerably cruel for weeks or months."

In *Wilson v. Seiter* (S.Ct.1991), the Supreme Court clarified that there is both an objective and a subjective requirement that must be met for conditions of confinement to be considered cruel and unusual punishment. In describing the objective component of the Eighth Amendment, the Court said that an inmate must have been deprived of an "identifiable human need," such as food, warmth, or exercise.

In *Overton v. Bazzetta* (S.Ct.2003), the Supreme Court held that rescinding for two years the visiting privileges of prisoners twice found guilty of violating a prison's substance-abuse regulations did not abridge the Eighth Amendment. The Court concluded that the visitation ban did not deprive inmates of "basic necessities." Because the restriction of visiting privileges was a commonly employed disciplinary sanction, the Court furthermore found that the ban did not constitute a "dramatic departure from accepted standards for conditions of confinement." At the same time, the Court intimated that its disposition of the case might have been different had prison officials instituted a more far-reaching visitation ban, such as a permanent ban on visiting privileges.

It is clear from the Supreme Court's decision in *Helling v. McKinney* (S.Ct.1993) that inmates need not currently be suffering injuries from the conditions of their confinement as a precondition to bringing an Eighth Amendment claim; sometimes a risk of future harm, if that risk is sufficiently high, will suffice.

The plaintiff in *Helling*, a nonsmoker, was confined in a 48–square-foot cell with another inmate who smoked five packs of cigarettes a day. While the Supreme Court did not itself resolve whether these conditions amounted to cruel and unusual punishment, the Court held that the objective requirement that had to be met to prevail on a claim of cruel and unusual punishment would be satisfied if, on remand, the plaintiff proved both that he was exposed to unreasonable amounts of tobacco smoke and that this exposure created a risk of harm so serious as to violate society's standards of decency. In other words, the risk could not be one that society has chosen to tolerate.

Elaborating on the subjective component of an Eighth Amendment claim challenging conditions of confinement in a correctional facility, the Supreme Court in *Wilson v. Seiter* said that a plaintiff must prove that a defendant acted with deliberate indifference in failing to rectify the deficiencies in those conditions. Four Justices on the Court strongly disagreed with this proposition, arguing that the effect on prisoners of inhumane prison conditions are the same, regardless of the state of mind of the officials maintaining those conditions. Another concern of the dissenters was that correctional officials might duck their responsibility under the Eighth Amendment to run safe and humane prisons by casting blame on legislatures for failing to appropriate requested funds needed to redress or avert problems in the prisons. The majority of the Court skirted this critical question of the extent to which, if at all, the costs of rectifying problems in prison conditions and the lack of funding to do so have a bearing on the existence of the deliberate indifference needed to sustain an Eighth Amendment claim.

C. USE OF FORCE AND
THE PROTECTION
OF INMATES

Correctional officials may use force in their dealings with inmates for a number of different reasons. Force may be used, for example, to end a prison riot, to stop a fight between two inmates, and to get a resisting inmate into or out of his or her cell. At some point, the use of force becomes excessive and violates constitutional strictures. The question is: How do we identify that point?

In *Whitley v. Albers* (S.Ct.1986), the Supreme Court was confronted with the question of when force employed to quell a prison riot or disturbance constitutes cruel and unusual punishment in violation of the Eighth Amendment. The plaintiff in *Whitley*, a prisoner, filed a § 1983 suit against several correctional officials after he was shot in the knee in the midst of a prison disturbance. During the disturbance, defiant prisoners refused orders to return to their cells, broke furniture, and seized a correctional officer as a hostage, placing him in a cell on the second tier of the cellblock.

When the prison security manager, Captain Whitley, visited the cellblock, the prisoners' ringleader, who had a knife, warned him that he would kill the hostage if a riot squad entered the cellblock. The ringleader also told Whitley that one inmate had been killed already. This latter statement, unbeknownst to Whitley, was not true, although one inmate had in fact been beaten by other inmates.

Whitley and his superiors eventually decided that they needed to storm the cellblock in order to save the hostage's life and protect other inmates. When they did so, a correctional officer fired a warning shot in accordance with the plan they had developed to retake the cellblock. When the plaintiff then began to run up the stairs in an attempt to get to the relative safety of his cell on an upper tier, the same correctional officer shot him in the knee, severely injuring him.

At the trial, expert witnesses offered conflicting testimony as to whether there was a need to use the force that had resulted in the plaintiff's injuries. Nonetheless, the trial court directed a verdict for the defendants, which means that the question of the constitutionality of the defendants' actions was not submitted to the jury.

The technical question before the Supreme Court was the propriety of entering this directed verdict, but to answer this question, the Court first had to clarify when the use of force would constitute cruel and unusual punishment under these circumstances. As in earlier cases, the Court noted that the "unnecessary and wanton infliction of pain" violates the Eighth Amendment. It is clear from *Whitley* that what constitutes the "unnecessary and wanton infliction of pain" depends upon the context in which a claim of cruel and unusual punishment is asserted.

In *Estelle v. Gamble* (S.Ct.1976), the Supreme Court had held that "deliberate indifference" to an inmate's "serious medical needs" represents the unnecessary and wanton infliction of pain that violates the Eighth Amendment. In *Whitley v. Albers*, however, the Supreme Court refused to apply a deliberate-indifference standard when examining correctional officials' use of force during a prison disturbance. The Court explained that the provision of needed medical care to inmates does not conflict with other important governmental responsibilities, so a standard of review which is less deferential to governmental officials is appropriate in the medical-care context. By contrast, when officials are deciding whether to use force to end a disturbance, they are often faced with a Hobson's choice: use force, which may lead to some inmates or hostages being harmed, or refrain from using force, leaving hostages and some inmates vulnerable to injuries and even death at the hands of other inmates.

The Court in *Whitley* ultimately concluded that to prevail on an Eighth Amendment claim contesting the force used to quell a prison disturbance, a prisoner would have to prove that the force was used " 'maliciously and sadistically for the very purpose of causing harm.' " Such unconstitutionally excessive force was to be contrasted with force used in " 'a good faith effort to maintain or restore discipline.' " The Court listed several factors to be examined when determining whether a correctional

official had acted with the malicious intent needed
for the use of force to be considered cruel and
unusual punishment: (1) the need to use force; (2)
the relationship between that need and the amount
of force that was used; (3) the gravity of the ensuing
injuries caused by the use of force; (4) the extent to
which, based on the facts known by the correctional
officials at the time they used force, inmates and
staff faced harm if force was not employed; and (5)
the steps, if any, taken by the correctional officials
to limit the amount of force used.

Having enunciated the applicable Eighth Amendment standard, the Supreme Court then turned to
the task of applying that standard to the facts of the
case before it. The Court acknowledged that there
was some evidence that the inmates had quieted
down somewhat by the time the riot squad entered
the cellblock. The Court also recognized that the
expert witnesses differed in their views as to whether the force employed in regaining control of the
cellblock was necessary. The Court concluded that
all of this evidence suggested, at most, that the
defendants had acted negligently in constructing
their rescue plan. The Court observed that in order
for this case to have been submitted to the jury, the
evidence adduced at trial would have to have supported an inference that the defendants acted wan-
tonly—either in the development of the plan for
regaining control of the cellblock and rescuing the
hostage or in the execution of that plan. But the
Court found the requisite evidence of wantonness
simply absent in this case. The Court underscored

how volatile and dangerous the situation remained when the correctional officials stormed the cellblock—a correctional officer was still held hostage, the most outspoken inmate was armed with a knife, and the inmates retained control of the cellblock. Under these circumstances, according to the Court, it could not be said that there was "no plausible basis" for believing that the use of force, as planned, was necessary to rescue the hostage and retake control of the cellblock.

The plaintiff in *Whitley* also contended that when he was shot, his right to substantive due process was violated. The Supreme Court summarily rejected this claim, simply noting that the Due Process Clause affords inmates no greater protection than the Eighth Amendment when they are contesting the constitutionality of the force used against them.

The Supreme Court has now clarified that the Eighth Amendment standard enunciated in *Whitley v. Albers* is to be applied, not just in cases involving the use of force during a prison riot, but whenever inmates claim that excessive force was used against them in violation of the Eighth Amendment. *Hudson v. McMillian* (S.Ct.1992). The line between an excessive-force claim, to which the *Whitley* standard applies, and a conditions-of-confinement claim, to which a deliberate-indifference standard applies, may not always be altogether clear. *Hope v. Pelzer* (S.Ct.2002) is a case in point. *Hope* involved a prisoner who was handcuffed two different times to a hitching post, once after arguing with a prisoner and the other time after failing to obey a correctional officer's order quickly enough. One of the times the inmate was shackled to the hitching post he was forced to stand with his hands raised slightly above his shoulders for seven hours in the baking sun without a shirt on. In concluding that the prisoner was subjected to the unnecessary and wanton infliction of pain prohibited by the Eighth Amendment, the Supreme Court applied the deliberate-indifference standard, not the malicious-intent test applied in excessive-force cases.

In *Hudson v. McMillian*, the Supreme Court rejected the notion that an inmate must have suffered a "significant injury" in order for the force used to be considered cruel and unusual punishment. The Court was concerned that to rule otherwise would leave prisoners vulnerable to forms of torture that cause no physical injuries or leave any lasting physical imprints. The Court emphasized in *Hudson*, however, that not every "malevolent touch" by a correctional officer gives rise to a constitutional grievance. The Court explained that *de minimis* uses of force do not rise to the level of cruel and unusual punishments unless the kind of force used is " 'repugnant to the conscience of mankind.' "

Although the Eighth Amendment contains no significant-injury requirement, the Prison Litigation Reform Act, enacted by Congress in 1996, included a provision that makes inmates', including pretrial detainees', access to federal courts contingent on the type of injury for which they are seeking redress in a suit for compensatory damages. That provision, codified at 42 U.S.C. § 1997e(e), prohibits prisoners from bringing civil suits in federal court for mental or emotional injuries suffered while confined in a correctional facility unless they can show that they also suffered a physical injury. An example of the type of claim for compensatory relief that now would be barred by this physical-injury requirement can be found in *Oses v. Fair* (D.Mass.1990). In that case, the district court held that a prisoner was subjected to cruel and unusual punishment when a correctional officer stuck a gun barrel in the prisoner's mouth and made him kiss the shoes of the correctional officer's wife.

At times, inmates sue correctional officials, not because the officials have hurt them, but because the officials have failed to protect them from being hurt by other inmates. The failure to protect an inmate from being harmed by other inmates can, in some circumstances, constitute cruel and unusual punishment. To violate the Eighth Amendment, the officials must have been more than just negligent in their failure to protect an inmate. The officials must have acted with deliberate indifference to a substantial risk that an inmate would be seriously harmed by another inmate. In other words, the officials must have been actually aware of the significant risk of serious harm and then failed to act reasonably to prevent the harm from occurring. *Farmer v. Brennan* (S.Ct.1994).

The failure to protect inmates, not from others but from themselves, may also in some circumstances violate the Eighth Amendment and, in the case of pretrial detainees, due process of law. Just because an inmate commits suicide does not mean that correctional officials will be held legally responsible for the death. As the courts have recognized, persons bent on killing themselves often will eventually succeed in doing so. When, however, officials act with deliberate indifference to the substantial risk that an inmate will commit suicide, a constitutional violation ensues. *Jacobs v. West Feliciana Sheriff's Dep't* (5th Cir.2000).

PART THREE

PRISONERS' RIGHTS LITIGATION

CHAPTER 18

THE MECHANICS OF LITIGATING INMATES' § 1983 SUITS

A. FILING A § 1983 COMPLAINT

The primary vehicle for redressing violations of inmates' constitutional rights by state or local officials is the federal civil-rights statute codified at 42 U.S.C. § 1983. Section 1983 provides in part as follows:

> Every person who, under color of any statute, ordinance, regulation, custom, or usage, of any State or Territory or the District of Columbia, subjects, or causes to be subjected, any citizen of the United States or other person within the jurisdiction thereof to the deprivation of any rights, privileges, or immunities secured by the Constitution and laws, shall be liable to the party injured in an action at law, suit in equity, or other proper proceeding for redress. . . .

The rules and procedures pertaining to the litigation of § 1983 suits are complex. This chapter focuses on some of the more basic points concerning § 1983 litigation. For more detailed information, the reader is encouraged to turn to additional resources that discuss § 1983 actions exclusively. *See, e.g.*, Sheldon H. Nahmod, *Civil Rights and Civil Liberties Litigation: The Law of Section 1983* (4th ed. 2004).

1. Elements of a Cause of Action Under § 1983

There are four key elements that must be established by an inmate to prevail in a § 1983 action. These elements are briefly described below.

1.   *Person*—First, a "person" must have violated the inmate's rights. The Supreme Court has not interpreted the word "person" literally; the "persons" who can be sued under § 1983 are not confined to human beings. Municipalities are, for example, "persons" within the meaning of § 1983. *Monell v. Department of Social Servs.* (S.Ct.1978). In *Monell*, the Supreme Court reached this conclusion due to the fact that at the time that § 1983 was enacted, another federal statute, known as the Dictionary Act, defined the word "person" to include political and corporate entities "unless the context shows that such words were intended to be used in a more limited sense." *See also Holloway v. Brush* (6th Cir.2000) (counties are "persons" subject to suit under § 1983).

According to the Supreme Court though, states are not "persons" subject to suit under § 1983. In *Will v. Michigan Dep't of State Police* (S.Ct.1989), the Court noted that Congress would have been aware of the immunity of states under the Eleventh Amendment when they are sued under § 1983 in a federal court. The Court thought it unlikely that Congress had nonetheless intended to make states subject to suit in § 1983 actions filed in state courts. The Court therefore interpreted § 1983 as not extending to states at all. U.S. territories are also not considered "persons" within the meaning of § 1983. *Ngiraingas v. Sanchez* (S.Ct.1990).

State officials, on the other hand, are sometimes "persons" who can be sued under § 1983 and sometimes not. When sued in their official capacity for damages, state officials are not considered "persons" in the legal sense, because the lawsuit, in effect, is one against the state. *Will v. Michigan Dep't of State Police* (S.Ct.1989). Any damages awarded would be paid out of the state's treasury.

However, state officials can be sued in their official capacity under § 1983 for injunctive relief. *Id.* This type of relief, which requires officials to take, or refrain from taking, certain actions in the future, is not considered to be directed at the state, even though in reality, compliance with an injunction will often require the expenditure of state funds.

State officials are also "persons" within the meaning of § 1983 when they are sued in their personal capacity. Personal-capacity suits, which are also called individual-capacity suits, are not considered suits against the state, because any damages awarded are payable by the officials themselves rather than the state. A state may still choose though to indemnify an official for damages paid to an inmate who prevails in a § 1983 suit.

2. *"Under Color of" State Law*—For an action to lie under § 1983, the "person" sued must have acted "under color of" state law—specifically, a state statute, ordinance, regulation, custom, or usage. To satisfy this under-color-of-state-law requirement, it is not necessary that a state law require, or even authorize, the defendant's unconstitutional actions. In fact, as was discussed in Chapter 10, the requirement can be met even if a state law specifically prohibits the defendant's actions. Thus, in *Monroe v. Pape* (S.Ct.1961), the Supreme Court concluded that police officers had acted "under the color of" state law when entering the plaintiffs' home without a warrant, even though the warrantless entry violated the state's constitution and certain state statutes.

The Court noted in *Monroe v. Pape* that for a person's actions to be deemed taken "under color of" state law, they need only reflect the " '[m]isuse of power, possessed by virtue of state law and made possible only because the wrongdoer is clothed with the authority of state law.' " The Court reasoned that § 1983 was enacted to provide a federal remedy for the violation of constitutional rights in part because states often had failed in the past to enforce their own laws.

In recent years, governments have increasingly turned to private contractors to provide specific services, such as medical care, at correctional facilities or to completely operate those facilities. The question that arises is whether these private contractors can be sued under § 1983 for violating the constitutional rights of inmates. Specifically, do these private contractors act "under color of" state law? The answer to these questions, after the Supreme Court's decision in *West v. Atkins* (S.Ct. 1988), is clearly yes. In *West*, the Court concluded that a private physician who worked in a state prison two days a week could be sued under § 1983. According to the Court, it did not matter that the defendant was not a state employee or that he only worked part-time within the prison. What mattered was his function; he had agreed to assume the government's responsibility, one that the state had delegated to him, of providing inmates with the medical care to which they were constitutionally entitled.

3. *Causation*—A third element that must be established to prevail in a § 1983 action is causation. Only a person who "subjects" another to a constitutional violation or "causes" another to be so subjected can be liable under § 1983.

Many of the questions concerning this causation requirement have arisen in cases concerning the liability of municipalities under § 1983. According to the Supreme Court, a municipality is not liable under § 1983 simply because one of its employees violated someone's constitutional rights. *Monell v.*

Department of Social Servs. (S.Ct.1978). In other words, the doctrine of *respondeat superior* does not apply in § 1983 actions. Under this doctrine, an employer generally is liable for torts committed by an employee that occurred when the employee was acting within the scope of his or her employment.

While the Supreme Court has definitively resolved that there is no *respondeat-superior* liability under § 1983, the Court has struggled in attempting to define exactly when municipalities will be held liable under § 1983. Most of the Supreme Court decisions discussing municipal liability have been fragmented into a confusing mix of plurality, concurring, and dissenting opinions. *See, e.g., St. Louis v. Praprotnik* (S.Ct.1988); *Pembaur v. Cincinnati* (S.Ct.1986); *Oklahoma City v. Tuttle* (S.Ct. 1985). A few clear requirements, however, emerge from these cases.

First, for a municipality to be liable under § 1983, the constitutional violation must have stemmed from an official policy or custom. Second, that policy or custom must have been the "moving force" behind the constitutional violation. Just because a municipality, for example, inadequately trains some of its employees, such as officials working in a local jail, does not mean that the municipality will necessarily be liable under § 1983 if one of those employees violates someone's constitutional rights. To give rise to § 1983 liability, the failure to train adequately must be accompanied by a "deliberate indifference" to the risk that the deficient training will result in constitutional violations. *Canton v. Harris* (S.Ct.1989).

The existence of such deliberate indifference can be established by showing, for example, that municipal policymakers ignored a very obvious need for more or different training even though deficiencies in the training of municipal employees created an apparent and substantial likelihood that they would act unconstitutionally. Alternatively, deliberate indifference may be manifested by the failure to augment training when recurring constitutional violations, such as repeated incidents involving excessive use of force by jail officials, make the need for more training "plainly obvious."

The indifference that will give rise to municipal liability under § 1983 is indifference to the risk that a constitutional violation will ensue from the municipality's actions or inaction. Thus, if a municipality is sued for hiring an unqualified person who then violated the plaintiff's constitutional rights, municipal officials' indifference to the job applicant's qualifications, or lack thereof, for the job will not suffice. For the municipality to be liable under § 1983, a municipal policymaker must have been indifferent to the obvious risk that a constitutional violation might ensue if the job applicant was hired. Consequently, a cursory review of a job applicant's credentials is not tantamount to deliberate indifference, because a full review of an applicant's background might reveal that the applicant is well-qualified for the job. Only if a "reasonable policymaker" would have concluded, after conducting an adequate review of the job applicant's background, that the "plainly obvious" consequence of hiring the applicant would be the violation of another person's constitutional rights is the deliberate indifference required for municipal liability present. *Board of the County Comm'rs v. Brown* (S.Ct.1997).

4. *Violation of Federal Rights*—Finally, to prevail in a § 1983 suit, the plaintiff must prove that the defendant violated his or her constitutional rights or other rights afforded by federal law. The constitutional rights of prisoners were discussed in earlier chapters of this book.

2. *Bivens* Actions

Section 1983 only authorizes the bringing of a lawsuit for the violation of constitutional rights that occurred "under the color of" state law. There is no federal counterpart to § 1983—no comparable statute to which federal prisoners can turn when their constitutional rights are violated. Nonetheless, these prisoners are not left remediless. In *Bivens v. Six Unknown Federal Narcotics Agents* (S.Ct.1971), the Supreme Court held that the Fourth Amendment implicitly authorizes suits for damages against federal officials who violate its requirements. The Court has since held that what has come to be known as a *Bivens* suit can be brought for the violation of other constitutional rights. *See, e.g., Carlson v. Green* (S.Ct.1980) (Eighth Amendment cruel and unusual punishment); *Davis v. Passman* (S.Ct.1979) (Fifth Amendment due process).

Bivens actions can only be brought against federal officials, not federal agencies. *Federal Deposit Ins. Corp. v. Meyer* (S.Ct.1994). In addition, private companies with which the Federal Bureau of Prisons contracts to provide housing and other services to inmates cannot be sued in a *Bivens* action. *Correctional Servs. Corp. v. Malesko* (S.Ct.2001).

3. Jurisdiction

State and federal courts have concurrent jurisdiction over § 1983 suits. *Felder v. Casey* (S.Ct.1988). In other words, a § 1983 suit can be filed in either a state court or a federal court. The decision regarding in which court to bring suit will depend on a number of factors, including the procedural rules, particularly the discovery rules, that apply in the two courts; the location of the courts; the time that it will take, because of docket loads, to move the case through the different courts; and the extent to which each court seems receptive to civil-rights claims—in this context, civil-rights claims filed by inmates.

After deciding in which court to file a § 1983 suit, a prisoner who files suit in federal court must decide whether to consent to a magistrate judge's assignment to the case if the district court has authorized the magistrate judge or judges in the district to handle such cases. If both parties consent to the magistrate judge's assignment, the magistrate judge can handle all proceedings in a case, even entering final judgment after a bench or jury trial. 28 U.S.C. § 636(c)(1).

Even if one or both parties refuse to consent to the assigning of a case to a magistrate judge, a magistrate judge can still be, and often is, heavily involved in the processing of a prisoner's civil-rights case. The magistrate judge can enter an array of what are called "nondispositive orders" in a case, including orders resolving discovery disputes. *Id.* § 636(b)(1)(A). The magistrate judge cannot enter dispositive orders, such as those resolving motions for summary judgment or involuntarily dismissing a case, but the magistrate judge can make recommendations to the district judge regarding the disposition of such motions. *Id.* § 636(b)(1)(B).

In addition, even if the parties have not consented to the referral of a case to a magistrate judge, the magistrate judge can still conduct a bench trial. The magistrate judge simply cannot render the final decision at the end of the trial. The magistrate judge must instead make proposed findings of fact and recommendations for the district judge's consideration. *Id.* Referral of a case to a magistrate judge for trial is, however, barred when a prisoner has a constitutional right to a jury trial (because the prisoner is suing for damages) and the prisoner has not waived that right. *McCarthy v. Bronson* (S.Ct. 1991).

4. Filing Fees

An indigent inmate who wants to file a lawsuit in federal court can seek leave under 28 U.S.C. § 1915(a)(1) to file a complaint *in forma pauperis*.

If the petition is granted, the inmate is excused from prepaying the full fees that normally must be paid when a lawsuit is filed in a federal district court. The indigent inmate is still responsible for paying the full filing fee at some point. The fee will simply be paid over time rather than at the outset of the lawsuit.

The Prison Litigation Reform Act (PLRA), which was enacted in 1996, established a mechanism for collecting filing-fee payments from prisoners unable to pay the full filing fee at the time a civil suit or appeal is filed in federal court. If a court determines that a prisoner cannot prepay the full filing fee, the court must assess an initial partial filing fee that represents the greater of: (1) the average monthly deposits in the prisoner's trust fund account; or (2) the average monthly balance in the account during the preceding six months. 28 U.S.C. § 1915(b)(1). If the prisoner has no means to pay this initial fee, the complaint or appeal can still be filed. *Id.* § 1915(b)(4).

The prisoner must then make monthly installment payments, when the funds are available to do so, until the full filing fee is paid. Each month, an amount equaling 20% of the income credited to the inmate's account the previous month is debited for payment of the balance of the filing fee. But no money to pay the filing fee can actually be sent to the court unless the amount of money in the account exceeds ten dollars. *Id.* § 1915(b)(2).

5. Sufficiency of the Complaint

Most prisoners' § 1983 complaints are filed *pro se*, which means that the prisoners are unrepresented and unassisted by counsel. A prisoner's *pro se* § 1983 complaint, like other complaints, will be dismissed if it fails to state a claim upon which relief can be granted. When determining whether a prisoner's *pro se* complaint states a cognizable claim, the lower courts have been instructed by the Supreme Court to liberally construe the complaint. *Haines v. Kerner* (S.Ct.1972). Only when it appears "beyond doubt that the plaintiff can prove no set of facts in support of his claim which would entitle him to relief" should the prisoner's *pro se* complaint be dismissed for failure to state a claim.

If feasible, a court must screen a prisoner's complaint against a governmental official or entity before it is docketed, or otherwise as soon as possible after docketing. If the court finds that a claim is frivolous, malicious, fails to state a claim for which relief can be granted, or seeks damages from a defendant who is immune from damages liability, the court must dismiss the claim. *Id.* § 1915A(a), (b). *See also* 42 U.S.C. § 1997e(c) (providing for *sua sponte* dismissals, which are dismissals on the court's own motion, for the same four reasons of prisoners' complaints brought under § 1983 or some other "Federal law" to contest the conditions of their confinement); 28 U.S.C. § 1915(e)(2)(providing for *sua sponte* dismissals for the same four reasons of federal lawsuits filed *in forma pauperis*).

The current standards governing the screening and dismissal of prisoners' complaints are different from those in effect before the PLRA was enacted in 1996. For example, before the PLRA's enactment, a court could *sua sponte* dismiss a frivolous claim that had been brought by a prisoner suing *in forma pauperis*, but a court could not *sua sponte* dismiss a complaint for failure to state a claim for which relief can be granted. To understand the significance of these changes in screening and dismissal procedures wrought by the PLRA, the distinction between a dismissal for frivolousness and a dismissal for failure to state a claim needs to be understood.

The standard applied when determining whether a complaint is frivolous is quite lax. A complaint will be considered frivolous only if it has no "arguable basis in law or in fact." *Neitzke v. Williams* (S.Ct.1989). By contrast, if a claim has an arguable basis in the law but the court decides that a disputed issue of law bearing on the claim's legal sufficiency should be resolved in the defendant's favor, a claim can be dismissed for failure to state a claim. The claim cannot, however, be considered frivolous.

The PLRA's practical repercussions stem from the fact that before the PLRA's enactment, a complaint could be dismissed for failure to state a claim for relief only upon motion of a defendant. A prisoner therefore had an opportunity to present arguments regarding whether the complaint stated a claim cognizable under the law. Because courts can now *sua sponte* dismiss prisoners' complaints for failure to state a claim, some prisoners may now be given no opportunity to respond to concerns about perceived legal deficiencies in a complaint.

6. The PLRA's "Three–Strikes" Provision

The PLRA also included what is known as the "three-strikes" provision. Under 28 U.S.C. § 1915(g), prisoners who have had civil complaints or appeals that they filed when they were incarcerated dismissed three or more times because they were frivolous, malicious, or failed to state a claim for which relief can be granted generally are prohibited from bringing further civil actions or appeals *in forma pauperis*. Only if an indigent prisoner is facing an imminent, serious, physical injury can suit be brought *in forma pauperis*. The practical effect of this provision is to foreclose indigent inmates who have accrued three "strikes" and do not have the funds to prepay the full filing fee from bringing many types of constitutional claims, such as First Amendment claims, that do not involve threats of physical injury.

Because the three-strikes provision does not apply to nonprisoners bringing suit *in forma pauperis*, prisoners have challenged its constitutionality on equal-protection grounds. Most courts have applied a rational-basis test in assessing the constitutionality of this differential treatment. This test requires that there be some "reasonably conceivable state of facts that could provide a rational basis for the classification" whose constitutionality has been contested. *FCC v. Beach Communications, Inc.* (S.Ct.

1993). Finding the requisite "rational basis" in Congress's supposition that prisoners are more likely than nonprisoners to file frivolous lawsuits, in part because prisoners have so much more spare time than nonprisoners, most courts have upheld the constitutionality of the three-strikes provision. *See, e.g., Higgins v. Carpenter* (8th Cir.2001) (listing cases).

7. Appointed Counsel

In addition to not having the funds to pay filing fees and costs, indigent inmates cannot afford to pay for the services of attorneys. These inmates are at a severe disadvantage when litigating their civil-rights claims unless a court appoints counsel to represent them. Title 28 U.S.C. § 1915(e)(1) authorizes courts to appoint counsel to represent indigent parties, including inmates, in federal lawsuits, but this authority is exercised in only a small fraction of prisoners' cases. The decision whether to appoint an attorney falls within the court's discretion, and the court's decision will be reversed on appeal only for an abuse of that discretion. Such reversals occur infrequently. Appellate courts typically have refused to find that the failure to appoint counsel was an abuse of discretion unless the following requirements were met: (1) the plaintiff was unable to procure, through his or her own efforts, the assistance of counsel; (2) because of the case's complexity or limitations on the plaintiff's ability to litigate the case, the plaintiff needed an attorney in order to "obtain justice"; and (3) the plaintiff had a "reasonable chance" of prevailing in the case if assisted by counsel. *Forbes v. Edgar* (7th Cir.1997).

B. AFFIRMATIVE DEFENSES

As is true in any lawsuit, defendants against whom § 1983 complaints have been filed can assert affirmative defenses to avoid liability. Some of the affirmative defenses that are most frequently raised in § 1983 lawsuits are discussed below.

1. Immunity

a. *Sovereign Immunity*

The United States cannot be sued without its consent. *United States v. Mitchell* (S.Ct.1983). Congress, however, has consented to the bringing of constitutional claims against the federal government, which means that federal prisoners can directly sue the government for violations of their constitutional rights. 28 U.S.C. § 1346(a)(2).

The assertion of constitutional claims against the states is more problematic. As mentioned earlier, states cannot even be sued under § 1983. *Will v. Michigan Dep't of State Police* (S.Ct.1989). If Congress were to amend § 1983 to specifically include states as suable defendants, however, the states, if sued, might not be able to successfully invoke an immunity defense. It is true that the Eleventh Amendment to the United States Constitution, as it has been construed by the Supreme Court, generally bars individuals from suing states in federal court. *Hans v. Louisiana* (S.Ct.1890). But Congress

has the power, stemming from § 5 of the Fourteenth Amendment, to override this Eleventh
Amendment immunity in order to effectuate the
provisions of the Fourteenth Amendment. *Fitzpatrick v. Bitzer* (S.Ct.1976). Although Congress did
not, according to the Court, exercise this power
when it enacted § 1983, *Quern v. Jordan* (S.Ct.
1979), it might choose to do so in the future.

Congress's exercise of its power under § 5, however, would face some constraints enunciated by the
Supreme Court in *Board of Trustees of the Univ. of
Alabama v. Garrett* (S.Ct.2001). In that case, the
Court held, in a 5–4 decision, that Congress had
exceeded its authority under § 5 when enacting the
part of the Americans with Disabilities Act that
prohibited the states from discriminating against
"qualified" prospective and current employees because of their disability. The Court cited two reasons for its holding. First, the Court stated that
Congress lacks the power to abrogate the states'
immunity under the Eleventh Amendment unless
Congress is responding to an established "pattern
of irrational state discrimination." According to the
Court majority, the fifty anecdotal accounts in the
ADA's legislative history of state discrimination
against the disabled were not enough evidence of
the requisite discriminatory pattern.

Second, the Court observed that even if the states
had engaged in such a pattern of discrimination
against the disabled, the federal remedy would have
to be "congruent and proportional" to the states'
constitutional violations in order to fall within the

scope of Congress's authority under § 5. The Court then concluded that the ADA provision did not meet these requirements; in other words, it was not narrowly tailored to prevent state discrimination against disabled employees and job applicants. The Court rested its conclusion on the fact that the statutory provision forbade the states from taking actions that have a disparate adverse impact on the disabled, while the Constitution does not forbid such differential treatment when there is a "rational basis" for the disparate treatment.

Another part of the Americans with Disabilities Act, Title II, prohibits state and local governments from discriminating against the disabled in the provision of services, programs, and activities. 42 U.S.C. §§ 12131–12165. Title II has enabled disabled inmates to participate in correctional programs and activities to which they previously had no access. Shortly before this book went to press, the Supreme Court granted certiorari in a case to determine whether the enforcement of Title II in state and local correctional facilities unconstitutionally encroaches on the authority of the states. *United States v. Georgia* (S.Ct.2005).

Although states cannot, as of now, be sued under § 1983, they can sometimes be liable for a plaintiff's attorney's fees incurred when litigating a § 1983 suit. The Civil Rights Attorney's Fees Awards Act of 1976, 42 U.S.C. § 1988(b), authorizes courts to award attorney's fees to prevailing plaintiffs in § 1983 suits. The Supreme Court has held that when enacting § 1988, Congress intended to exercise its authority under the Fourteenth Amendment to abrogate the states' Eleventh Amendment immunity. *Hutto v. Finney* (S.Ct.1978). The states can therefore be required to pay the tab for a plaintiff's attorney's fees when state officials were sued in their official capacity under § 1983, litigated their case in good faith, but lost. *Id.*

b. Personal Immunity

Section 1983 says that *"[e]very* person" who violates another's constitutional rights while acting under the color of state law *"shall* be liable." Despite the all-encompassing and mandatory language of § 1983, the Supreme Court has held that it does not mean what it says. Even when officials have violated the constitutional rights of others, there will be times when they can successfully invoke an immunity defense.

Personal-immunity defenses can be raised by officials sued in their personal capacities for damages. They cannot be invoked by officials sued in their official capacities. *Kentucky v. Graham* (S.Ct.1985).

There are two types of personal immunity—absolute and qualified. Absolute immunity, as its name suggests, totally protects an official from damages liability. Qualified immunity, on the other hand, provides more limited protection. If an official violated "clearly established statutory or constitutional rights of which a reasonable person would have known," a qualified-immunity defense will fail. *Harlow v. Fitzgerald* (S.Ct.1982). In determining whether a defendant is entitled to qualified immunity, the "salient question," according to the Supreme Court, is whether the "state of the law" at the time of the constitutional violation provided the defendant with "fair warning" of the illegality of his or her actions. *Hope v. Pelzer* (S.Ct.2002). If the law provided the requisite "fair warning," the defendant cannot prevail on the defense of qualified immunity.

The purpose of personal immunity, both absolute and qualified, is to prevent the fear of being sued, as well as the attendant burdens of litigation, from unduly hampering official decisionmaking. Another interest is implicated though when decisions are being made regarding the scope of immunity, if any, that should be extended to a particular type of governmental official—the interest in vindicating constitutional rights. The Supreme Court has balanced these competing interests by holding that generally, executive officials can avail themselves of only a qualified-immunity defense. *See, e.g., Procunier v. Navarette* (S.Ct.1978) (prison officials, including the director of the department of corrections and the warden, were entitled to qualified immunity). If executive officials seek even greater protection from damages liability, they have the burden of proving their entitlement to absolute immunity.

In *Cleavinger v. Saxner* (S.Ct.1985), the defendants, who were members of a prison disciplinary committee, contended that they were entitled to absolute immunity from damages liability when sued for violating inmates' constitutional rights.

They argued that, like judges, they should be accorded absolute immunity, because they too perform an adjudicatory function.

The Supreme Court conceded that prison disciplinary committees perform an adjudicatory function of sorts when they decide whether inmates have violated prison rules. Nonetheless, the Court concluded that the prison disciplinary committee members differed from judges in some important respects. For one thing, the disciplinary committee members, unlike judges, were not independent. They were employees of the Federal Bureau of Prisons. In the course of making disciplinary decisions, they had to choose between their fellow employees and inmates when deciding who was telling the truth, and obviously, they would feel pressure to find in favor of their colleagues.

The Supreme Court highlighted another important distinction between prison disciplinary committee members and judges: differences in the procedural safeguards surrounding their decisionmaking processes. These safeguards are relevant because they reduce the risk of constitutional errors occurring when decisions are rendered. While a whole gamut of procedural safeguards attend court proceedings, the Supreme Court noted in *Cleavinger v. Saxner* that most of these safeguards were not included in the disciplinary process in federal prisons. Prisoners faced with disciplinary charges were not represented by counsel or by any other independent nonstaff assistant. They had no discovery rights, no right to confront and cross-examine adverse witnesses, and no right to receive a transcript of the hearing. There was no prescribed standard of proof that had to be met before prisoners could be found guilty of disciplinary misconduct, and the prison disciplinary committee could consider hearsay evidence.

The Supreme Court therefore concluded in *Cleavinger* that the prison disciplinary committee members who had been sued in that case were only entitled to invoke a qualified-immunity defense. At the same time, the Court observed that prison disciplinary processes can be structured in a way that permits disciplinary decisionmakers to be afforded absolute immunity. Administrative law judges can, for example, be used to adjudicate prison disciplinary charges.

Because one of the purposes of an immunity defense is to insulate officials from the burdens of litigation, an official's entitlement to immunity normally will be resolved before discovery in a case commences. *Harlow v. Fitzgerald* (S.Ct.1982). For the same reason, an official can often, though not always, immediately appeal an order denying a motion to dismiss on immunity grounds and need not wait until a case is over in the trial court before taking that appeal. *Mitchell v. Forsyth* (S.Ct.1985). When the immunity issue is the purely legal one of whether a right was "clearly established" when the defendant allegedly violated the right, the defendant can immediately appeal a district court's order ruling that the right was "clearly established." On the other hand, if the immunity issue is a factual one, no interlocutory appeal will lie. Thus, if a defendant concedes that a right was clearly established but claims an entitlement to qualified immunity because there is not enough evidence that the defendant actually violated that right for the case to go to trial, the defendant cannot immediately appeal the district court's order rejecting the qualified-immunity defense. *Johnson v. Jones* (S.Ct. 1995).

Municipalities, unlike states, cannot invoke the immunity afforded by the Eleventh Amendment when they are sued in a federal court. *Will v. Michigan Dep't of State Police* (S.Ct.1989). In addition, while municipal employees may be able to successfully invoke a qualified-immunity defense, municipalities cannot use this defense to insulate themselves from damages liability. *Owen v. City of Independence* (S.Ct.1980). Reading § 1983 against its common-law backdrop, the Supreme Court has explained that at common law, such qualified immunity was not the norm for municipalities. In addition, the Court has stated that making a municipality fully responsible for the damages caused by its violation of constitutional rights furthers the two objectives of § 1983—to compensate individuals for the violation of their constitutional rights and to deter such violations through the imposition of liability.

Based on the Supreme Court's construction of the common law in effect at the time § 1983 was enacted, however, municipalities are immune from punitive-damages awards. *Newport v. Fact Concerts, Inc.*

(S.Ct.1981). While the Court has said that it is fair to spread the loss caused by a constitutional violation amongst all of the taxpayers in a municipality, the Court has qualms about punishing taxpayers for the wrongdoing of others by requiring them to pay a punitive-damages award.

While correctional officers employed by the government may invoke a qualified-immunity defense, those employed by private entities currently cannot. Holding that § 1983 does not implicitly include a qualified-immunity defense for correctional officers employed by the private sector, the Supreme Court, in *Richardson v. McKnight* (S.Ct.1997), observed that there was no " 'firmly rooted' tradition,'' at the time § 1983 was enacted, of according immunity to such privately employed correctional officers.

Because Congress can always amend § 1983 to include a qualified-immunity defense for private corrections companies and their employees, the important question, over the long term, is whether, as a policy matter, the qualified-immunity defense should be extended to private organizations and their employees. In addition, the Supreme Court in *Richardson* specifically left open the question whether a private corrections company or its employees can assert a good-faith defense to a § 1983 claim. The Court did not elaborate on the parameters of this potential defense.

2. Statute of Limitations

As is true with other lawsuits, a suit under § 1983 must be brought within the time frame prescribed by the applicable statute of limitations. There is no federal statute that dictates a time limit for bringing a § 1983 action, so federal district courts are directed by 42 U.S.C. § 1988 to apply the statute of limitations in effect in the state where a lawsuit is brought, unless the application of that statute would conflict with the Constitution or federal law. The statute of limitations to be applied is the one governing actions to recover damages for personal injuries. *Wilson v. Garcia* (S.Ct.1985). If there are two statutes of limitations in the state— one covering the intentional infliction of personal injuries and a catch-all statute that encompasses all other personal-injury actions, the more general statute of limitations is to be applied. *Owens v. Okure* (S.Ct.1989).

3. Mootness

If a case becomes moot while it is being litigated, the case must be dismissed, even if the case is on appeal. Mootness issues arise with some frequency in prisoners' cases because of the release or transfer of inmates from prisons where a cause of action arose. *See, e.g., Hewitt v. Helms* (S.Ct.1987); *Vitek v. Jones* (S.Ct.1980). There are at least two ways, however, for a prisoner to thwart a motion to dismiss on mootness grounds. First, a transfer or release from a prison will not moot a claim for damages relief if such a claim is included in the complaint. *Boag v. MacDougall* (S.Ct.1982). Second, if the prisoner has brought a class-action suit and the class has been certified by the court, the prisoner's departure from the prison will not moot the case. *Sosna v. Iowa* (S.Ct.1975).

4. Exhaustion of Remedies

Over the years, the Supreme Court has repeatedly held that there is, at least generally, no exhaustion-of-remedies requirement subsumed within § 1983. See the cases cited in *Patsy v. Florida Bd. of Regents* (S.Ct.1982). In other words, most persons do not have to exhaust available state judicial or administrative remedies before bringing suit under § 1983. However, Congress has carved out a statutory exception to this no-exhaustion rule for prisoners, pretrial detainees, and juveniles charged with being, or adjudicated, delinquent. These persons are forbidden from bringing any lawsuits under § 1983 or any other "federal law" unless they have exhausted "available" administrative remedies. 42 U.S.C. § 1997e(a).

In *Booth v. Churner* (S.Ct.2001), the Supreme Court held that this exhaustion requirement generally applies even when a prisoner is seeking damages and monetary relief cannot be recovered through the grievance process. As long as the prisoner can obtain some kind of relief through that process or it would culminate in the taking of "some responsive action" to the grievance, the prisoner must first pursue his or her claim through the grievance process before seeking redress in a lawsuit.

CHAPTER 19

REMEDIES

A. § 1983 SUITS

1. Damages

Damages are frequently sought as a form of relief by individuals who bring suit under § 1983. Damages can be awarded in § 1983 actions to compensate individuals for the harm they have suffered due to the violation of their constitutional rights. To recover such compensatory damages, plaintiffs must prove that they were actually injured by the violation of their constitutional rights.

In *Carey v. Piphus* (S.Ct.1978), two students filed a lawsuit under § 1983 after they were summarily suspended from school. The students contended that their suspensions had been effected without following certain procedures required by due process. The federal district court agreed that their constitutional rights had been violated, but refused to award the plaintiffs any compensatory damages because they had failed to introduce any evidence as to how they had been harmed by the violation of their rights.

The plaintiffs contended that the introduction of such evidence was unnecessary—that a court can appropriately presume that injuries have ensued from the violation of the right to procedural due process. They based this argument, in part, on the fact that one purpose of the procedural safeguards required by due process is to ensure that people deprived of their life, liberty, or property feel that the deprivations have occurred in processes that are fair. The plaintiffs argued that when an individual has not been afforded the "process" that is constitutionally "due," a court can assume then that the individual has felt distress stemming from the perception of unfair treatment.

The Supreme Court felt that such an assumption is unwarranted. The Court pointed out that sometimes a person will not even be aware of procedural irregularities that attended a deprivation, so these irregularities will not have caused that individual any distress. In addition, even when distress is felt, often that distress is due to a deprivation that was in fact justified, even though effected without proper procedural safeguards.

The Supreme Court added that no compensation is due for injuries stemming from such a justified deprivation. For example, assume that an inmate was confined in disciplinary segregation and that because of the duration of his confinement, was deprived of a liberty interest. If the disciplinary hearing that resulted in his confinement in segregation did not comport with the requirements of due process, the inmate could not recover damages for being confined in the segregation unit if he still would have been found guilty of misconduct and received the segregation sanction after a disciplinary hearing that met the requirements of due process. The inmate could, however, recover damages for any emotional or mental distress caused by the failure to afford him his procedural-due-process rights.

The point of *Carey v. Piphus* is that plaintiffs have to prove that they actually suffered such distress; the existence of such distress or other types of injuries will not be presumed. In the absence of such proof of actual injury, plaintiffs who have established that their procedural-due-process rights were violated can be awarded only nominal damages. Consequently, the Supreme Court directed that the plaintiffs in *Carey* receive no more than one dollar if the district court, on remand, concluded that the school suspensions were justified.

Although the Supreme Court said in *Carey v. Piphus* that plaintiffs who bring § 1983 suits can recover compensatory damages for emotional or mental distress that they prove was caused by the violation of their constitutional rights, the Prison Litigation Reform Act limits the recoverability of damages for this kind of harm. The PLRA prohibits prisoners from bringing civil suits in federal court for mental or emotional injuries suffered while confined in a correctional facility unless they first show that they also suffered a physical injury. 42 U.S.C. § 1997e(e).

The lower courts are split regarding the applicability of the physical-injury requirement to certain kinds of constitutional claims. Some courts have held that the requirement does not apply, for example, to First Amendment, due-process, and equal-protection claims. *See, e.g., Canell v. Lightner* (9th Cir.1998). These courts have reasoned that these kinds of claims are brought to vindicate a constitutional right rather than to obtain recompense for mental or emotional injuries.

Other courts disagree with this narrow construction of the scope of the physical-injury requirement, holding that it extends to all constitutional claims, even those that typically don't cause a physical injury. *See, e.g., Royal v. Kautzky* (8th Cir.2004) (listing cases). The practical result of this latter construction of the physical-injury requirement has been to effectively foreclose prisoners bringing certain types of constitutional claims from recovering compensatory damages in federal court for mental or emotional distress suffered as a result of a violation of their constitutional rights while in custody. These prisoners, however, can still recover nominal and punitive damages. In addition, the physical-injury requirement does not foreclose inmates from obtaining injunctive and declaratory relief.

To be liable for punitive damages, a defendant need not have acted with a malicious intent to harm the plaintiff, although such a malicious intent will certainly support a punitive-damages award. Punitive damages can be awarded as long as the defendant acted with "reckless or callous indifference to the federally protected rights of others." *Smith v. Wade* (S.Ct.1983). A plaintiff who recovers only nominal damages in a § 1983 suit can still be awarded punitive damages. *See*, *e.g.*, *Walker v. Bain* (6th Cir.2001).

The Prison Litigation Reform Act effected other changes in the recovery of damages by prisoners. When damages are awarded a prisoner in a case, such as a § 1983 suit, in which attorney's fees are recoverable under 42 U.S.C. § 1988, a portion of the award, but no more than 25%, must be used to pay the attorney's fees awarded against the defendant. 42 U.S.C. § 1997e(d)(2). In addition, any compensatory damages awarded against correctional officials must be used to pay any outstanding restitution order to which the prisoner is subject. *See* 18 U.S.C. § 3626 note. The prisoner gets whatever, if any, is left after full payment of the restitution due.

2. Equitable Relief

Plaintiffs who bring suit under § 1983 often seek some form of equitable relief, either alone or in addition to damages. The relief sought may come in several different forms. A declaratory judgment is one form of equitable relief. An example of a declaratory judgment would be one finding a state statute or regulation to be unconstitutional. If a court provides the plaintiff with some type of injunctive relief, the court goes even further—directing a defendant to refrain from taking certain unconstitutional actions in the future or requiring the defendant to take certain steps to avoid future violations of the Constitution.

Injunctive relief can come in the form of a temporary restraining order, a preliminary injunction, or a permanent injunction. The rules governing the issuance of these orders are quite complex. *See* 1 Dan B. Dobbs, *Law of Remedies* 223–76 (2d ed. 1993). Certain key points concerning equitable relief, particularly equitable relief in the correctional context, bear noting here.

First, while a court is vested with equitable discretion to remedy ongoing constitutional violations, it must try, at least generally, to limit its interference with correctional operations by first allowing governmental officials the opportunity to develop a plan to alleviate unconstitutional conditions found to exist in a correctional facility. *Lewis v. Casey* (S.Ct.1996). If the officials fail to submit a plan or an adequate plan to the court, the court will then intervene, if need be quite forcefully. Court orders going so far as to place a population cap on a correctional facility or even to direct the release of some inmates from a facility whose conditions were unconstitutional have been upheld on appeal. *See, e.g., Harris v. Angelina County, Texas* (5th Cir.1994)(population cap); *Duran v. Elrod* (7th Cir. 1983) (affirming order directing the release of pretrial detainees incarcerated only because they could not pay low bonds).

The Prison Litigation Reform Act places some restrictions on the issuance of prisoner release orders. Under 18 U.S.C. § 3626(a)(3), no prisoner release order can be entered unless three requirements are met: (1) less intrusive relief has failed to remedy the violation of a federal right; (2) the defendant has had a reasonable amount of time to comply with the previous orders; and (3) a three-judge court, comprised of two district judges and one judge from the court of appeals, finds that crowding is the "primary cause" of the violation and that no other relief will remedy the violation. The court orders subject to these requirements are defined as those having the "purpose or effect" of limiting a correctional facility's population and those which direct that prisoners be released from, or not be admitted into, such a facility. *Id.* § 3626(g)(4). Thus, population caps are subject to these requirements.

The second principal point to remember concerning equitable relief is that despite the equitable discretion that a court can wield when enforcing the provisions of the Constitution, there are still limits on the steps that can be taken by a court to redress a constitutional violation through the exercise of its equitable powers. *Missouri v. Jenkins* (S.Ct.1990) is a case in point. In that case, a federal district court was confronted with a school district where unconstitutional segregation had persisted for many years. To redress this problem, the school district had proposed a magnet-school program that would cost $380 million to implement. The school district, however, was hamstrung in implementing this plan because the state's constitution limited the school district's ability to raise property taxes to pay for the program. The federal district court responded by raising property taxes to obtain the funds necessary to implement the desegregation plan.

The Supreme Court held that in raising property taxes, the district court had abused its equitable discretion, because there was a less intrusive alternative to a court-directed tax increase. That alternative was to order the school officials themselves to raise the taxes needed to pay for the magnet-school program and then enjoin enforcement of the state constitutional provision that stood in the way of this tax increase. To the Supreme Court, the difference between these two remedies was not just a matter of form, since the school officials themselves, rather than the court, now would have the primary responsibility to take the steps needed to rectify constitutional violations in the operation of the school district.

In addition to some inherent limitations on the scope of a court's equitable powers, the Prison Litigation Reform Act has placed some restrictions on the prospective (nonmonetary) relief available in cases contesting conditions of confinement in federal, state, and local prisons, jails, and juvenile correctional facilities. The prospective relief must: (1) extend no further than necessary to correct the violation of the federal right; (2) be "narrowly drawn"; and (3) be the "least intrusive means" of redressing the violation. In addition, the court must give "substantial weight" to any adverse effects the relief will have on public safety or the criminal-justice system. 18 U.S.C. § 3626(a)(1)(A).

These restrictions potentially can have the greatest effect in cases that the parties normally would settle through entry of a consent decree. When a court enters a consent decree, it usually does not render a finding that the defendants have been violating the Constitution. In fact, defendants typically insist that a consent decree include a statement that their agreement to the terms of the decree does not signify an admission of liability. This caveat is inserted to protect the defendants from being inundated with suits filed by inmates for damages stemming from the conditions the consent decree is designed to ameliorate.

The PLRA restrictions on the scope of prospective relief in conditions-of-confinement cases therefore may lead to trials in some cases that would, in the past, have been settled. On the other hand, it is possible that trials that none of the parties want can be avoided through stipulations that essentially say: "The defendants do not agree that they have violated the rights of any plaintiffs to this action. However, the defendants stipulate that there is sufficient evidence to support a court finding that the relief set forth in this consent decree is narrowly drawn, extends no further than necessary to correct violations of federal rights of the plaintiffs, and is the least intrusive means necessary to correct the violations." A court might then enter an order finding that, based on this stipulation, the consent decree extends no further than necessary to correct the violations of the plaintiffs' federal rights, is narrowly drawn, and is the least intrusive means of correcting those violations.

Nothing in the Prison Litigation Reform Act precludes parties from entering into private settlement agreements not subject to the requirements of § 3626(a). 18 U.S.C. § 3626(c)(2). The plaintiffs might, for example, agree to dismiss a case on the condition that the defendants take certain steps to remedy allegedly unconstitutional prison conditions. However, if the defendants fail to abide by the agreement, it is not enforceable in federal court. The plaintiffs' possible options are to reinstate the federal lawsuit or to seek relief for the breach of the agreement in state court. *Id.* § 3626(c)(2)(A), (B).

A third important point to understand about the exercise of a court's equitable discretion in a § 1983 suit is that while, in an unusual case, a court may order the release of inmates from a correctional facility to redress unconstitutional conditions of confinement, a court has no authority under § 1983 to release a prisoner who is challenging, not the conditions of his or her confinement, but the fact or duration of that confinement. In *Preiser v. Rodriguez* (S.Ct.1973), a prisoner brought suit under § 1983 seeking the restoration of good-time credits that he claimed had been revoked unconstitutionally. Issuance of an injunction directing that these good-time credits be restored would have led to the inmate's immediate release from prison. The Supreme Court concluded that the relief that the inmate was seeking was not obtainable in a § 1983 action. Instead, the inmate, and any other inmates challenging the fact or duration of their confinement who sought immediate or earlier release from confinement, would have to attempt to secure relief in a habeas corpus action filed under 28 U.S.C. § 2254.

The Supreme Court was concerned that to permit a prisoner to seek release from confinement in a § 1983 suit would undermine the comity considerations that underlie the requirement in § 2254(c) that a prisoner first exhaust available state court remedies before pursuing habeas corpus relief in a federal court. The purpose of this exhaustion requirement is to limit the intrusion into the state's domain that ensues when federal courts take the rather drastic step of ordering the release of a person from state or local confinement.

State prisoners challenging the fact or duration of their confinement also cannot seek damages in a § 1983 suit stemming from their allegedly unconstitutional confinement unless and until one of three events has occurred: the conviction or sentence has been reversed or set aside by an order of a state court; the conviction or sentence has been expunged by an executive order; or a federal court has issued a writ of habeas corpus, thereby raising doubts about the validity of the conviction or sentence. *Heck v. Humphrey* (S.Ct.1994). These restrictions on the bringing of a § 1983 suit also apply to prisoners seeking damages or a declaratory judgment because of allegedly unconstitutional procedures used during certain prison disciplinary hearings. When those hearings resulted in the revocation of good-time credits and a court finding in favor of the prisoner would "necessarily imply" that the revocation of the credits was invalid, the prisoner first must seek and obtain redress in one of the alternative forums identified in *Heck v. Humphrey* before pursuing damages relief in a § 1983 suit. *Edwards v. Balisok* (S.Ct.1997).

It is evident from a series of Supreme Court cases that courts need to examine a plaintiff's § 1983 claim with care to determine whether *Heck*'s favorable-termination requirement applies. *Muhammad v. Close* (S.Ct.2004) is one of those cases. The prisoner who filed a § 1983 suit in that case charged that a correctional officer unconstitutionally retaliated against him for filing lawsuits and grievances by charging him with "threatening behavior." This charge required that the prisoner be detained pending the disciplinary hearing. The prisoner ultimately was found guilty of insolence, a lesser-included disciplinary infraction, a finding that he admitted was warranted. But since prehearing detention was not authorized for that kind of disciplinary infraction and the plaintiff was seeking damages only for his prehearing confinement, the Supreme Court held that his retaliation claim was cognizable under § 1983. *Muhammad* confirms that just because a prisoner's claim relates to the prison's disciplinary process does not necessarily mean that the prisoner is foreclosed from bringing the claim under § 1983.

A majority of the Justices on the Supreme Court indicated in another case, though in a *dicta*, that a § 1983 suit for damages is not barred if it would be impossible for the plaintiff to satisfy the favorable-termination requirement set forth in *Heck v. Humphrey. See Spencer v. Kemna* (S.Ct.1998) (Souter, J., with O'Connor, Ginsburg, and Breyer, J.J., concurring; Stevens, J., dissenting). These Justices are concerned that without this exception to the favorable-termination requirement, some persons whose constitutional rights had been violated would be left without a remedy.

Spencer is an example of the kind of case in which this exception might be triggered. In that case, a former prisoner filed a habeas corpus petition in which he alleged that the procedures followed when revoking his parole failed to meet constitutional requirements. The Supreme Court ruled that his petition was moot because he had completed serving his criminal sentence. Consequently, unless he were permitted to file a § 1983 suit for damages, the alleged violation of his constitutional rights would go unremedied.

Wilkinson v. Dotson (S.Ct.2005) is another case that illustrates the limits of the favorable-termination requirement. The prisoners who filed suit under § 1983 in that case contended that the state's parole procedures were unconstitutionally flawed. As relief, they sought new parole hearings and an injunction commanding officials to revamp the parole process to comport with constitutional requirements. The Supreme Court conceded that the prisoners obviously hoped that the end result of the recontoured parole process would be their expedited release from prison. But the Court noted that since the decision whether to release the prisoners on parole still fell within the board's discretion, they might not be successful in that endeavor. Because a judgment for the prisoners would not, as the *Heck* rule requires, "necessarily demonstrate the invalidity of confinement or its duration," the Court held that the constitutionality of the parole process could properly be challenged in a § 1983 suit.

The fourth and final point that bears highlighting regarding equitable relief in conditions-of-confinement cases is that the Prison Litigation Reform Act has placed a significant time limit on the duration of preliminary injunctive relief. Under 18 U.S.C. § 3626(a)(2), preliminary injunctions automatically expire ninety days after their entry unless a court makes the findings required by § 3626(a)(1)(A)—that the relief is "narrowly drawn," extends no further than necessary to correct the federal-right violation, and is the least intrusive means of remedying the violation.

3. Attorney's Fees

a. *General Rules*

i. *Prevailing Party*

Plaintiffs who prevail in § 1983 suits can, in the discretion of the court, recover "reasonable" attorney's fees under 42 U.S.C. § 1988. Section 1988 refers to the recovery of attorney's fees by any "prevailing party" in such a lawsuit, but the Supreme Court has held that only in an unusual case should attorney's fees be assessed against a plaintiff. Otherwise, the private enforcement of civil-rights laws would be discouraged, in contravention of the purpose of § 1988. A plaintiff can therefore be required to pay a defendant's attorney's fees only when the plaintiff's lawsuit was " 'frivolous, unreasonable, or without foundation, even though not brought in subjective bad faith.' " *Hughes v. Rowe* (S.Ct.1980). In addition, because of the difficulties inmates face in understanding the complexities of the law, the Supreme Court has counseled courts to be particularly hesitant to award attorney's fees against prisoners who have represented themselves in § 1983 suits. *Id.*

To be considered a "prevailing party" within the meaning of § 1988, a plaintiff need not have won the central claim asserted in a § 1983 suit. All that is necessary is that the plaintiff succeeded on " 'any significant issue in litigation which achieve[d] some of the benefit the parties sought in bringing suit.' " *Texas State Teachers Ass'n v. Garland Indep. School Dist.* (S.Ct.1989). That benefit may, but need not, have been reaped after taking the case to trial. In *Maher v. Gagne* (S.Ct.1980), the Supreme Court concluded that the plaintiffs were entitled to attorney's fees even though their lawsuit was resolved through the entry of a consent decree.

Just because a plaintiff's lawsuit prompts the defendants to implement changes to rectify the illegalities alleged in the complaint does not mean that the plaintiff is a "prevailing party" within the meaning of § 1988 or other fee-shifting statutes. In

414 PRISONERS' RIGHTS LITIGATION Pt. 3

Buckhannon Bd. & Care Home, Inc. v. West Virginia Dep't of Health & Human Res. (S.Ct.2001), the Supreme Court rejected the "catalyst theory" for awarding attorney's fees. In that case, after the state legislature amended several state statutes in a way that addressed the concerns that were the focus of the plaintiff's complaint, the complaint was dismissed as moot. The Court, in a 5–4 decision, held that even though the plaintiff's lawsuit may have catalyzed these changes in state law, the plaintiff was not a "prevailing party" in the legal sense. According to the Court, to be considered a prevailing party entitled to attorney's fees, the plaintiff's lawsuit must have culminated in the obtaining of "some relief by the court," whether in the form of a judgment on the merits or a consent judgment enforceable by the court.

ii. Reasonable Attorney's Fee

In determining what is a "reasonable" attorney's fee to be awarded under § 1988, what is known as the lodestar figure must first be computed. This figure is calculated by multiplying the number of hours "reasonably expended" by an attorney working on a case times a "reasonable" hourly rate. *Hensley v. Eckerhart* (S.Ct.1983). If the parties cannot agree on what is an appropriate fee award, then the plaintiff has the burden of proving the reasonableness of the time expended on a case and the hourly rate charged.

The lodestar figure represents the baseline figure from which the final fee award is calculated. One or more of several factors may lead to an award of attorney's fees that is higher or lower than the lodestar figure. For example, the extent of a plaintiff's success in a lawsuit may lead to an upwards or downwards shift in the fee award. *Hensley v. Eckerhart* (S.Ct.1983). Thus, while a plaintiff awarded only nominal damages is technically the prevailing party, the court normally should not award the plaintiff attorney's fees. *Farrar v. Hobby* (S.Ct. 1992). At times, though, an award of nominal damages will justify a fee award. Examples of relevant factors to be considered by the court when determining whether to award attorney's fees to a plaintiff who recovered only nominal damages include: the significance of the legal issue on which the plaintiff prevailed; the public benefits from the lawsuit, such as the deterrence of future unconstitutional conduct; and the difference between the amount of damages the plaintiff sought and the nominal damages awarded.

The fee award can also be adjusted to compensate the plaintiff's attorneys for the delay in receiving payment for their work. *Missouri v. Jenkins* (S.Ct. 1989). One way in which to make such an adjustment is to compute the fee award using the current market rate for the attorneys' services rather than the rate in effect when the work for the plaintiff was performed.

Sometimes an attorney will represent a client on a contingent-fee basis. Under a contingent-fee agreement, the attorney does not charge the client on an hourly basis as work is being performed on a case. Instead, if the client wins the case and recovers damages, the attorney is entitled to a certain percentage, such as one third, of the damages recovered. If the plaintiff recovers no damages, on the other hand, the attorney is left with no compensation for the work done on the case.

In *City of Burlington v. Dague* (S.Ct.1992), the Supreme Court concluded that a fee award should not be shifted upwards to compensate an attorney for assuming the risk of nonpayment when representing a client under a contingent-fee agreement. The dissenters argued that such an upwards adjustment was appropriate and in keeping with the purpose of the fee-shifting statutes to attract counsel to represent plaintiffs who might not otherwise be able to bring suit because of their lack of funds to pay an attorney up front. The majority responded that much of the risk of nonpayment is already subsumed within the lodestar figure. The risk of nonpayment is in part a function of the difficulty of proving that the plaintiff's claim has merit. Surmounting this difficulty will lead to the expenditure of more time on a case, which is reflected in the lodestar, or the hiring of an attorney whose experience and ability in handling such claims lead to a higher hourly rate, which is also factored into the lodestar. To adjust the fee award upwards because of the risk of nonpayment therefore would result, in the Supreme Court's opinion, in double-counting.

While the existence of a contingent-fee agreement will not justify the elevation of a fee award under § 1988, a fee award will not be diminished because of such an agreement either. *Blanchard v. Bergeron* (S.Ct.1989). Consequently, the plaintiff's attorney sometimes may receive more money under § 1988 than the attorney is entitled to under a contingent-fee agreement. On the other hand, if the fee award under § 1988 is less than the attorney's fees to be paid under the contingent-fee agreement, the plaintiff can be required to pay additional money to the attorney. *Venegas v. Mitchell* (S.Ct.1990) (plaintiff awarded $117,000 in attorney's fees under § 1988 required to pay attorney 40% of judgment for 2.08 million dollars, offset by the fee award, in accordance with the terms of the contingent-fee agreement).

The "reasonable attorney's fee" awardable under § 1988 includes compensation for more than just the work of attorneys. The work of paralegals and law clerks is also compensable under § 1988. *Missouri v. Jenkins* (S.Ct.1989). In addition, a prevailing party can be reimbursed under § 1988(c) for the services of expert witnesses who provided assistance in preparing and presenting the case.

b. Restrictions Under the Prison Litigation Reform Act

The Prison Litigation Reform Act placed significant restrictions on the attorney's fees that can be awarded prisoners and pretrial detainees under § 1988. For one, the hourly rate that can be charged when an inmate seeks attorney's fees under § 1988 is now capped. The hourly rate cannot exceed 150% of the rate at which court-appointed counsel in federal criminal cases are paid under the Criminal Justice Act, 18 U.S.C. § 3006A(d). What that means, as a practical matter, is that attorneys can be awarded, at most, $169.50 an hour for their work on behalf of prisoners who prevailed in their § 1983 suits.

Under the PLRA, the attorney's fees awarded in prisoners' cases must be "proportionately related" to the court-ordered relief. 42 U.S.C. § 1997e(d)(1)(B)(i). By contrast, the attorney's fees awarded nonprisoners under § 1988 do not have to be proportionate to the amount of damages recouped by the plaintiff. In *City of Riverside v. Rivera* (S.Ct.1986), the Supreme Court refused to read a proportionality requirement into § 1988, because such a requirement fails to take into account the nonpecuniary benefits to individuals and the public of vindicating constitutional rights and the deterrence of future constitutional violations that occurs when plaintiffs prevail in civil-rights suits. The Court also observed that many meritorious civil-rights claims would never be brought if a proportionality requirement were adopted, because attorneys would be unwilling to represent plaintiffs in cases where such a requirement was applied.

Section 1997e(d)(2) fleshes out the meaning of the proportionality requirement now applied when calculating the attorney's fees to be awarded prisoners under § 1988. That provision limits the fee award to no more than 150% of the amount recovered by a prisoner in damages. Some courts have held that this 150% cap does not place an absolute limit on the attorney's fees recoverable when an inmate has secured both monetary and injunctive relief. *See Dannenberg v. Valadez* (9th Cir.2003) (listing cases). But if, for example, a prisoner is solely awarded $100 in damages in a § 1983 suit, the fee award is capped at $150. In addition, as mentioned earlier, a portion of the damages awarded—not to exceed 25%—must be applied to pay this fee award for which the defendant, in a case involving a nonprisoner, would be completely responsible.

Prisoners have filed a number of lawsuits contending that the disparate treatment of prisoners compared to nonprisoners in the awarding of attorney's fees under § 1988 violates their constitutional rights, in particular, their right to be afforded the equal protection of the law. Thus far, most courts have rejected these constitutional challenges to the PLRA's fee restrictions. *See Johnson v. Daley* (7th Cir.2003) (listing cases).

B. MODIFYING AND TERMINATING COURT ORDERS

Like other types of lawsuits, some inmates' civil-rights suits are resolved through a settlement—an agreement between the parties regarding the disposition of the case. Some of these settlement agreements, particularly in class-action suits, are embodied in consent decrees. A consent decree, as mentioned earlier, is a binding court order that reflects the parties' agreement.

At times, one of the parties may wish to be relieved of an obligation under a consent decree because meeting that obligation has become burdensome or perhaps even impossible. It is clear that final court orders and judgments can, in certain circumstances, be modified. Rule 60(b) of the Federal Rules of Civil Procedure, for example, authorizes a court to modify a final judgment or order "upon such terms as are just" when "it is no longer equitable" to enforce the judgment or when there is "any other reason justifying relief from the operation of the judgment."

In *Rufo v. Inmates of the Suffolk County Jail* (S.Ct.1992), the Supreme Court elaborated on when modification of a consent decree entered in a case involving operations or conditions in a prison, jail, or other public institution is appropriate. *Rufo* involved a consent decree entered after years of sparring in court between pretrial detainees confined in an old, dilapidated, and extremely crowded jail and correctional and other governmental officials. The consent decree, entered in 1979, permitted the defendants to continue to house detainees in the old jail while a new jail was being constructed. The consent decree outlined the agreed-upon design of the new facility and provided for the construction of cells designed to hold only one inmate.

The defendants dragged their heels in implementing the requirements of the consent decree, and as time passed, it became evident that the jail contemplated by the consent decree would not be big enough to meet the county's space needs. The consent decree, with the concurrence of the parties, was then modified in 1985 to permit construction of a larger jail as long as certain other requirements of the consent decree were still adhered to, such as single celling.

Construction of the new jail finally began in 1987. In 1989, while construction of the new jail continued, the sheriff who oversaw the jail's operation moved once again to modify the consent decree, this time to permit the housing of two inmates in a cell. The plaintiffs, however, balked at this proposed change.

The Supreme Court began its analysis of the standards to be applied to consent-decree modifications by noting that the party seeking modification of a consent decree has the burden of proving that the modification is warranted. To meet that burden, the party seeking modification must surmount two hurdles—first, by establishing that there has been a "significant change" in the facts or the law since entry of the consent decree; and second, by demonstrating that the proposed modification is "suitably tailored" to the changed circumstance that is prompting modification of the consent decree.

The Supreme Court identified three instances when changed factual conditions might justify modification of a consent decree. The first was when a change in the facts has made compliance with the consent decree "substantially more onerous." The Court hastened to add that modification is not justified when a party is simply finding it inconvenient to live up to the terms of the agreement.

Second, the Supreme Court said that modification of a consent decree might be in order when enforcement of the decree would be "detrimental to the public interest." As an example of an instance when the public interest might dictate modification of a consent decree, the Court cited a lower-court case in which a consent decree had been modified to avert the release of pretrial detainees charged with committing violent felonies.

Finally, the Supreme Court noted the appropriateness of modifying consent decrees that have proven to be "unworkable" because of "unforeseen obstacles." The Court rejected the plaintiffs' argument that modification of a consent decree should not be allowed if the impediments to the decree's implementation were foreseeable, even if not actually foreseen. The Court was reluctant to burden the process through which consent decrees are entered into by in effect asking the parties to provide for every possible contingency that might arise during the years and even decades while the consent decree was in effect. The Court added that if a party, at the time the agreement was entered into, actually had anticipated the possibility of the problem occurring in the decree's implementation that had now actually occurred, modification would usually not be appropriate because of the change in the facts. The party seeking modification would have a "heavy burden" of demonstrating that despite the fact that the change in circumstances was anticipated, the party had agreed to entry of the consent decree in good faith and had made a "reasonable effort" to meet the requirements of that decree.

As mentioned earlier, a significant change in the law might also, in some circumstances, support the modification of the terms of a consent decree. For example, if a consent decree requires a party to do something which is now illegal, the consent decree must be modified. The rules that pertain when the change in the law makes legal what the consent decree prohibits are a bit more complex.

The sheriff in *Rufo* argued that the Supreme Court's decision in *Bell v. Wolfish* (S.Ct.1979), which was rendered after entry of the consent decree, justified the modification of that decree. In *Bell v. Wolfish*, you will recall, the Supreme Court held that the double celling of pretrial detainees is not *per se* unconstitutional. *See* page 358.

The Court in *Rufo* responded that just because it becomes evident from a change in the law that the parties have obligated themselves to do something more than the Constitution requires does not mean that a consent decree can and should be modified. The Court pointed out that parties entering into consent decrees have the prerogative to, and often do, take steps that go beyond the minimal requirements of the Constitution. A change in the law that clarifies that the parties in fact did so when they entered into a consent decree is therefore not adequate grounds for unsettling the parties' agreement. Otherwise, consent decrees would be on tenuous grounds, and the incentive of parties to resolve their differences through entry of a consent decree would be substantially diminished. On the other hand, if the parties actually misunderstood the law—in this case, believing that single celling was constitutionally mandated—and based their consent decree on this misunderstanding, then this misunderstanding might, according to the Supreme Court, support modification of the consent decree.

Once a party seeking modification of a consent decree has proven that there has been a significant change in the facts or the law that warrants changing the terms of the consent decree, the party, as mentioned earlier, must then establish that the proposed modification is "suitably tailored to the changed circumstance." The Court emphasized in *Rufo* that just because the terms of a consent decree might need to be changed somewhat does not mean that the consent decree should then be rewritten to reflect only the minimal requirements of the Constitution. Instead, the changes should be limited to those needed to respond adequately to the change in circumstances. In other words, the consent decree should be reopened "only to the extent that equity requires."

At the same time, the Court observed that trial courts should treat with some deference the judgment of governmental officials regarding how to best respond to the change in circumstances. In addition, the courts should take into account the interests of the public when modifying consent decrees. Finally, while a lack of funds will not justify a failure to rectify a constitutional violation, financial constraints can properly be considered when determining the best way in which to modify a consent decree.

The Supreme Court added in *Rufo* that the two-part test that it was enunciating for consent-decree modifications pertained to the modification of provisions that were at least arguably related to rectifying a constitutional violation. This somewhat rigorous test did not apply to insignificant changes in "extraneous details in the decree," such as the color a building would be painted. While the Court anticipated that normally the parties would agree to such minor changes, the Court noted that if they did not, all that the party seeking modification would have to establish is that there is a "reasonable basis" for the proposed modification.

Many of the court orders that are designed to bring conditions in a correctional facility into compliance with the Constitution govern many different facets of the facility's operation. The question is: What happens when the constitutional violations in one or more areas of the facility's operations being overseen by a court have been rectified, but constitutional problems remain in other areas subject to court supervision?

It is clear that courts may properly end their supervision of some areas of a correctional facility's operations while continuing to supervise other areas. When a court is exercising its discretion to partially end its supervision in a case, the Supreme

Court has said that the court should be guided by "the purposes and objectives of its equitable power." Some of the factors that should inform the court's decision include: whether there has been "full and satisfactory" compliance in the area in which the withdrawal of supervision is contemplated; whether ongoing supervision in this area will be needed or helpful to secure compliance in other areas; and whether the governmental officials have demonstrated their commitment to abide by the requirements of the Constitution. *Freeman v. Pitts* (S.Ct.1992).

Even if a court ends its active supervision over some areas of a prison's operations subject to a court order, it still retains jurisdiction over those areas. Consequently, if there is an unconstitutional relapse, the court can resume its supervision in that area. Once the problems that are the focus of a court order have been resolved and the purposes of the order "fully achieved," a court may then withdraw its jurisdiction over the entire case. According to the Supreme Court, the termination of jurisdiction should occur only when a court finds both that an institution is being operated in conformance with the Constitution and that it is unlikely that the defendants will resume their unconstitutional conduct in the future. On this latter question, courts need not necessarily believe the protestations of officials that they have learned their lesson and will now obey the Constitution. Instead, the courts should look at the extent to which the officials actually have acted in good faith in their attempts to abide by the requirements set forth in the court's orders. *Board of Educ. v. Dowell* (S.Ct.1991).

The Supreme Court's decisions in *Rufo*, *Freeman*, and *Dowell* describe equitable limitations on a federal court's power to modify or terminate injunctive relief. Provisions in the Prison Litigation Reform Act governing the termination of prospective relief in conditions-of-confinement cases have added some nettlesome complexities to the law bearing on the exercise of this power. If these provisions are constitutional, as most lower courts have held, their primary impact will be felt in cases where, but for the PLRA, the prospective relief would remain in effect because termination of the relief would be inequitable under the circumstances.

Under one PLRA provision, defendants are entitled, with one exception, to the immediate termination of prospective relief if a court order providing such relief was entered without a court finding that the relief was narrowly drawn, was necessary to correct a federal-right violation, and was the least intrusive means of redressing the violation. *Id.* § 3626(b)(2). The exception to which the termination provision is subject provides that the prospective relief will remain in effect if the court adjudicating the termination motion makes written findings that the relief is still necessary to remedy a violation of a federal right, is no broader than necessary to correct the violation, is "narrowly drawn," and is the least intrusive means of correcting the violation. *Id.* § 3626(b)(3). Unless this exception applies, the prospective relief embodied in a consent decree entered before the PLRA's enactment will likely be terminated, because consent decrees in the past were not normally attended by the court findings required by § 3626(b)(2).

Another PLRA provision provides for the termination of prospective relief after a specified time lapse. Subject to the exception outlined above, prospective relief will remain in effect no longer than two years if the defendants move to terminate the relief. *Id.* § 3626(b)(1). The prospective relief generally is terminable two years after the relief was granted or one year after a court has entered an order refusing to terminate the relief. But again, if the court finds, in writing, that the relief is needed to rectify a violation of a federal right, is "narrowly drawn," and is the least intrusive means of remedying the violation, the court will not abate the prospective relief.

The critical question concerning the termination provisions is: Are they constitutional? One legal issue upon which much litigation has focused is whether the termination provisions violate the constitutional separation of powers.

One of the primary cases upon which prisoners have relied in support of their contention that the termination provisions are unconstitutional is *Plaut v. Spendthrift Farm, Inc.* (S.Ct.1995). In that case, the Supreme Court considered the constitutionality of a federal statute that directed the federal courts to reinstate certain civil actions for securities fraud that had previously been dismissed because they had not been filed within the then-applicable limitations period. The Supreme Court struck down the statute on separation-of-powers grounds, holding that Congress had no power to reopen a final judgment rendered before the law's enactment.

Most lower courts have distinguished *Plaut* on the grounds that it involved a suit for damages. *See Gilmore v. California* (9th Cir.2000) (listing cases). The Supreme Court's decision in *Miller v. French* (S.Ct.2000) provides some support for the decisions holding that the PLRA's termination provisions comport with separation-of-powers principles.

In *Miller*, the Supreme Court addressed the question whether the PLRA's "automatic stay" provision abridges the constitutional separation of powers. Under that provision, a defendant's motion to terminate prospective relief in a conditions-of-confinement case operates to stay that relief—in other words, to put the remedial order on hold—thirty days after the date the defendant filed the motion. 18 U.S.C. § 3626(e)(2). For "good cause," the court can defer the initiation of the stay for up to sixty additional days. *Id.* § 3626(e)(3). But once the stay is triggered, it remains in effect until the court has ruled on the termination motion. The stay provision applies regardless of the likelihood, or lack thereof, that a defendant will prevail on the termination motion and regardless of whether the plaintiffs will suffer irreparable harm during the period of time the stay is in effect.

The Supreme Court in *Miller* rejected the prisoners' argument that the stay provision unconstitutionally usurps judges' authority by suspending a final judgment. Because an injunction is subject to a court's ongoing supervision and may be modified by the court over time, the Court said that an injunction is not the "last word of the judicial department," impervious to modification under new standards issued by Congress. And the stay provision, according to the Court, is simply a mechanism that enables the modified standards set forth in the PLRA's termination provisions to be applied to existing injunctions that, under those standards, may no longer be enforceable.

C.   ENFORCING COURT ORDERS THROUGH CONTEMPT PROCEEDINGS AND OTHER MEANS

Lawyers who specialize in prisoners' rights litigation recognize that winning a judgment that requires correctional officials to change operations or conditions in a correctional facility is just the beginning of the litigation battle. What often follows are years of haggling over the defendants' compliance with the court's orders.

The defendants are responsible, under 42 U.S.C. § 1988, for the plaintiff's attorney's fees incurred in enforcing the court's orders in a §' 1983 suit. 42 U.S.C. § 1997e(d)(1)(B)(ii). One of the ways in which the plaintiff may seek to secure the defendants' compliance is by asking the court to hold the defendants in contempt. If the defendants are found to be in contempt of a court order, one common court response is to impose a fine, which continues to accrue until the defendants meet their constitutional obligations. If the defendants have been found in civil contempt, the fine will be paid to the plaintiff, because the purpose of the fine is simply to induce the defendants to comply with the court's orders. On the other hand, if the defendants have been held in criminal contempt, the fine usually will be paid to the court, because the purpose of the fine is to punish the defendants for their recalcitrance.

Courts may take other steps to ensure that defendants comply with their orders. Federal district courts, for example, sometimes invoke their authority under 18 U.S.C. § 3626(f) and Rule 53 of the Federal Rules of Civil Procedure and appoint what is called a "special master." The special master is responsible for reporting to the court at designated intervals about the defendants' compliance with the court's orders, and the master may also assist in the development of remedial plans.

D.   OTHER REMEDIES

In addition to civil-rights actions brought by prisoners, there are other means by which prisoners' constitutional rights may be enforced. For example, the Civil Rights of Institutionalized Persons Act (CRIPA) authorizes the United States Attorney General to bring suit on behalf of the United States to enjoin the maintaining of "egregious or flagrant" unconstitutional conditions in a state or local correctional facility that are causing inmates "grievous harm" and are the product of a "pattern or practice" of violating the Constitution. 42 U.S.C. § 1997a(a). The Attorney General also has the authority to intervene in civil-rights suits brought by inmates which involve such unconstitutional conditions. *Id.* § 1997c(a)(1).

The Constitution is not the sole source of protection for inmates. In fact, because of the contracted scope of prisoners' rights under the Constitution, as it has been interpreted by the Supreme Court, the Constitution may be one of the least important sources of prisoners' rights. Prisoners also have rights under state constitutions and federal and state statutes, all of which can accord rights that go beyond the federal constitutional minima. In addition, inmates may be able to bring state common-law claims for the tortious conduct of correctional officials, such as for assault, battery, or negligence. However, state immunity statutes may insulate correctional officials from liability or limit their liability under state law.

Litigation to enforce constitutional or other rights is not the only means of ensuring that correctional facilities are safe, humane, and sanitary. States can, for example, adopt health and safety standards for state and local correctional facilities and implement inspection schemes to monitor compliance with those standards. In addition, correctional officials can operate their facilities in conformance with professional standards and then seek accreditation of those facilities from such accrediting bodies as the Commission on Accreditation for Corrections and the National Commission on Correctional Health Care. Finally, inmates may be able to seek redress for injurious conditions or practices through inmate grievance procedures. If the need for litigation is to be dissipated and its costs and burdens diminished, it is imperative that steps be taken to ensure that these alternative modes of making correctional facilities safe, humane, and sanitary are effectual.

*

INDEX

References are to Pages

ACCESS TO THE COURTS
Generally, 252–69
Attorneys, appointment of, 259–62, 387–88
Inspection, mail to and from attorneys, 254–56
Interviews by law students and paralegals, 256–58
Jailhouse lawyers, 258–60
Law libraries, 262–67
Legal assistance, 258–67
Legal documents, refusal to forward, 253
Retaliation for pursuing litigation, 267–69
Standing to claim denial of, 263–64
Turner test, applicability of, 266–67

ACCREDITATION
Correctional facilities, 432–33

ADMINISTRATIVE SEGREGATION
Liberty interest, 285, 287
Procedural safeguards, 294–96, 298–302

AFFIRMATIVE DEFENSES
Generally, 388–98
Exhaustion of remedies, 398
Immunity,
Eleventh Amendment, 388–91, 395
Official immunity, absolute and qualified, 391–96
Private contractors, 396
Sovereign immunity, United States, 388

435

AFFIRMATIVE DEFENSES—Cont'd
Mootness, 397–98
Statute of limitations, 396–97

AMERICAN BAR ASSOCIATION
Model Adult Community Corrections Act, 123–25, 184
Standards for Criminal Justice,
    Collateral sanctions and discretionary disqualifications, 212
    Economic sanctions/assessments, 121–22

AMERICANS WITH DISABILITIES ACT
Constitutionality, 389–90
Disabled, discrimination against, 353

ASSAULTS BY OTHER INMATES
Cruel and unusual punishment, 371
Due process, 339–40

ASSOCIATION, FREEDOM OF
    Generally, 239–44
Visitation rights, 239–44

ATTORNEYS
Appointment,
    Indigent defendants, sentencing, 45–46
    Indigent prisoners,
        Civil-rights actions, 259–60, 262, 387–88
        State postconviction proceedings, 261–62
Disciplinary hearings, 273–74
Effective assistance,
    Death penalty, 147
    Guilty pleas, 22–23, 26–27
    Sentencing, 46–48
Inspection, mail to and from attorneys, 254–56
Monitoring communications with, 255–56
Prisoner, involuntary administration of psychotropic drugs, 306
Prisoner transfer, to mental institution, 297–98
Psychiatrist interviews, 49
Revocation, parole and probation, 170–73
Sentencing hearings, 45–46
Waiver of, 21–22

ATTORNEY'S FEES
    Generally, 390–91, 403, 412–19
Catalyst theory, 413–14
Enforcing court orders, 430
Expert witnesses, 417

ATTORNEY'S FEES—Cont'd
Paralegals, 417
Prevailing party, 412–14
Prisoners' payment of, 403
Prison Litigation Reform Act, restrictions under, 403, 417–19
Proportionality requirement, 418–19
Reasonable attorney's fee, 414–17
States, liability for, 390–91

BIVENS **ACTIONS**
Generally, 380–81

CAPITAL PUNISHMENT
See Death Penalty

CIVIL RIGHTS OF INSTITUTIONALIZED PERSONS ACT
Attorney General, enforcement by, 431–32

COLLATERAL SANCTIONS AND CONSEQUENCES
See also Convicted Offenders, Rights of
Guilty plea, awareness of when entering, 19

COMMUNITY–BASED SANCTIONS
Generally, 107–29
Public opinion, 125–26
Sentencing options, 109–22

COMMUNITY-CORRECTIONS ACTS
ABA Model Act, 123–25, 184

COMMUNITY SERVICE
Generally, 122

COMPLAINT
Pro se inmate complaints, liberal construction of, 384
Sua sponte dismissal of, 384–86

CONDITIONS OF CONFINEMENT
See Cruel and Unusual Punishment

CONFRONTATION AND CROSS–EXAMINATION
Disciplinary hearings, 275–77
Mental hospitals, inmate transfers to, 297
Parole-revocation hearings, 168–69
Sentencing hearings, 56–57

CONSENT DECREES
See also Injunctive Relief
Attorney's fees, 413

CONSENT DECREES—Cont'd
Modification, 420–25
Prospective relief, limitations on, 404–08

CONTACT VISITS
Body-cavity searches after, 321–24
Right to, 239–43

CONTEMPT OF COURT
Civil, 431
Criminal, 431

CONVICTED OFFENDERS, RIGHTS OF
Collateral consequences, restrictions on imposition of, 212
Criminal records, expungement or sealing of, 210–11
Deportation, 19, 28
Discrimination, bans against, 211–12
Employment, 195–96, 198, 209–12
Government benefits, 120–21, 198
Jury, right to serve on, 199
Pardons, 209–10
Restoration-of-rights procedures, 210
Sex offenders,
 Civil confinement, 204–09
 Community notification, 201–04
 Registration, 201–04
Voting, 199–201, 212

CORRESPONDENCE
See Mail

COUNSEL
See Attorneys

COURT
Drug, 127–28
Jurisdiction, termination of, 426–27
Mental-health, 128
Prospective relief,
 Stay of, 429–30
 Termination of, 427–29
State or federal,
 Section 1983 suits, 381
Supervision, withdrawal of, 425–26

CRIMINAL RECORDS
Expungement or sealing of, 210–11

CRUEL AND UNUSUAL PUNISHMENT
    See also Death Penalty; Privacy, Right of; Shame Sentences
Assaults by other inmates, 371
Body searches, 326
Castration, 162
Conditions of confinement,
    Length of time subjected to, 362
    State-of-mind requirement, 364
Disproportionate sentences in noncapital cases, 148–58
Double celling, 358–61
Force, use of, 365–70
Medical care,
    Deliberate indifference, 348–51
    Psychiatric or psychological care, 352–53
    Serious medical needs, 351–53
    Systemic problems, 350–51
Pretrial detainees, 347–48, 351, 371
Rehabilitative programs, lack of, 361
Secondhand smoke, 363–64
Suicide, 371–72
Visiting privileges, withdrawal of, 363

DAMAGES
    Generally, 399–403, 409–11
Attorney's fees, payable towards, 403
Compensatory, 399–403
Confinement, fact or duration of, 409–11
Mental or emotional injuries, 401–02
Nominal, 401–02
Punitive, 402–03
Restitution, payable towards, 403

DAY REPORTING CENTERS
Generally, 111–12

DEATH PENALTY
    Generally, 130–62
Counsel, ineffective assistance of, 147
Double jeopardy, 66–67
Errors in imposition of, 146–47
Felony murder, 142–43
Guilty plea to avoid, 19–20, 27
Individualized sentencing determination, 139–41
Insane prisoner, 146

DEATH PENALTY—Cont'd
Jury,
Instructions,
Executive clemency, 141
Parole, eligibility for, 141
No right to, 62
Right to finding of aggravating circumstances by, 62–63
Juveniles, 144–46
Mandatory imposition, 137–40
Mentally retarded defendant, 143–44
Racial bias, 135–37
Rape, 142
Vagueness, 137

DECLARATORY JUDGMENTS
Generally, 403, 409

DELIBERATE INDIFFERENCE
Conditions of confinement, 364
Failure to protect inmates,
Assaults by other inmates, 371
Suicide, 372
Medical care, 348–51
Municipalities, 378–80

DISABILITIES
Americans with Disabilities Act, 353, 389–90
Rehabilitation Act of 1973, 353–54

DISCIPLINARY PROCEEDINGS
Generally, 270–82
Assistance, 273–74
Confidential information, use of, 277–78
Confrontation and cross-examination, 275–77
Counsel, right to, 273–74
Documentary evidence, 272
Good-time credits, loss of, 270–71, 408–09
Impartial decisionmaker, 275
Miranda warnings, statements made without, 279–81
Notice of charges, 271
Punitive segregation, 271, 289–92
Reasons,
For decision, 274
For not calling witness, 272–73
Silence, evidence of guilt, 281–82
Standard of proof, 277

DISCIPLINARY PROCEEDINGS—Cont'd
Statutes and regulations, rights under, 279
Witnesses, presentation of, 272
Written decision, 274

DISCRIMINATION/DISPARITY
See also Equal Protection
Disabled, 353, 389–90
Ex-offenders, 211–12
Gender,
Correctional officers, discrimination against, 327, 329–36
Inmates, discrimination against, 313–15, 332–33
Racial,
Death penalty, 135–37
Segregation in prisons, 309–13
Sentencing, 11–12, 93
Voting rights, 200–01

DNA TESTING
Fourth Amendment, 181

DOUBLE CELLING
Constitutionality, 358–61

DOUBLE JEOPARDY
Capital sentences, 66–67
Civil commitment, 207–09
Crimes of which not convicted, consideration at sentencing of, 67–68
Guilty pleas, 24–25
Noncapital sentences, 67
Revocation, parole and probation, 173–74

DRUG OFFENDERS
Drug courts, 127–28
Drug treatment, crime-control benefits of, 5
Incapacitation of, 4
Use of drugs, impact on deterrence, 220

DRUGS, INVOLUNTARY ADMINISTRATION OF
Procedural due process, 305–07
Substantive due process, 354–57

DUE PROCESS
See also Access to the Courts; Sentencing
Administrative segregation, 285, 287, 294–96, 298–302

DUE PROCESS—Cont'd
Antipsychotic drugs,
    Involuntary administration of, 305–07, 354–57
Balancing test, 50, 193–94, 298–304, 307
Capital cases, jury instructions in, 141
Civil commitment, 204–07
Courts, access to, 253
Deprivation, 337–40
Disciplinary proceedings, 270–78, 289–92
Executive clemency, 187–88
Guilty pleas, 16–21, 23–41
Liberty interests, 166, 185–89, 271, 284–93, 305
Mail censorship, 226
Mental hospital, transfer to, 285–87, 296–99
Parole and probation revocation, 165–73
Parole release, 185–94
Postdeprivation remedies, 340–43
Pretrial detainees,
    Punishment proscribed, 240
Sex offenders, community notification about, 203

EFFECTIVE ASSISTANCE OF COUNSEL
Capital cases, 147
Guilty pleas, 22–23, 26–27
Sentencing, 45–46

EIGHTH AMENDMENT
See Cruel and Unusual Punishment; Death Penalty

ELECTRONIC MONITORING
Generally, 112–13

ELEVENTH AMENDMENT
Municipalities, 395
States, 388–91

EMPLOYMENT
Compensation of prisoners for,
    Fair Labor Standards Act, 344–45
    Thirteenth Amendment, 343
Ex-offenders, discrimination against, 211–12

**EQUAL EMPLOYMENT RIGHTS OF CORRECTIONAL OFFI-
CERS**
Generally, 327, 329–36

EQUAL PROTECTION
See also Discrimination/Disparity
Gender discrimination, 313–15, 332–33
Indigent inmates' access to courts, 253–54
Prison Litigation Reform Act,
    Attorney's fees, restriction on, 419
    Three-strikes provision, 386–87
Racial discrimination,
    Death penalty, 135–37
    Segregation in prisons, 309–13
Union activities, 315–16
Voting, convicted offenders, 199–201

EXCLUSIONARY RULE
Parole-revocation hearings, 181–83
Sentencing hearings, 79–80

EXECUTIVE CLEMENCY
See also Restoration of Rights
Capital cases, jury instructions in, 141
Due process, 187–88

EXHAUSTION OF REMEDIES
Generally, 398

EXPERT WITNESSES
Fees, 417

EX POST FACTO LAWS
Civil commitment, 207–09
Unconstitutionality, 103–06

FEES
Sanctions/assessments, 121–22

FIFTH AMENDMENT
See Self–Incrimination, Privilege Against

FILING FEES
In forma pauperis petitions, 382–83, 386–87

FINES
Generally, 114–19
Day fines, 115–16
Excessive, prohibition of, 159
Indigent defendants, 116–19
Probation revocation, indigent defendant's failure to pay, 117–19
Tariff system, 114

FIRST AMENDMENT
See also, Association, Freedom of; Religion, Freedom of;
    Speech, Freedom of
Courts, access to, 253
Prisoners' rights under, 223–24, 226–49, 251
Sentencing,
    Gang membership, evidence of, 73
    Racial motive, admissibility of, 73–74

FORCE, USE OF
Correctional officers, by,
    Eighth Amendment, 365–70
    Significant injury, 370

FOURTEENTH AMENDMENT
See Due Process; Equal Protection

FOURTH AMENDMENT
    See also Privacy, Right of
    Generally, 79–80, 178–81, 318–25
Balancing test, "special needs" searches, 179–80, 322, 324
Body searches, 321–25
Cell searches, 318–19
DNA testing, 181
Exclusionary rule,
    Parole-revocation hearings, 181–83
    Sentencing hearings, 79–80
Probationers, rights of, 178–81
Seizure of inmates' property, 319–20

GENDER
See Discrimination/Disparity; Equal Protection; Privacy, Right of

GOOD–TIME CREDITS
Ex post facto laws, 104
Length of incarceration, 89–90
Procedures when revoking, 271–79
Restoration of, 408–09

GOVERNMENT BENEFITS
Denial of, 120–21, 198

GRIEVANCE PROCEDURES
    See also Exhaustion of Remedies
Alternative to litigation, 433
Alternative to prisoner union, 230
Retaliation for invoking, 268

GUILTY PLEAS
See also Plea Bargains
Generally, 14–44
Acceptance, 29
Appeal,
Notice of right to, 26–27
Waiver of, 42–43
Blind guilty plea, 14
Collateral attacks on, 17–18, 23–25
Collateral consequences, awareness of, 19, 28
Conditional plea, 26
Counsel,
Ineffective assistance of, 22–23, 26–27
Role of, 15–16, 19
Waiver of, 21–22
Death penalty, avoidance of, 19–20, 27
Double jeopardy, 24–25
Exculpatory evidence, awareness of, 20–21
Factual basis, 27–28
Innocence, protestations of, 27–28
Negotiated, 14–15
Sentence increase after, 38–40, 59
Voluntary and intelligent, 16–21, 23–25, 27

HABEAS CORPUS
Confinement, release from, 408–09
Jailhouse lawyers, petitions prepared by, 258–60
Petition for writ,
Prison officials, initial submission to, 253

HANDS–OFF DOCTRINE
Reasons for, 214–15
Reasons for abandonment of, 215–18

HISTORY
Prisoners' rights, 214–19

HOME CONFINEMENT
Electronic monitoring devices, 112–13

IMMUNITY
Generally, 388–96
Eleventh Amendment, 388–91, 395
Official immunity,
Absolute, 391–94
Qualified, 391–96
Private contractors, 396

IMMUNITY—Cont'd
Sovereign immunity, United States, 388
State statutes, 432

INCARCERATION
Purposes of, 2–7, 10, 219–22
    Conflict between, 10
Rate, 11

***IN FORMA PAUPERIS* PETITIONS**
Filing fees, 382–83, 386
Frivolousness, dismissal for, 384
Three strikes, 386–87

INJUNCTIVE RELIEF
    Generally, 403–09, 411–12, 419–30
Confinement, release from, 404–05, 408–09, 411–12
Modification of, 420–25
Preliminary injunctions, duration of, 412
Requirements for, 404–08
Stay of, 429–30
Taxes, raising of, 405–06
Termination of, 426–29

INTERNATIONAL LAWS AND PRACTICES
Death penalty, 145–46
Fines, 115

JAILHOUSE LAWYERS
Incompetent, 260
Prohibition against, 258–60
Reasonable alternative assistance, 259–60

JURISDICTION
    Generally, 381–82
Termination of, 426–27

JURY, RIGHT TO
Sentencing, 61–65

LAW LIBRARIES
Access, adequacy of, 263, 266–67
Collections, adequacy of, 263

LAW STUDENTS
Interviews of prisoners, 256–58

LAWYERS
See Attorneys

INDEX 447
References are to Pages

LIBERTY INTERESTS
See also Due Process
Generally, 166, 185–89, 271, 284–93, 305

MAGISTRATE JUDGES
Prisoner cases, adjudication of, 381–82

MAIL
Alternative to media interviews, 227
Attorneys, correspondence with, 254–55
Books and magazines, 230–31, 236–39
Court documents, withholding of, 253
Due process, 226
Inmate-to-inmate, 231–35, 267
Nonprisoners, 223–26, 236–37
Publications, censorship of, 236–39
Union materials,
  Equal protection, 315–16
  First Amendment, 229–30

MANDATORY–MINIMUM SENTENCES
Generally, 59–61, 92–95, 157
Eighth Amendment, constitutionality under, 157
Sentencing factors, 59–61

MARRIAGE
Prisoners, 235–36

MEDIA
Interviews,
  Freedom of speech, 226–28
  Freedom of the press, 228–29

MEDICAL CARE
Generally, 348–57
Deliberate indifference, 348–51
Disabilities, 353–54
Pretrial detainees, 351
Psychiatric or psychological care, 352–53
Right to refuse, 305–07, 354–57
Serious medical needs, 351–53
Systemic problems, 350–51

MENTALLY ILL PRISONERS
Involuntary medication, 305–07, 354–57
Psychiatric care, right to, 352–53
Suicides, 371–72

MENTALLY ILL PRISONERS—Cont'd
Transfers to mental hospitals, 285–87, 296–99

MINIMUM WAGE
Fair Labor Standards Act, 344–45

***MIRANDA* WARNINGS**
Criminal cases,
    Statements of prisoners, 280–81
    Statements of probationers, 175
Disciplinary proceedings, statements of prisoners, 279–80

MOOTNESS
Prisoners' civil-rights suits, 397–98

MUNICIPAL LIABILITY
Eleventh Amendment, 395
Failure to train, 378–79
Hiring decisions, 379–80
"Person" under § 1983, 374
Policy, 378–80
Punitive damages, 395–96
Qualified immunity, 395
Respondeat-superior liability, 377–78

PARALEGALS
Attorney's fees, 417
Interviews of prisoners, 256–58

PAROLE RELEASE
    See also Supervised Release
  Generally, 86–88, 163–65, 184–94
Conditions,
    Sex-offender treatment, 177–78
Ex post facto laws, 104–06
Guidelines, 88, 163
Liberty interest, 185–89
Process due, 189–94

PAROLE REVOCATION
    See also, Probation; Supervised Release
  Generally, 165–78, 181–84
Counsel, right to, 170–73
Due process,
    Liberty interest, 166
    Preliminary hearings, 167–69
    Revocation hearings, 169–73

PAROLE REVOCATION—Cont'd
Exclusionary rule, 181–83
Standard of proof, 173

PERSONAL PROPERTY
Seizure or destruction of,
    Due process, 337–43
    Fourth Amendment, 319–20

PLEA BARGAINS
    Generally, 15–16, 29–38, 42–44
Benefits, 16
Breach,
    Defendant, by, 32–33
    Prosecutor, by, 30–32
Codefendant, reduced charge, 37
Criticisms, 15–16
Impeachment, statements made during plea negotiations for, 42
Inducements,
    Legislative, 40–41
    Prosecutorial, 33–37
Release-dismissal agreements, 43–44

POSTCONVICTION PROCEEDINGS
    See also Habeas Corpus
Attorney, assistance of, 261–62

PRESENTENCE INVESTIGATION REPORT
Right of access to, 50–52
Right to respond to, 52–53

PRETRIAL DETAINEES
Attorneys, monitoring communications with, 255–56
Body searches, 321–25
Cell searches,
    Right to observe, 320–21
Contact visits, 239–43
Credit for time incarcerated, 67
Cruel and unusual punishment, 347–48, 351, 371
Disciplinary segregation, 293
Double celling, 358–59
First Amendment, 230–31
Medical care, 351
Punishment proscribed, 240
Thirteenth Amendment, 343

PRISON LITIGATION REFORM ACT
Attorney's fees, restrictions on, 403, 417–19
Filing fees, 383, 386–87
Physical-injury requirement, 370–71, 401–02
Preliminary injunctions, duration of, 412
Prospective relief,
    Restrictions on, 404–08
    Stay of, 429–30
    Termination of, 427–29
Remedies, exhaustion of, 398
Restitution, 403
Sua sponte dismissals, 384–86
Three strikes, 386–87

PRISONS
Crowding, 358
Incarceration, increase in, 11, 358
Programs, gender discrimination in, 313–15
Supermaximum-security, 292–93

PRIVACY, RIGHT OF
    See also Fourth Amendment
    Generally, 325–33
Bodily functions, view of, 327–32
Emergencies, 328–29
Equal employment opportunities, correctional personnel, 327, 329–36
Genitals, view of, 327–32
Marriage, 325–26
Patdown searches, 329–32
Source of, 325–26
Strip searches, 327, 332

PRIVATE CONTRACTORS
Bivens actions, 381
Immunity, 396
Section 1983 liability, 377

PROBATION
    See also Shame Sentences
    Generally, 109–11, 165–74
Conditions of, 110–11
Incarceration, combined with,
    Shock incarceration, 111
    Split sentence, 111
Incarceration, in lieu of, 89

PROBATION—Cont'd
Intensive supervision probation, 110
Revocation,
    Indigent defendant's failure to pay fine, 117–19
    Model Community Corrections Act, 184
    Process due, 166–73
Searches, 178–81
Self-incrimination, privilege against, 174–78

PUBLICATIONS
See Law Libraries; Mail

PUBLIC OPINION
Community sanctions, 125–26
Death penalty, 132

RACIAL SEGREGATION
    See also Discrimination/Disparity; Equal Protection
Prisons, 309–13

RECIDIVISM
Boot camps, 111
Drug treatment, 5
Family ties, impact of, 244
Rates, 3, 5, 196, 220
Unemployment, 195

RELIGION, FREEDOM OF
    Generally, 244–51
Constitutional, 244–49
Religious Freedom Restoration Act, 249–50
Religious Land Use and Institutionalized Persons Act, 250–51

REMEDIES
    See also Attorney's Fees; Injunctive Relief
    Generally, 399–433
Attorney's fees, 390–91, 403, 412–19
Damages,
    Attorney's fees, payable towards, 403
    Compensatory, 399–403
    Confinement, fact or duration of, 409–11
    Mental or emotional injuries, 401–02
    Nominal, 401–02
    Punitive, 402–03
    Restitution, payable towards, 403
Declaratory judgments, 403, 409
Enforcement of court orders, 430–31

REMEDIES—Cont'd
Equitable relief, 403–09, 411–12
Exhaustion of, 398
Grievance procedures, 433
Master, appointment of, 431
Modification of consent decrees, 420–25
State common law, 432
State constitutions, 432
Statutes, 432

RESTITUTION
    Generally, 119–20
Damages awards payable towards, 403
Seventh Amendment, 119
Victim-offender mediation programs, 8

RETALIATION
For litigation, 267–69
Increased sentences, 38–40, 58–59

SEARCHES AND SEIZURES
See Fourth Amendment

SECTION 1983
    See also Affirmative Defenses; Attorney's Fees; Court; Ex-
        haustion of Remedies; Immunity; Jurisdiction; Munici-
        pal Liability; Remedies
Causation, 377–80
Complaint, sufficiency of, 384–86
Elements, 374–80
Federal rights, violation of, 380
Person,
    Municipalities, 374
    State officials, 375–76
    States, 375
Private contractors, 377, 396
"Under color of" state law, 217–18, 376–77

SEGREGATION
See Administrative Segregation; Cruel and Unusual Punishment;
    Disciplinary Proceedings

SELF–INCRIMINATION, PRIVILEGE AGAINST
Disciplinary hearings, applicability at, 281–82
Probation meetings, 174–77
Rule 11 hearings, 29
Sentencing hearings, applicability at, 71–72

SELF–INCRIMINATION, PRIVILEGE AGAINST—Cont'd
Sex-offender treatment, 177–78, 307–09

SENTENCING
See also Death Penalty
Allocution, 54–55
Appellate review, 159
Confrontation and cross-examination, 56–57
Cooperation with criminal investigators, 71
Counsel,
    Effective assistance of, 46–48
    Right to, 45–46
Criminal history,
    Acquitted, 69–70
    Nonadjudicated, 67–70
    Sentencing enhancements, 65–66
Disproportionate sentences in noncapital cases, 148–58
Enhanced sentence, uncounselled conviction as basis for, 72–73
Exclusionary rule, 79–80
Factors,
    Generally, 59–66, 68–84
    Versus elements, 59–66
False information, 74–75
Gang membership, 73
Jury trial, 61–65
Multi-tiered system, 126–127
Nonviolent offenders, 124, 184
Notice, right to,
    Right to appeal, 26–27
    Upward departure, 53
Perjury, 70–71
Presentence investigation reports,
    Right of access to, 50–52
    Right to respond to, 52–53
Purposes of,
    Deterrence, 2–3, 219–20
    Incapacitation, 3–5, 10, 219–20
    Just deserts, 6–7, 221–22
    Least restrictive alternative, 6–7
    Rehabilitation, 5–6, 10, 221
    Restorative justice, 7–10
    Retribution, 5–7, 10, 221–22
Real offense, 101–03
Reasons for, 57–59
Standard of proof, 59–64

SENTENCING—Cont'd
Unconstitutional conviction, 75–79
Victim-impact statements, 80–84
Witnesses, 55–56

SENTENCING GUIDELINES
Generally, 95–103, 128–29
Capacity-based, 100
Circumvention, 101–03
Ex post facto constraints, 103–04
Federal, 65, 99–103
Jury trial, right to, 63–65
Minnesota, 95–101
Non-imprisonment guidelines, 101, 128–29
North Carolina, 101
Standard of proof, 63–65

SENTENCING STATUTES
Generally, 85–95
Community-corrections acts, 123–25, 184
Determinate,
    Determinate-discretionary, 89–91
    Mandatory, 59–61, 92–95, 157
    Presumptive, 91–92
Indeterminate, 86–88

SEPARATION OF POWERS
Injunctive relief,
    Stay of, 429–30
    Termination of, 428–29

SEVENTH AMENDMENT
Restitution, 119

SEX DISCRIMINATION
See Discrimination/Disparity; Equal Employment Rights of Correctional Officers; Equal Protection; Privacy, Right of

SEX OFFENDERS
Castration, 162
Civil confinement, 204–09
Community notification, 201–04
Registration, 201–04
Self-incrimination, privilege against, 177–78, 307–09

SEXUAL ABUSE
Prisoners, by correctional officers, 335

SHAME SENTENCES
Generally, 160–61
Historical use of, 160
Sex offenders, community notification about, 201–204

SIXTH AMENDMENT
Counsel,
    Effective assistance of,
        Guilty pleas, 22–23, 26–27
        Sentencing, 46–48
Monitoring attorney/pretrial detainee communications, 255–56
Psychiatrist interviews, right to during, 49
Sentencing, right to at, 45–46
Waiver of, 21–22

SPEECH, FREEDOM OF
Generally, 223–39
Nonprisoners, 223–26, 236–37
Prisoners, 226–39

STANDING
Right-of-access claims, 263–64

STATUTES OF LIMITATIONS
Section 1983, 396–97

SUPERMAXIMUM-SECURITY PRISONS
Liberty interests, 292–93
Procedural safeguards, 302–05

SUPERVISED RELEASE
See also Shame Sentences
Sentence, 164–65
Violation of, 165

THREE STRIKES
Cruel and unusual punishment, 158
Habitual-offender laws, 92
Prison Litigation Reform Act, 386–87

TRANSFERS
Administrative segregation, 285, 287, 294–96, 298–302
Disciplinary segregation, 271, 289–93
Mental hospital, 285–87, 296–99
Other prison, 284–87, 292–93, 302–05
Retaliatory, 267–68
Supermaximum-security prison, 292–93

VICTIM–IMPACT STATEMENTS
Constitutionality, 80–84

VICTIM–OFFENDER MEDIATION PROGRAMS
Restorative justice, 7–10

VISITATION RIGHTS
Generally, 239–44
Contact visits, 239–43
Cruel and unusual punishment, 363
Liberty interest, 287–89

VOTING RIGHTS
Convicted offenders, 199–201, 212

†